"A student-centered book by a gifted classroom instructor, thoroughly clear and relentlessly dialogical. It will introduce students to every important issue facing the church today. The inclusive dialogue will provide them with the resources to think their way through these issues. Beginning from and grounded in the documents of Vatican II, this text is comprehensive in its treatment of the church. It should become a college-level standard for courses on the church."

William L. Portier
Mount Saint Mary's College, Maryland

"*The Church Emerging From Vatican II* is an accessible and balanced textbook on contemporary Catholic teaching and practice. By his focusing on the center which conservatives and progressives share, Doyle gives a nuanced and generous portrayal of the issues that unite and divide us, from the place of Mary to social justice to religious pluralism. This stimulating and readable text does not give 'the answers' to contemporary problems, but enables the readers to understand what is involved in finding resolutions of those problems. This book should be considered as a text by anyone who teaches undergraduate courses in modern Catholicism or contemporary ecclesiology."

Terrence W. Tilley
Florida State University

"Using the documents of Vatican II as its guide, this book not only underlines the precise significance of the council, but also discusses with clarity and sensitivity a broad range of important theological topics—from God to inter-religious dialogue—that have engaged reflective Christians in the intervening years. The author writes out of deep love for and commitment to the church, and he skillfully interweaves some of the story of his own spiritual journey with the story of the Roman church's journey since Vatican II. The breadth and balance of this work makes it a very fine introduction to contemporary Catholicism."

William Madges
Xavier University

"Dennis Doyle has a finely tuned ear. He has listened carefully to the questions American Catholics voice about themselves, their lives, and the church. He has listened critically to the documents of Vatican II as they address those questions. He has listened with an open mind and heart to a broad band of voices and their views about those questions and the official church teachings. He has responded with a remarkably useful book: honest, challenging, balanced, and easy to read. It is the best available introduction to the documents of Vatican II for college students. It will be very valuable for other adults."

Francis J. Buckley, S.J.
University of San Francisco

"Dennis Doyle's book, the fruit of long classroom experience, reflects, on every page, his deep conviction that to be an informed Catholic today one must not only live the fruits of the council but connect, in some deep way, with the entire witness to the church in space and time. That conviction is set forth with clear writing, wide learning, and a great spirit of Christian generosity."

Lawrence A. Cunningham
University of Notre Dame

"I am astonished at how much basic and important information can be found in this book; and yet it is consistently presented in a very personal, engaging way. Doyle presents sophisticated theological reflection in a form that accurately gauges the needs and abilities of a large portion of the undergraduate audience in the United States. The author's personal/confessional commentary, coupled with excellent questions for reflection at the end of each chapter, encourage students to find their own reaction or image or personal example, thus making the vital connection between experience and theology. I will certainly use this book for my Church in the Modern World course; I also think it would be ideal in a parish study group."

David M. Hammond, Ph.D.
Wheeling Jesuit College

"Doyle draws on solid scholarship, personal experience, and pedagogical savvy to paint a picture of the emerging Roman Catholic church that is enlightening, engaging, inspiring, and sometimes unsettling. He handles the issues in a way that is neither liberal nor conservative; his manner of treating such sticky questions as feminism, church authority, liberation theology, religious pluralism can best be described as open and sensitive, both to church tradition and to the new questions.

"Given the book's solid content, its clarity, and the way Doyle appeals to his own and the reader's experience, ministers and teachers will find it eminently useful and enjoyable in both undergraduate classrooms and religious education programs."

Paul Knitter
Xavier University
co-author of *Faith, Religion & Theology*

"This is just the book I have been looking for to use as a text in my undergraduate course on the church. It deals with almost all of the topics which arise in that course and it uses non-technical language that undergraduates can understand. Doyle shows the connections between theological theory and issues that students may read about in the newspaper or see on TV, and he treats divisive questions in an even-handed way. His frequent personal illustrations will help students and teachers relate the book's concerns to their own experience."

William J. Collinge
Mount Saint Mary's College, Maryland

"Dennis Doyle's book will be an excellent tool for helping Catholic college (and even high school) students to think about the church and their role within it. The presentations are clear and balanced, nicely combining concrete and personal experiences with historical and theological seriousness. Brief bibliographies and questions for reflection increase the value of this book, which I hope will find wide use."

Rev. Joseph A. Komonchak
The Catholic University of America

The

CHURCH EMERGING

from

VATICAN II

A popular approach to contemporary Catholicism

DENNIS M. DOYLE

TWENTY-THIRD PUBLICATIONS
Mystic, Connecticut 06355

Sixth printing 1999

Twenty-Third Publications
185 Willow Street
P.O. Box 180
Mystic CT 06355
(860) 536-2611
(800) 321-0411

ISBN 0-89622-507-0
Library of Congress Catalog Card Number 91-67714

PREFACE

This book can be used as an introduction to Roman Catholicism. Since it focuses on the topic of "church" from a Catholic perspective, it can also be used as a text in "ecclesiology," understood in a broad sense. In a classroom setting, I recommend that it be used in conjunction with two Vatican II documents, *Lumen Gentium* and *Gaudium et Spes.* The organization of these documents provides the basic framework for this book.

The church is an interpersonal reality. For this reason, I intend this book to be also about you and about me, about our fears and our hopes, our sorrows and our joys, our needs and our satisfactions. The church exists within the context of our life stories, and it cannot be adequately understood apart from them. For this reason I include throughout references to my own life and to the lives of others. When I use this material in a classroom, I begin the semester by having my students write an autobiographical statement concerning their own faith and value development and where the church does or does not fit for them. For students who are non-Catholic, "church" can be interpreted as it suits them.

I have found that many of my non-Catholic students feel by the end of the course that they have learned not only about Catholicism but also about their own denomination or religion and their own personal faith. I try to facilitate this in several ways. First of all, I stress the ecumenical nature of contemporary Catholicism and the open attitude toward other denominations and religions. Today one cannot be a faithful Catholic without being ecumenically-minded. Second, I spend significant time near the beginning of the course covering ecumenism. We discuss various ecumenical issues in the New Testament, the Reformation, and current inter-faith dialogues. Throughout the course I treat the divisions among Christians as stemming from complex causes with many rights and wrongs on both sides. Third, I encourage non-Catholic students to do their term projects on topics related to their own denominations or religions. Fourth, I try to encourage ecumenical sensitivity in classroom discussion. I know from very early on the religious affiliation of each student, and I respectfully make this part of the ongoing conversation. There may be some teachers who feel that a student's personal background is irrelevant in an academic course. I am not one of them.

Often in this book I use the phrase, "the church," to refer to specifically the Roman Catholic church. This usage reflects my own particular perspective. I have found in the Catholic church my spiritual home. I have many significant relationships outside my own denomination and religion, but within my own I find a core community centered around a tradition without which I could not do. I belong to the Catholic church, with all its marvels and glories, as well as its bruises and even warts. I think it only fair to tell you that I write from this perspective, although I believe that my commitment to the church makes me neither uncritical toward it nor disinterested in questions of truth.

It is my hope that whoever reads this book may find it useful in their own personal faith-journey.

ACKNOWLEDGMENTS

I wish to thank first of all my wife, Patricia, who read and critiqued several versions of the entire manuscript. Her editorial advice and loving support were of immense help to me throughout the entire project.

Thanks also to Mike Barnes, my colleague and jogging partner, whose insights and criticisms throughout this process were invaluable.

Thanks too to Jeff Staub, my graduate assistant, who spent many hours helping with research and editing.

Thanks to several of my colleagues who gave me good comments on selected chapters: John Bregenzer, Una Cadegan, Bob Hater, and Jack McGrath.

Thanks to Bill Madges of Xavier University in Cincinnati for his helpful criticisms.

Thanks to the University of Dayton and its administration for giving me both encouragement and financial support for this project, especially Jim Heft, John Geiger, Tom Martin, and the committee for the Fund for Educational Development.

Thanks to my publisher, Neil Kluepfel, who gave me good advice at key moments. Thanks to my editor, Dan Connors, for help with style, ideas, and for the elimination of several would-be gaffes and blunders.

Thanks to my children, Thomas, Michael, Patrick, and Christopher, for sparing me for many extra hours at work.

Thanks especially to my students at the University of Dayton over the last seven years. When I began this book, I asked myself, should I address this work more to Monica Tylinski, who is interested, or to the infrequent attenders who sit in the back? Thanks to Monica for being the one in my imagination to whom I addressed this text.

I wish I could mention all my students. I will limit myself to the members of Religion 340: The Church, Winter 1991, who read a xe-roxed version of this book and gave me many helpful suggestions:

Bill Auxer	Jennifer Ivory
Monica Gates	Jenny Parrili
Karen McCoach	Dixie Caporal
Jenny Bell	Bernardo Izaguirre
Lisa Gonzales	Paul Romanello
Chris McKiernan	Andrea Carrano
Susie Breitenstein	Jennie Linz
Steve Grimberg	David Schnittger
Steve Michel	Mike Cavanaugh
Michael Byrnes	Christine Lombardo
Emily Holtel	John Thompson
Matt Parker	Angie Coterel
Brian Caperton	Debbie Maus
Mark Engert	Mark Wittich

CONTENTS

SECTION EIGHT
MARY AND THE CHURCH

PART THREE
GAUDIUM ET SPES:
THE CHURCH ENGAGING THE WORLD

SECTION ONE
CHURCH AND WORLD

SECTION TWO
PRINCIPLES, FAMILY CULTURE

SECTION THREE
ECONOMICS, POLITICS, PEACE, ECOLOGY

The
CHURCH
EMERGING
from
VATICAN II

Part One

Introductory Chapters

CHAPTER 1

THE CATHOLIC CHURCH TODAY

I t was a steamy September afternoon when John Paul II emerged from his plane in Miami to begin a week-long tour of the United States. This 1987 visit, his second as pope, took place just twenty-two short years after the Second Vatican Council had ushered in a new era in the history of the Catholic church. As reporters crowded around with microphones, one question caught the pope's attention: "How do you feel about all of the dissent and protest awaiting you?" With a deep grin, John Paul II replied, "I am accustomed to that. It would be, I could say, not quite normal not to have that—especially in America."

Throughout his trip, the pope was greeted by a mixture of adulation, questioning, and protest. Although the adulation seemed to far outweigh the questioning both in quantity and in enthusiasm, the challenges posed were not any less serious or important.

The mixed reception the pope received on this journey symbolizes the explosive drama of the Catholic church as it struggles to continue in the direction set for it by Vatican II. What is it about the present pope and the Catholic church that can make some Catholics so enthusiastic, others so upset, and many a bit of both?

This Chapter

The Second Vatican Council, or Vatican II, was a meeting of Catholic bishops from throughout the world that took place intermittently between 1962 and 1965. This council was one of the most significant events in the history of the Catholic church. Its purpose was to bring the church up to date by opening it to dialogue with the modern world.

The council attempted to define the nature and mission of the church for the twentieth century and beyond.

The purpose of this book is to explore the many issues faced by the Catholic church today against the background of the developments of Vatican II. The book takes its basic outline and structure from two of the council's major documents: the Dogmatic Constitution on the Church (*Lumen Gentium*) and the Pastoral Constitution on the Church in the Modern World (*Gaudium et Spes*). Contemporary issues are examined against the background of the actual positions taken at Vatican II.

This chapter will address the current state of the Catholic church. Is the church polarized between liberals and conservatives? Is there any middle ground? We conclude by exploring reasons why a careful study of contemporary issues against the background of Vatican II should lead to a deeper understanding of the many complex religious questions that Catholics, as well as other Christians and perhaps all human beings, face today.

One View of the Issues

What are some of the more important issues faced by the Catholic church today? In the wake of the many changes that have flowed from Vatican II, different groups of Catholics define the issues differently.

Some groups have as their main concern a list of further changes that they believe still need to be made. These groups tend to think that the general thrust of Vatican II is not being carried forth sufficiently by church leadership. Such is the stance of a Chicago-based organization of lay Catholics who label themselves "Call to Action." In a large ad taken out in the *New York Times* on February 28, 1990, this group called for major reforms in the church. Their ad was accompanied by the signatures of 4505 Catholics.

Among the reforms called for were:
- more involvement of women on all levels of ministry and decision making;
- allowing married priests;
- consulting the laity extensively when formulating teaching on sexual matters;
- participation of the laity, religious, and clergy in the selection of bishops;
- open dialogue, academic freedom, and due process for theologians;
- concrete movement for resolving differences with other Christians;
- movement away from an authoritarian style of leadership.[1]

The ad claimed that without these and other reforms in its structure, the church cannot effectively carry out its mission to the world. Because the church is failing to address justice issues within itself, it is more of a stumbling block than a help.

This statement was echoed later that year by a statement of the distinguished Catholic Theological Society of America, a group of 1400 theologians.[2] Although the CTSA's statement was less sweeping and more theologically nuanced than the *New York Times* ad, its basic message was one of concern that the spirit of the Second Vatican council was being stifled by the conservatism and lack of openness of present church leadership. The theologians' complaints included excessive centralization of authority, lack of freedom for theological inquiry, an attitude of suspicion toward feminism and women's issues, and a negative role taken by church leaders in relation to ecumenical progress.

Another View of the Issues

Other groups of Catholics believe that too many changes have already taken place, and that the entire tradition may be lost if something is not done to reverse the tide of change. These groups tend to believe that liberal reformers have read changes into Vatican II that were never there. Such is the stance of a conservative organization called The Fellowship of Catholic Scholars with a membership of nearly a thousand Catholic academics from various fields. In September 1990 this group issued its own statement: "Vatican II: Promise and Reality—The Catholic church in the United States Twenty-Five Years After Vatican II."

The basic thesis of this document is that many of the liberal reforms done in the name of Vatican II have been counterproductive for Catholicism in the United States. The Fellowship expressly disagrees with those who say that the major problems in the church today are authoritarianism, the repression of theologians, a lack of openness to women's ordination, and a refusal to implement the results of ecumenical dialogue. The Fellowship sees, instead, a different set of problems:
- serious decline among Catholics in active affiliation with the worshiping community;
- widespread ignorance among Catholics of the teaching and discipline of the church;
- deterioration among Catholics in marital stability and family life;
- slippage among Catholics into secular and relativistic mindsets;
- growing incidence among Catholics of divorce and invalid remarriage;
- radical decline of the Catholic elementary and secondary school systems;

•continuing downturn in priestly and religious vocations;

•inability of many Catholic colleges and universities to support the faith, devotion, and orthodoxy of the young men and women entrusted to their care.[3]

The statement goes on to call for a renewed dedication to promoting personal holiness and for a restoration of discipline within the church.

A Polarized Church?

Is it accurate to picture the Catholic church as full of division and even polarization? During the pope's 1987 visit, each of the three major television networks broadcast news specials about the Catholic church in the United States. As news media are inclined to do, the networks focused on controversy and division. The clear message was that the Catholic church is polarized between the ultra-traditional pope and the wildly rebellious Catholics of the United States.

Such a picture, however, may be more misleading than revealing. A close analysis of the ABC program, "The Pope in America" (which I personally found to be the least offensive of the three), shows the use of many journalistic techniques that generate more controversy than accuracy. For example, flashing images presented the United States through scenes of bright lights, sexy women, flamboyant gays, and futuristic nightclub acts with rock music blaring in the background; the Vatican was presented through scenes of magnificent domes, marble halls, grand assemblies, and solemn liturgies against the background of angelic choir harmonies. Liberal U.S. Catholic positions were represented by attractive teenagers and dynamic priests dressed in suits; positions supportive of the Vatican were represented by older priests and religious dressed in traditional garb who were limited to one-liners that emphasize that the church is not simply free to change with the times. Polls were taken that were limited to only the most controversial questions and that posed complex matters in a simplistic "agree/disagree" format. Two extremes, then, were presented throughout the program as if they constituted the whole reality of the church.

Many in the Middle

It is easy to find opposing groups in the Catholic church today. However, this is not the whole picture. I was part of a group studying the positions of Catholic theologians in a national professional society, and of Catholic parishioners in a parish in Dayton, Ohio. Although our sample was too small to be statistically conclusive, we found evidence that neither theologians nor parishioners were simply clustered toward either extreme. We found a good deal of diversity in the church, with parishioners tending to be rather traditional, and with theologians most often endorsing nuanced middle positions. We concluded that a large group of Catholics exists who do not fall simply under the categories of traditional or liberal. Although this group can be easy to overlook, it includes the highest number of theologians and a significant number of parishioners. In other words, whereas the media focus on the extremes on either side, a great many people are somewhere in the middle. They neither regret the changes that have taken place nor want to push for more change too rapidly. Rather than a divided church moving simultaneously in opposite directions, a picture can be drawn of a church developing more and more nuanced positions in response to contemporary developments.[4]

This conclusion may be overly optimistic, and it has been criticized as such.[5] I have no wish to deny the importance of either the many controversial issues in the church today or of the divisions and the hard feelings that they cause. In spite of their overall distortions, the media can do us a great service by highlighting real tensions and points of disagreements, but we need to remember that such is not the whole picture nor even the greater part of the whole picture.

The Big Picture

A careful study of the Catholic church as it is emerging from Vatican II can be helpful for at least a couple of important reasons.

For one thing, such a study can examine the controversial issues of today within a historical and systematic framework that can shed light instead of just stirring up heat. It can help us explore a spectrum of diverse opinions instead of a false dichotomy of artificially opposed views. People can thus come to grips with a range of options in the church today without being forced into one or another camp.

Perhaps even more significantly, such a study can delve deeply beneath the surface of the hot issues to consider more basic matters of what the Catholic church has to offer today. What is the message of Vatican II, and how does it express in its own way the two-thousand-year-old tradition of Christianity? What does the Catholic church have to say to contemporary people who struggle with their personal spiritual journey? It is my hope that this book will be helpful not only to Catholics and other Christians, but to anyone who asks questions of a religious nature.

Some of the topics addressed in this book include:

• various positions taken at Vatican II and differing ways of interpreting them;
• the history of ecumenical divisions and the current state of ecumenical dialogue;
• the changing roles of bishops and priests in the church;
• the existence of legitimate disagreement among Catholics and the current emphasis on religious freedom;
• the importance of the laity and their mission in the world;
• contemporary themes in spirituality;
• liberation theology;
• gender issues and the ordination of women;
• atheism and religious pluralism;
• the new focus on social and economic issues;
• the religious significance of peace and ecology.

Any presentation of such issues will reflect to some degree the biases and opinions of the author. I have tried as much as possible to present fairly a range of positions on each issue.

Summary

In this chapter we have raised some basic questions about the state of the Catholic church in the United States as a way of suggesting why a study of contemporary issues in the light of Vatican II might be helpful. In the next chapter we will explore in their historical context some of the challenges faced by the Catholic church that led to the calling of the council.

FOR FURTHER REFLECTION

1. Do you tend to identify yourself more with the conservatives, the liberals, or the middle? Why do you think you are this way?

2. Which issues facing the Catholic church today do you think are the most important?

3. Why might the news media have a tendency to present a distorted picture of the Catholic church?

4. What might a Catholic hope to gain from a study of the church?

5. What might a non-Catholic hope to gain from a study of the church?

SUGGESTED READINGS

National Catholic Reporter (a somewhat liberal Catholic newspaper), any recent issue.

The Wanderer (a highly conservative Catholic newspaper), any recent issue.

CHAPTER 2

CHALLENGES FOR THE CHURCH

I magine, for a moment, that you are a powerful king living in a large castle somewhat isolated from the modern world. One day there is a note at your doorstep telling you that your worldview is inadequate. The next day there is another note, this one saying that you are thoroughly corrupt. That note is followed the next day by a message telling you that you are not very important any more. In succeeding days you find notes that say that you really don't know anything, that you are a ruthless dictator who will not listen to reason, and that you are a degenerate ruler who sides with the establishment against the poor. Under these circumstances, you might tend to become a bit suspicious of the outside world and somewhat defensive about its accusations.

The king in this story can be taken to represent the Catholic church. The notes represent the many challenges posed to the church through various developments in Western civilization. The suspicion and defensiveness represent the posture of the church in the period immediately preceding Vatican II.

How did the Catholic church come to be somewhat like this king? The following paragraphs are broad and general in their scope, yet they are intended to represent how a church that often thinks more in terms of centuries than of days could see the threats piling up on its doorstep one by one.

Christianity began as an underground, sometimes persecuted religion. For much of the first three centuries, it was illegal not to worship the Roman gods. In 313, Constantine issued the Edict of Milan that declared freedom of religion. By 380, Christianity had become the official religion of the Roman empire. Over the years, the Catholic church adopted many of the structures and trappings of the Roman empire and the feudal society of the Middle Ages. By the thirteenth century, not only was most of the Western world Christian, but the Catholic church was by far the single most important influence on Western civilization. Western culture had itself become Christian, and offered a completely integrated view of the cosmos, nature, faith, and everyday life. Although theological debates raged hot and heavy throughout the Middle Ages, they took place within a Christian worldview with rock-certain premises: that the world had been saved through the Incarnation of Christ; that Christ founded the church; that the church and the sacraments provided people with access to the saving grace of Christ. *How* this was so was often debated; that it *was* so was not often challenged.

Over the centuries, however, the medieval synthesis of the Catholic church faced many challenges that made it start to unravel. In the fourteenth century, the bubonic plague, or the Black Death, devastated much of the world, wiping out about one-third of the European population, and raising many questions about God, suffering, and the purpose of life. In the fifteenth century, widespread corruption in the Catholic church gave rise to many serious calls for reform. In the sixteenth century, some of these reform movements took institutional form as Protestant denominations. Their growth was aided by a concomitant rise of nationalism, the formation of new economic arrangements, and the growth of literacy and education brought about by the printing press. These developments also paralleled the emergence of a "secular" world that had no direct need for a Catholic church. This constituted quite a change from the medieval world that depended wholly on the church and in which a "secular" world simply did not exist.

In more recent centuries the development of the natural and social sciences have posed additional challenges to the Catholic church. The seventeenth century witnessed astronomers such as Galileo challenging the cosmic view of the world that was taught by the church as depicted in the book of Genesis. The eighteenth century saw an even deeper emphasis on human reason, fostering new experiments in revolutionary politics that sought to put democratic authority in the hands of common people liberated from traditional tyrannies. In the nineteenth century, a new industrial society emerged, bringing with it new forms of human exploitation; many social analysts and reformers interpreted the church's role in negative terms, seeing it as a traditional reinforcer of the structures of oppression.

Somewhat like the king in the opening story, the church saw the accusations piling up on what seemed to be a daily basis. By the period immediately preceding Vatican II, the church had developed what some have called a "fortress mentality" or a "ghetto mentality," somewhat defensively isolated from developments in the modern world.

This Chapter

The purpose of this chapter is explore within a historical context some of the many challenges that the church had to address at Vatican II. After placing Vatican II within the context of the history of earlier councils, we will discuss the challenges posed to the church by the modern world. We will then mention briefly some of the ways that Vatican II responded to these challenges; such responses will be investigated in more detail in later chapters.

Twenty-One Councils Accepted by Catholics

Vatican II is one of twenty-one ecumenical councils affirmed by Catholics as authentic. Of these councils, only the first seven are affirmed by Greek Orthodox Christians, who have since added some of their own.[1] Protestant denominations differ in how many councils they accept.

Although it is not listed as an "ecumenical" council, the council of Jerusalem referred to in Acts 15 involved the earliest church leaders deciding the basic question of whether or not a gentile becoming a Christian also had to become a Jew and observe the Mosaic law completely. Some argued strongly that such should be the case, but the decision was otherwise.

The first seven ecumenical councils passed judgments on scriptures and creeds and calendars, but were mainly occupied with clarifying what it is that Christians believe about Jesus. The Council of Nicaea in 325 condemned the Arian heresy that Jesus, though higher than human beings, is somewhat less than God. It declared that Jesus is "one in being with the Father." The Council of Chalcedon in 451 argued against those who would reduce Jesus either to only a human being or to only God. It declared that Jesus is one person with two natures, fully human and fully divine.

The next eight councils affirmed as ecumenical by Catholics (councils 8–15) often concerned relations between the Greek Orthodox and the Roman Catholic churches. Constantinople IV in 869–70, for example, deposed a Patriarch of Constantinople and played a role in the coming schism between Greeks and Romans. Lyons II in 1274 established a short-lived reunion between the two.

One council during that time period, Lateran III in 1179, condemned the early Protestant movements known as the Waldenses and the Albigenses, and also called for some church reform. The condemnation of Protestants and attempts at church reform became a major thrust of councils 16–19. The Council of Constance in 1414–18, most famous for settling a controversy over who of three claimants was to be pope, issued decrees against the early reformers John Hus and John Wycliffe. Lateran V in 1512–17 tried to correct abuses in the face of many calls for reform, but lacked the decisive action to stem the tide of the coming Reformation. The Council of Trent, 1545–63, condemned the positions of the Protestant reformers while taking strict measures to improve the quality of pastoral care in the church. In its sharp reaction against anything Protestant, this council brought about an emphasis on rules and regulations that would remain with the church until the 1960s and the Second Vatican Council.

The First Vatican Council (Vatican I) in 1869–70 had a document on the church on its agenda, but the document was not passed before the council ended prematurely because of the Franco-Prussian war. The council did manage, though, to pass two very important documents: a document on faith and reason that expressed how for Catholics the two are ultimately compatible, and a document (originally a segment of the document on church) defining the primacy and infallibility of the pope.

The Second Vatican Council (Vatican II) took place between 1962 and 1965. The council did not meet continuously, but rather gathered together for about two months in each of the four years. Vatican II was the twenty-first council. Except for the unfinished Vatican I, an ecumenical council had not met for four hundred years.

Modern Challenges

The Catholic church faced many challenges in the period immediately preceding Vatican II. Some scholars now refer to the entire four hundred years prior to Vatican II as the "Counter-Reformation Period," characterized by an overemphasis on rules and regulations stemming from the Council of Trent. In order to move beyond this Counter-Reformation period through Vatican II, the church needed to reverse its extreme anti-Protestantism and to balance its top-heavy hierarchical structure of authority. It needed to redress its mutual grievances with the Greek Orthodox church. Also, it needed to come to terms with its relations with the Jews and with other world religions in the emerging global community.

Challenges at least as serious, however, were posed from outside the religious realm. The church had established an ambivalent relationship with science: On the one hand, it had acknowledged in theory the basic validity of human reason; on the other hand, it had shown hesitancy over and even rejection of some scientific breakthroughs in the name of defending the faith. By the 1960s, what many perceived as a war between science and religion seemed to have been won handily by science. Technological developments had brought cures for diseases, space exploration, mass transportation, skyscrapers, and increased food production. It was an age of unparalleled optimism in human progress in which the authority of the church was beginning to lack credibility for many.

The most intense challenges were posed by respected voices that were quite vocally atheist. Karl Marx, the nineteenth-century philosopher who had predicted and encouraged worldwide communist revolution, interpreted religion as false promises about an afterlife that hold people back from doing something about their oppressive situations here and now.[2] Sigmund Freud, the founder of psychoanalysis, believed that God and religion were things that should be abandoned by the mature individual and culture. Freud held that science is the only way that we can know things.[3] The French existentialist philosopher Albert Camus argued that religion is powerless to address the basic questions that face humankind.[4] The sufferings and evil that people endure seem to reveal not an all-good and all-powerful loving God, but rather an absurd universe in which the human heart cries out for meaning but finds no response.

Even for those who are not attracted to the various forms of atheism, these critiques of religion are important because they articulate the doubts and questions of ordinary people. Many in the modern world, while not atheists, had become increasingly agnostic, secularist, and humanistic. To be agnostic is to take the position that one does not know if there is a God or not; to be secularist is to live in a world in which the church is experienced as irrelevant; to be humanistic is to hold a fundamental belief in the goodness of human endeavors without necessarily connecting them to supernatural purposes. It appeared to some that the Catholic church was trying to stand its ground on a down escalator while the rest of the world was moving onwards and upwards.

Vatican II as a Pastoral Council

Like the first twenty ecumenical councils, Vatican II needed to address many challenges both internal and external. Unlike the previous councils, however, Vatican II was not intended to condemn heretics through dogmatic pronouncements. Rather, it was to proceed in a more positive vein by formulating a new self-definition and by engaging the modern world in dialogue.

It is for this reason that Pope John XXIII said that the main purpose of Vatican II was *aggiornamento*, that is, bringing the church up to date. He called for the council to be "pastoral" in that it would define no new dogmas, but rather explore how the teaching of the church might be communicated more fully and put to use more effectively. He said:

> The substance of the ancient doctrine of the deposit of faith is one thing, and the way in which it is presented is another. And it is the latter that must be taken into great consideration with patience if necessary, everything being measured in the forms and proportions of a magisterium which is predominantly pastoral in character.[5]

In other words, this council was called so that the Catholic church might renew itself in order to carry out more effectively its mission in the world.

It would be misleading, however, to ignore the challenge-response dimension of the council altogether. Although Freud and Marx and Camus are not mentioned in the documents by name, there are clear attempts to address the issues that they and many other critics had raised. Moreover, Vatican II established a direction and a momentum through which the church has continued to explore such issues in an ongoing manner.

One of the great things about Vatican II is that it did not simply refute such challenges and then dismiss them; rather, although it does ultimately reject the atheism of Freud, Marx, and Camus, it allows their critiques to have a positive impact on the church's self-understanding. That is, in Vatican II there is much evidence that the church has not simply defended itself but has grown from the challenges.

This point is important because the critiques of Freud, Marx, Camus, and others represent not just historical arguments but the very doubts and concerns that any person, believer or unbeliever, might face in our society today. Many people wonder at some point in their lives if religion might not be a psychological crutch, a controlling tool of social leaders, or a set of answers when all we really have are good questions.

The church emerged from Vatican II with more explicit concern for individual autonomy and maturity of faith, for human progress and transformation of social structures, for the unfathomable mystery of life and a sense of the need for the church to engage in self-criticism. Although the pre-Vatican II version of Catholicism had many wonderful aspects, the post-Vatican II church is much better equipped to deal with the critiques of religion, to take seriously their legitimate concerns, and to grow from the encounter.

Summary

In this chapter we have considered how the church developed its "fortress mentality" prior to Vatican II. We then tried to view Vatican II against the background of previous ecumenical councils and the challenges of modern times. Finally we discussed Vatican II as a pastoral council that needed to address various challenges in its attempt to bring the church up to date. In the next chapter we will become acquainted with the sixteen documents of Vatican II, with particular attention to *Lumen Gentium* (Dogmatic Constitution on the Church) and *Gaudium et Spes* (Pastoral Constitution on the Church in the Modern World), the two documents that will provide the organizational plan for the rest of the chapters of this book.

FOR FURTHER REFLECTION

1. What images and ideas do you most associate with the pre-Vatican II church? Do they tend to be more positive or more negative?

2. Which of the many challenges that have been posed to the Catholic church do you find to be the most serious?

3. Which of the many challenges posed to the church most represent your own questions, doubts, and concerns?

4. Would some people be better off if they did not know about the many challenges posed to the church?

5. How is it that the Catholic church can benefit by taking seriously the criticisms posed by atheists?

SUGGESTED READING

Camus, Albert. *The Myth of Sisyphus.* New York: Vintage Books, 1955 [1942].

Freud, Sigmund. *The Future of an Illusion.* Garden City, New York: Doubleday/Anchor, 1957 [1927].

Küng, Hans. *Does God Exist?* N.Y.: Vintage Books, 1981 [1978].

Marx, Karl, and Friedrich Engels. *On Religion.* Moscow: Foreign Languages Publishing House, 1955.

CHAPTER 3

THE DOCUMENTS OF VATICAN II

I t would be hard to underestimate the impact Vatican II has had on the Catholic church. For the first couple of decades after the council, its story was often told in a "before and after" mode: Before Vatican II, all was darkness and guilt and repression; after Vatican II, all was sunshine and renewal and openness. Perhaps some people needed to tell that story for a time. There is no question that Vatican II brought about many significant and much needed changes. It is perhaps natural to want to focus on these changes.

At the same time, however, there are many Catholic voices today who are asking that the "before and after" story of Vatican II be told within the deeper context of the ongoing story of the church. For all of the changes, there is a larger, bedrock substratum that remains. In what follows, it is hoped that Vatican II will be understood not only in terms of the great changes that it brought about, but also in terms of its articulation of the Catholic faith in a manner continuous with the larger Catholic tradition.

This Chapter
The purpose of this chapter is to offer an overview of the sixteen documents of Vatican II. We will first list the documents along with a very brief description of each. Then we will discuss the relative importance of the documents. Finally, special attention will be paid to *Lumen Gentium* and *Gaudium et Spes,* the two main documents on the topic of church that will provide the underlying structure for the remainder of this book.

Documents of Vatican II

Many of the sixteen documents of Vatican II are related to the topic of church. Drafts of each document were prepared by commissions of bishops and theologians and put forth for vote by the bishops at the council.[1] The original preparatory commissions were highly traditional; during the very first session of the council, a vote was taken to reject a prepared list of commission members in favor of electing new ones. This vote was very significant, for it launched the council from its very beginning on the path of change and renewal. Most of the documents went through several drafts and the final results were very different from the originals. The following list in intended to be only a most general overview of the documents.

Documents from 1963

Constitution on the Sacred Liturgy: expresses principles for liturgical renewal that laid the groundwork for the many liturgical reforms that have followed the council.

Decree on the Means of Social Communication: discusses the importance of communications for continuing human progress and the contribution that Catholics in particular might make.

Documents from 1964

Dogmatic Constitution on the Church (*Lumen Gentium*, "Light of Nations"): promotes an understanding of the church that highlights mystery, ecumenism, shared authority, the laity, and the need for reform and renewal.

Decree on the Catholic Eastern Churches: praises the theological and liturgical heritage of those churches in the East that have remained united with Rome.

Decree on Ecumenism: acknowledges blame on all sides for the controversies underlying divisions among Christians; seeks dialogue and unity with "our separated brethren."

Documents from 1965

Decree on the Pastoral Office of Bishops in the Church: defines the authority and duties of bishops in their own dioceses, in their regional gatherings, and in the church as a whole.

Decree on the Up-to-Date Renewal of Religious Life: calls for reforms in institutional structures and regulations, but sees the key to renewal as the practice of the vows of poverty, chastity, and obedience.

Decree on the Training of Priests: calls for sound formation of priests, including particular attention to high standards in academic, spiritual, and pastoral training.

Declaration on Christian Education: affirms the importance of Christian education in home, school, and church and calls for an updating of methods in line with the social sciences.

Declaration on the Relation of the Church to Non-Christian Religions: calls for openness toward and cooperation with the major religions of the world.

Dogmatic Constitution on Divine Revelation: defines how Scripture and Tradition function as the primary expressions of Christian revelation; notable for its acceptance of up-to-date methods in Scripture study and in theology.

Decree on the Apostolate of Lay People: encourages the laity to live a spiritual life and to proclaim the gospel through family, work, and social action.

Declaration on Religious Liberty: argued that the basic dignity of human beings demands freedom from coercion in matters of religion. All people should be free to worship according to their own conscience.

Decree on the Church's Missionary Activity: stresses the importance of the missionary outreach of the church, particularly through the formation of community in local churches.

Decree on the Ministry and Life of Priests: clarifies the duties of priests and their relations with bishops and lay people.

Pastoral Constitution on the Church in the Modern World (*Gaudium et Spes*, "Joy and Hope"): portrays the church as being in service to the world; presents in particular the church's positions concerning family, culture, economics, politics, and peace.

The Relative Importance of the Documents

The above list is arranged simply in the order in which the documents were released. The question of which documents are the most important is a debatable matter.

Many theologians see *Lumen Gentium*, the Dogmatic Constitution on the Church, as the centerpiece of the council. It is in this document that the Catholic church articulates its own identity for the twentieth century. Many of the most important changes of the council can be found in it. Several of the other documents, such as the ones on Ecumenism, Non-Christian Religions, Bishops, Religious Life, Priests, Priestly Formation, and Laity, can be read as extensions of points made in *Lumen Gentium*.

Other theologians like to point out that one cannot have a full understanding of what Vatican II said about the church without studying *Gaudium et Spes*, the Pastoral Constitution on the Church in the Modern World. This is the great social justice document of the council and represents what many think is the most profound change from being a church in conflict with the world to being a church making a contribution to the world.

Yet other theologians will argue that the document on Revelation represents the most profound statement of the council. This document has implications for the most basic ways that Catholics think about the Christian message as it is communicated through Scripture and Tradition. It acknowledges the way that the expression of the church's teaching changes within the changing contexts of history. It affirms the Catholic openness to modern tools of biblical study and contemporary methods in theology.

Although few would claim that the document on Religious Liberty is the most important, it stands for many as the clearest symbol of change at Vatican II. The church reversed an earlier stand that encouraged Catholic countries to restrict the religious practices of others. The acknowledgment that people must follow their consciences in religious matters represents a profound growth with many possibilities for further development.

The document on Missionary Activity is a candidate for being the one most relevant to contemporary developments in the church. In recent years, the most important areas of renewal have centered around evangelization and the development of local faith communities.

The document on the Liturgy is notable for being the first one released. The changes in our understanding of sacraments set the initial pattern for later changes that were to come. The most obvious effects of the council in the early years had to do with changes in the liturgy, such as having the priest face the people and the use of local languages rather than Latin.

These documents continue to have a profound impact on the church. Virtually every document released in recent years by a pope, papal office, bishop, or bishops' conference can find a direct predecessor at Vatican II.

Lumen Gentium (Light of the Nations)

One of the reasons that a council needed to be called was to complete the unfinished agenda of Vatican I (1869–70). Vatican I had on the table a proposed document on the church that defined the duties of the pope and the bishops. This document reflected many juridical concerns about the distribution of power in the church. Segments of the document regarding the primacy and infallibility of the pope were passed. Before Vatican I could finalize the parts of the document dealing with bishops, however, the council was interrupted and then adjourned because of the Franco-Prussian war. The result was a tendency to emphasize the power of the pope to the neglect of the bishops, since the bishops' powers remained relatively undefined.

In retrospect, many Catholics are relieved that the full document on the church did not pass at Vatican I. If it had, official Catholic teaching about the church would today remain extremely traditional and conservative. The document put forth a vision of the church much less open than the vision of Vatican II. The language and concepts of the document reflected the defensive institutional focus of a church struggling to fight against Protestantism and secularism.

Some sense of the evolution of Vatican II's *Lumen Gentium* can be gained by examining the progress of its three major drafts. The first draft of the document on the church proposed at Vatican II was written by a highly traditional preparatory commission. It contained some very significant advances, but in many ways it had more in common theologically with the unpassed Vatican I document than it did with the final version of *Lumen Gentium*. Even from its chapter titles one can gain a sense of the archaic language and stark tone of the document:

First Draft, 1962

1. The nature of the church militant.

2. The members of the church and the necessity of the church for salvation.

3. The episcopate as the highest grade of the sacrament of orders; the priesthood.

4. Residential bishops.

5. The states of evangelical perfection.

6. The laity.

7. The teaching office (magisterium) of the church.

8. Authority and obedience in the church.

9. Relationship between church and State and religious tolerance.

10. The necessity of proclaiming the gospel to all peoples and in the whole world.

11. Ecumenism.

Appendix: "Virgin Mary, Mother of God and Mother of Men."[2]

In a famous address at the council, Bishop Emile De Smedt of Bruges denounced this first draft for its clericalism, juridicism, and triumphalism.[3] Clericalism is the attitude that grants too much emphasis to priests, bishops, and other clergy; juridicism is the attitude that focuses too much on the legal and the organizational; triumphalism is the attitude that focuses uncritically on one's achievements and potentials to the neglect of one's problems and need for growth. A new draft was called for that stressed more the call to holiness throughout all the people of the church, the mystery of the church in the plan of salvation, and the need for the church to tread the path of reform and renewal.

A second draft, written by a new commission set up by Pope John to represent traditional and progressive views equally, was put forward in 1963. It contained many of the sweeping changes that would characterize the third and final draft. The topics of chapters 9, 10, and 11 in the first draft were seen as so important as to call for separate documents on each (Religious Liberty, Missionary Activity, and Ecumenism). The strictly institutional concerns of chapters 3, 4, 7, and 8 in the first draft were collapsed into one segment and therefore received relatively less emphasis in the second draft. The term "People of God" emerged as a title of one segment addressing the laity. The call to holiness in the church received its own section. The second draft was organized as follows:

Second draft, 1963
Section 1:

I. The Mystery of the Church.

II. The hierarchical constitution of the church and the episcopate in particular.

Section 2:
   III. The people of God and the laity in particular.
   IV. The call to holiness in the church.[4]

The second draft was accompanied by a supplement that suggested that "the People of God" should become its own chapter. This change was accepted at once almost unanimously. This was extremely significant insofar as it signified a shift away from an emphasis on the hierarchical nature of the church to a new emphasis on the church as made up in a primary sense of all of its members. In the final version of *Lumen Gentium* the chapter on the People of God appeared second, right after the opening chapter that stressed the mysterious (more than juridical) nature of the church:

Final Version, 1964
1. The Mystery of the Church.
2. The People of God.
3. The Hierarchical Structure of the Church, with Special Reference to the Episcopate.
4. The Laity.
5. The Call of the Whole Church to Holiness.
6. Religious.
7. The Eschatological Nature of the Pilgrim Church and Her Union with the Heavenly Church.
8. The Role of the Blessed Virgin Mary, Mother of God, in the Mystery of Christ and the Church.

This final version of *Lumen Gentium* is helping to set the course of the church as it moves into the twenty-first century. The document's eight chapters provide the basic structure for the following twenty-four chapters of this book. For each chapter of *Lumen Gentium*, there are three chapters that discuss the document and explore related contemporary themes.

Gaudium et Spes (Joy and Hope)
The idea for fifteen out of sixteen of the documents of Vatican II originated in preparatory commissions. *Gaudium et Spes* is the one document that emerged directly out of discussion that took place on the floor of the council. On December 4, 1962, Cardinal Léon-Joseph Suenens urged that the council find a central vision that would articulate how the church conceived of its relation to the world of today. His remarks

were echoed the next day by Giovanni Battista Montini, who within the year would become Pope Paul VI.[5] Paul VI promoted the theme of human progress throughout his pontificate.

Much of the impetus for *Gaudium et Spes*, however, can be traced to Pope John XXIII. The central vision for which Suenens called had already been expressed in an initial way in John XXIII's opening address to the council. The actual text of *Gaudium et Spes* draws heavily upon John XXIII's social encyclicals, *Mater et Magistra* (Mother and Teacher, 1961) and *Pacem in Terris* (Peace on Earth, 1963). *Gaudium et Spes* maintains the basic posture associated with these encyclicals: Instead of simply proclaiming to the world how it should be run, it offers to the world the services of the church for contributing to dialogue and ongoing human progress.

Gaudium et Spes is in one sense a summation of the growing tradition of papal social teaching that finds its beginnings in Leo XIII's *Rerum Novarum* (On the Condition of Workers, 1891). This tradition has been continued in recent years by Paul VI in *Populorum Progressio* (On the Development of Peoples, 1967) and by John Paul II in *Laborem Exercens* (On Human Work, 1981), *Sollicitudo Rei Socialis* (On Social Concerns, 1987), and *Centesimus Annus* (On the Hundredth Anniversary [of *Rerum Novarum*], 1991).

Following a brief introduction, there are two major sections in *Gaudium et Spes*. Part one consists of four chapters that examine basic principles that underlying the relationship between the church and human progress. Part two consists of five chapters that address particular cultural and social issues:

Preface
Introductory Statement
Part One: The Church and Humankind's Calling
   1. The Dignity of the Human Person
   2. The Community of Humankind
   3. Humankind's Activity throughout the World
   4. The Role of the Church in the Modern World
Part Two: Some Problems of Special Urgency
   1. Fostering the Nobility of Marriage and the Family
   2. The Proper Development of Culture
   3. Economic and Social Life
   4. The Life of the Political Community
   5. The Fostering of Peace and the Promotion of a Community of Nations

Gaudium et Spes, by far the longest of the council's documents, attested to the importance of the tradition of Catholic social teaching and stamped a direction of openness and dialogue upon that teaching. The structure of the document provides the inspiration for the final nine chapters of this book. Part one gives rise to chapters 28–31; part two gives rise to chapters 32–36.

Summary

In this chapter we have taken an overview of the documents of Vatican II, focusing especially on the two major documents on the church. We have initiated a discussion concerning how Vatican II brought about many changes as it struggled to express faithfully the Catholic tradition. The next three chapters will take chapter one of *Lumen Gentium* as their basic point of departure as they explore contemporary issues facing the church today.

FOR FURTHER REFLECTION

1. Do you think of Vatican II more as a turning point in a "before and after" story, or more as a significant event in a long, continuous tradition?

2. If you could read only one of the sixteen documents of Vatican II, which one would you choose?

3. Why was it important for *Lumen Gentium* to focus on the church as a "mystery" and as the "People of God" rather than just as a structured organization?

4. In what ways have you been aware of the renewed stress in the Catholic church on social and political matters?

5. Is it time for Vatican III?

SUGGESTED READINGS

Albergio, Giuseppe, Jean-Pierre Jossua, and Joseph A. Komonchak, eds. *The Reception of Vatican II.* Washington, D.C.: The Catholic University of America Press, 1987.

Flannery, Austin, ed. *Vatican Council II: The Conciliar and Post-Conciliar Documents*. Northport, N.Y.: Costello Publishing Company, 1975. (This is one of several different editions of the Vatican II documents.)

Latourelle, René, ed. *Vatican II: Assessment and Perspectives*. Vol. 1. Mahwah, N.J.: Paulist Press, 1988.

O'Connell, Timothy E., ed. *Vatican II and Its Documents: An American Reappraisal*. Wilmington, Del.: Michael Glazier, 1986.

Stacpoole, Alberic, ed. *Vatican II: By Those Who Were There*. London: Geoffrey Chapman, 1986.

Vorgrimler, Herbert, ed. *Commentary on the Documents of Vatican II*. 5 Vols. New York: Herder and Herder, 1967–69.

PART TWO

LUMEN GENTIUM:
A NEW SELF-DEFINITION
FOR THE CHURCH

SECTION ONE

THE MYSTERY OF THE CHURCH

4. The Nature and Mission of the Church

5. God and the Church

6. The Symbolic Character of the Church

CHAPTER 4

THE NATURE AND MISSION OF THE CHURCH

D uring my college years I went through a period when I was apart from the church. For a time I was agnostic; for a time atheist; for a time I was interested in philosophies of the East as well as American transcendentalism. When I first came back to the church I was somewhat embarrassed and more than a little defensive. For a while I could hardly get into a conversation without trying to turn it into a debate about the Catholic church. My understanding of my own faith lacked depth, yet I still felt compelled to justify my return by arguing against anything that was not distinctly Catholic.

Today, after many years of study and trying to live my faith, I am much less defensive. My faith remains the single most important thing in my life. I am more inclined, however, to be open to other viewpoints and not perceive them as necessarily threatening my worldview. I am not only a member of the Catholic church, but I am also a participating citizen of a global society, and I look toward other points of view to enrich my own. This *doesn't* mean that I accept everything without hesitation or that there is no opinion that I would patently reject. It is just that my basic attitude has changed from one of being suspiciously disposed toward rejection of other stances to being appreciatively open toward them.

This Chapter
I think this change in my own life is a microcosmic reflection of the

growth in the Catholic church that had its high point at Vatican II. *Lumen Gentium*, the Dogmatic Constitution on the Church, signaled a shift in Catholic understanding of the church. This chapter will examine, first, an example of how the church was understood prior to Vatican II, and then several contemporary models of the church that offer alternative understandings.

This chapter is related to *Lumen Gentium* in two ways. First, it is an exploration of the nature and mission of the church as mentioned in the first paragraph of the document. Second, the models of the church discussed here are present throughout *Lumen Gentium* in various ways.

The Baltimore Catechism

Many Catholics in the United States received instruction from the Baltimore Catechism, a religious education text first published in 1884 and used extensively from 1910 through 1965. A catechism is a text that explains the basics of the Christian faith in question and answer form. "Who made us?" asks the Baltimore Catechism. "God made us" is the response that it gives. "Who is God?" asks the next question. "God is the Supreme Being, infinitely perfect, who made all things and keeps them in existence," we are told. The Baltimore Catechism has major sections on beliefs, commandments, and sacraments.

Martin Luther, the Protestant reformer, had published the first catechism in Germany in 1529 in order to help put the faith into the hands of the common people. Many Catholic catechisms followed in response, such as the one by Peter Canisius in 1555, the Catechism of the Council of Trent (known as the Roman Catechism) in 1566, and the catechism of Robert Bellarmine issued in 1599.

The period in which these first Catholic catechisms appeared is known as the Counter-Reformation. This period and the texts it spawned reflect a diametric opposition to anything Protestant. Many of the early Catholic catechisms told one as much about how not to be a Protestant as how to be a Catholic. The same is true in reverse of the Protestant versions.

The Baltimore Catechism is a direct descendant of these Counter-Reformation texts. One of its main purposes was the preservation of the Catholic faith in the United States, a Protestant country with a secular school system. While one could find without much difficulty a reasonable account of the truth of the Christian faith in the Baltimore Catechism, it was marred by an air of defensiveness and a disproportionate treatment of issues. For example, there are several pages of questions and answers concerning which church is the one, true church within which one could be assured of eternal salvation. There is little, however, on the life and teaching of Jesus. The resurrection, which St. Paul calls the foundation of our faith, receives but one short question and answer. This is because the resurrection was not an issue of major debate during the Counter-Reformation, whereas the questions of how one is saved and to which church one must belong were hotly disputed.

The defensive stance of the Baltimore Catechism reflects something of the theological and pastoral climate of the church in the pre-Vatican II period. It was a church concerned with maintaining internal unity and sacramental integrity, while casting suspicious and sometimes hostile glances toward outsiders who did not accept the Catholic faith.

Models of the Church

An air of openness in inquiry characterizes the documents of Vatican II. *Lumen Gentium* states its own purpose as unfolding the "inner nature and universal mission" of the church (*LG*, 1). The document did not simply present the church as a monolithic institution established by God for the salvation of its members; several models and images of the church were put forward. In his now classic work, *Models of the Church,* Avery Dulles explored several of the underlying guiding concepts of church in contemporary Catholic theology.[1] Each of these models finds significant support in the Vatican II documents. Dulles discussed the following five overlapping models, each with its own distinct nature and mission.

Dulles's Models of the Church		
Nature		Mission
institution	—>	offer salvation to members
mystical communion	—>	provide spiritual support
sacrament	—>	make Christ present
herald	—>	preach the gospel
servant	—>	transform society

The *institution* model, as Dulles characterized it in the original version of his book, is the view that makes primary the institutional elements of the church, such as offices, doctrines, laws, and ritual forms. The people, their relationship with God, the Scriptures, and justice issues become subordinate. This model, then, unlike the other four, is by definition a limited starting point. Dulles states that any of the models could be a good starting basis for one's view of church, except this one. He does add, though, that whatever one's model of church, one needs to incorporate and appreciate the institutional elements.

In a chapter added to a later edition of his book, Dulles admits that he was somewhat too severe in his portrayal of the institution model. He stills holds that institutional structures should not be taken as primary, but he adds that some of the problems with the institution model could be overcome if one thinks not simply in sociological terms but in terms of "what God 'instituted' in Christ" (p. 205). In other words, there are ways of thinking of the church as basically an institution without pitting the structural elements over against the people and their spirituality. This clarification is important because the institution model is the one most directly associated with pre-Vatican II views of the church.

The *mystical communion* model places its emphasis on the people who make up the church and their connectedness with each other and with God. This model, while not necessarily rejecting institutional elements, places more stress upon spirituality, community, and fellowship. The church in this view is something of a spiritual support group that aids people in their quest to live holy lives.

Dulles associates two images with this model, the Body of Christ and the People of God. These images, although they can be harmonized, stand in conflict with each other in contemporary theological debates. Both functioned prominently at Vatican II as images for church renewal. The Body of Christ image is often used today to support a strong role for the hierarchy as the particular "member" that functions in the place of Christ as the "head" of the body. The People of God image tends to be favored by those who push for continuing reform in the church by granting larger roles in ministry and decision making to women and to lay people.

The *sacrament* model is the view that focuses on the church as the continuing presence of Christ in the world. Sacrament is understood as a way of making a sacred reality present and active. As Christ can be thought of as the sacrament of God, so the church can be thought of as the sacrament of Christ.

Dulles sees the sacrament model as especially useful in that it reconciles elements that were in tension in the previous models. The institution model stresses the visible organization to the neglect of the spiritual; the mystical communion model can leave one wondering why a visible organization is necessary at all. The sacrament model explains how visible realities mediate invisible realities. A thing or word or gesture that is present can make available something that is otherwise not present.

The sacrament model also allows the believer to maintain a critical distance from the symbols themselves. The church is the sacrament of Christ, but the church must also be clearly distinguished from Christ. The sacraments make real the saving action of Christ, but the forms and words are not the reality. The sacrament model is the most theoretical of the models. As Dulles points out, it is the most useful model for theologians, but the most difficult one for anyone else to understand.

The *herald* model emphasizes the primacy of the Bible. The church consists of those who hear the word and are converted. The mission of the church is to preach the word to the ends of the earth.

Those who accept the primacy of Scripture over all other forms of tradition and authority are known as evangelical Christians. Many evangelical Christians are also fundamentalists who interpret the Scriptures as historical fact that is inerrant in every way. There are some evangelicals, however, who insist on the primacy of Scripture while accepting basic historical-critical approaches to it. Rudolf Bultmann, for example, is a famous liberal Protestant whose existential methods of interpreting the Scriptures fit with the evangelical herald model yet are not fundamentalist.

The herald model, more than any of the other models, can be directly associated with Protestantism. Karl Barth, the great twentieth-century evangelical theologian, exemplified the herald model when, drawing upon the thought of Martin Luther, he distinguished between a theology of glory and a theology of the cross. A church that proclaims its own glory is working counter to the gospel; the task of the church is to point humbly away from itself toward its Lord and Redeemer. Hans Küng, a Catholic theologian who has been censured by the Vatican, takes a similar position when he emphasizes that the church is not the kingdom of God but rather its proclaimer or herald. The official Catholic position, in contrast, holds that the church is the seed of the kingdom but not the fullness of the kingdom.

When Dulles wrote *Models of the Church* in 1974 he was able to comment accurately that those who subscribe to some form of the herald model tend not to be politically engaged. This situation changed dramatically in the United States in the 1980s, when evangelicals in great numbers turned their efforts toward political reform. In 1989, evangelical leader Jerry Falwell disbanded his political group, the Moral Majority, proclaiming that the organization had accomplished its objective of making evangelical Christians politically involved. Evangelical Christians were prominently involved in the social and political movements that supported the Reagan and Bush presidencies. Though most evangelical Christians have been strongly conservative, not all are. The magazine *Sojourners* represents the voice of evangelical Christians who are committed to more radical social change.

The *servant* model emphasizes the need for the church to be engaged in social transformation. If traditionally the church had been presented as a refuge from a world of vice and temptation, this model presents a church that should be at the service of a world that is basically good. Members of the church are seen as part of the larger human family. God is known not simply through the church but also through human experience and the things of this world. Culture and science are recognized as having their own legitimate autonomy apart from the dominance of the church.

Dulles links this last model both with Vatican II's Pastoral Constitution on the Church in the Modern World and with the pioneering work of Pierre Teilhard de Chardin. Chardin, a Jesuit priest as well as a paleontologist, is best known for his attempt to reconcile evolutionary theory with Christianity. He envisioned the church as a progressive society intended to function as the spearhead of evolution. The Pastoral Constitution on the Church in the Modern World incorporated some of Chardin's basic themes by affirming the importance of Catholics working together with people of various backgrounds for the betterment of the human community.

The most striking contemporary example of a servant model today can be found in the liberation theology being developed in Latin America. The original edition of *Models of the Church* had but one scant allusion to this then young phenomenon; the added chapter in the expanded edition has a more substantial reference. In the thirteen years between the editions, liberation theology exploded onto the world scene. Gustavo Gutierrez's *A Theology of Liberation* [English version 1973; Spanish original 1971] is a now a classic text. Liberation theology begins with the experience of political, social, and economic oppression of the people of Latin America. It exemplifies a version of the servant model in that it places a strong emphasis on the need for the church to be involved in social change. It differs from other forms of the servant model, however, in that it does not begin with an optimistic view of the basic goodness of human beings and of human progress. Instead, it focuses on the structures of sin that seem to dominate human affairs.

These five models—institution, mystical communion, sacrament, herald, and servant—formed the basis of Dulles's original text. *Models of the Church* was an important book in that it made clear that Catholics have several legitimate starting points for thinking about the church. In the first decade after Vatican II, most Catholics not only still operated out of some form of institution model, but did not know that other visions that reflected the council were available. These models were also useful for labeling some of the issues that might otherwise have polarized the church. Instead of simply arguing back and forth about conceptions of the church, with no resolution in sight, many Catholics were relieved to find that there may be many acceptable views. Today the models remain an important tool for helping Catholics who wish to examine where they themselves stand.

Community of Disciples

In the expanded edition of *Models of the Church*, Dulles added a new category, the *community of disciples* model. He took the phrase from a passing comment made by Pope John Paul II in his first encyclical, *Redemptor Hominis* (1979). The community of disciples is not just another model to be added to the others, but a more inclusive model intended to integrate what is best in the other five. Dulles says that it is in a sense a version of the mystical communion model, but without the tendency to be satisfied with internal mutual support. Rather, this model focuses on discipleship. What does it mean to follow the Lord and to carry out the implications of this seriously in one's life? This model is intended to illuminate the purposes of the institutional structures and the sacramental aspects of the church, and to ground the missionary thrust toward evangelization and social transformation.

Dulles calls the community of disciples a "contrast community" in that it socializes people into choosing higher values in the face of a secularized society that promotes pleasure, wealth, and power. A stress is placed on the formation of Christians in communities small enough to foster networks of close interpersonal relationships that will shape the attitudes and feelings of the members. Christian formation should take place within communities that can invoke the memory of Jesus together with the twelve apostles. Such communities will be filled not with alienated or merely communal Catholics but with those who are truly committed to evangelization and service.

Critical questions can be raised about this model. Are the only good Christians the ones who center their lives around the church? Do people go through different stages in their life, some of which often legitimately entail alienation from the church? Are Catholics to turn their backs on the good dimensions of the secular world just a few decades after Vatican II recognized them?

Dulles himself argues that some tension between church and world seems inevitable. Although he is a pioneer in offering Catholics various options that have emerged from Vatican II, Dulles is now taking a strong stand that although there may be a legitimate pluralism of starting points and styles, not just anything goes if one is to talk in a comprehensive sense about the nature and mission of the church. The community of disciples model is therefore not just another option, but an attempt at a higher synthesis of the best elements of the earlier models.

Summary

In this chapter we have considered how the church appeared in the pre-Vatican II Baltimore Catechism, and then examined several models of the church that serve as optional starting points for constructing a more contemporary view. On the whole, the Catholic church has grown less defensive and more open over the years. The challenge today is to find ways to appreciate and maintain our distinctive identity in a world that takes pluralism for granted and that seems inclined to reduce everything to a common denominator.

In the next chapter we will discuss ways in which the church is linked with and yet quite distinct from God.

FOR FURTHER REFLECTION

1. Have you ever met anyone who seemed defensive about their religion?

2. What types of textbooks were used in your own childhood religious education? What models of the church did these texts reflect?

3. Which of the models of the church discussed holds the most appeal for you? Which holds the least appeal?

4. How would you construct your own model of the church?

5. Should the church raise its standards for membership, or should the church include people at various levels of participation and even non-participation?

SUGGESTED READINGS

Dulles, Avery. *Models of the Church*. Expanded edition. Garden City, N.Y.: Image Books, [original 1974], 1987.

Baltimore Catechism. New York: Benzinger Brothers. Original 1884 with various revisions and editions over the years.

CHAPTER 5

GOD AND THE CHURCH

W hen I was a small child in Philadelphia in the 1950s, I grew up in Holy Mother Church. That was not the name of my parish; it was the way I was socialized into thinking of the church itself. The church was not just a building, nor was it the congregation, any combination of congregations, or even the hierarchy. The church was the whole array of everything that was associated in any way with my religion. The church was the Bible, the Creed, the sacraments, the commandments, salvation, and, above all, God. To be in church was to be in the House of God. To disagree with the church was to disagree with God. To leave the church was to abandon God.

Many Catholics today are fond of pointing out that the church is not God. And how right they are! The church is *not* God, and anyone who thinks that it is is making a big mistake.

And yet I cannot help but wonder if some contemporary Catholics might not emphasize this crucial point with just a bit too much zeal. Just as many Catholics failed to distinguish adequately between the church and God before Vatican II, some Catholics today seem hard pressed to see the connection.

This Chapter

This chapter will first examine the link between church and God, then the relationship between church and kingdom in the teaching of Jesus, and finally the importance of both distinguishing and connecting God and the church. In chapter 1 of *Lumen Gentium*, sections 2, 3, and 4 address the links between God, church, and kingdom. Section 8 speaks of the intermingling of human and divine elements in the church.

Making the Connection

The title *Lumen Gentium*, "Light of the Peoples," applies directly to Christ. A close reading of section 1 of the document reveals this. The church is *lumen gentium* to the extent that the light of Christ "is brightly visible on the countenance of the church." That is, the light that the church has to offer is not, strictly speaking, of itself, but is rather a reflection of Christ shining through it. So, right from the beginning, *Lumen Gentium* lays solid grounds for distinguishing between the church and Christ, and thus between the church and God.

This important distinction, however, should not obscure the main thrust of the opening sections, which is to highlight the connections between God and the church. Section 1 emphasizes that since the light of Christ is brightly visible on the countenance of the church, the church itself is of the nature of a sacrament, "a sign and instrument both of a very closely knit union with God and of the unity of the whole human race." To call the church itself a sacrament is to link it with God. A sacrament, as Avery Dulles points out, "is more than just a sign. It betokens the actual presence, in a hidden way, of that to which it points."[1]

Sections 2, 3, and 4 address respectively the connections between the church and the Father, the Son, and the Holy Spirit. These sections place the church within the context of the Christian story. The church is part of the mysterious plan of the Father; the church is the kingdom of God present in mystery that was inaugurated by the Son; the church is kept continually fresh and sanctified by the Holy Spirit. There is no attempt in these sections, nor should there be, to distinguish between the literal and the symbolic, between images and realities. The point is to situate the church within the cosmic/historical dimensions of the Christian story in a simple manner that allows people of various levels of sophistication to enter into the story on their own terms.

God and the Church		
Father	—>	church in plan of salvation
Son	—>	inaugurates kingdom/church
Holy Spirit	—>	keeps church fresh and holy

These points are of tremendous significance, because one of the great Catholic insights has been the importance of the connection between the church and God. The French philosopher Albert Camus has said that the world is absurd because the human heart cries out for meaning but the universe gives no response. Catholics have claimed throughout their history that God has given us a response through Christ, and that Christ can be encountered through the church, which is informed by the Holy Spirit.

Preaching the Kingdom, Founding the Church

The way *Lumen Gentium* draws out the relationship between the church and the kingdom of God further highlights the church's connection with God. Prior to Vatican II, such church documents as Pius XII's 1943 encyclical *Mystici Corporis*, as well as the writings of many theologians, identified the church with the kingdom of God. There was no distinction whatever between the kingdom of God that was the central focus of the teaching of Jesus and the church that Jesus founded. As sophisticated a scholar as Yves Congar, a French theologian whose work helped lead to Vatican II, could quote Jesus talking about the kingdom and go on to explain what point Jesus was making about the church. When Catholics were taught that Jesus founded the church, the implication was that Jesus intentionally envisioned the institution of the Catholic church with its offices and its seven sacraments.

Such beliefs about Jesus' explicit intentions are difficult to justify today in the light of scriptural scholarship. What Jesus meant by the kingdom of God seems broader and more inclusive than any concept of an organized church. Also, while it is defensible to claim that the church that emerged is continuous with the community that Jesus founded, Catholics have acknowledged that much of what has developed as Catholicism over the centuries, though guided by the Spirit, cannot in its complete structure be literally traced back to an explicit intention of Jesus.

Lumen Gentium itself clearly operates with a distinction between the church and the kingdom. The church is not the "completed kingdom" but is rather "the initial budding forth of the kingdom" (*LG*, 5). The kingdom is not finally established but it has been "inaugurated." Some scholars, such as Hans Küng, have focused emphatically on this distinction between the church and the kingdom. Küng has gone so far as to portray the church not as embodying the kingdom, but rather as simply being its proclaimer or herald. The intention of *Lumen Gentium*, however, is to highlight the connection between the church and the kingdom at the same time that it acknowledges the distinction between the two. The church is not the fullness of the kingdom, pure and simple, but the church *is* the seed of the kingdom, which is now present in mystery.

Some Christians are out and out anti-institutional in their approach to church. They see the church as counter to the kingdom and think that each individual must relate to God on his or her own through prayer and Scripture reading. Such a position is completely foreign to the Catholic mindset that stresses the social and communal context that makes the fruitful lives of individuals possible. For the Catholic, there is no such thing as Christianity without church.

Importance of the Distinction

Before exploring why the connection between church and God is so important, it will be helpful to examine why it is also important to distinguish between the two. First of all, when God is exclusively connected with church there may be a tendency to underemphasize or ignore the experience of God that is available in the everyday lives of people. Christ is present not only in church, but can be encountered in peak moments in our lives, in deep relationships, in the midst of our suffering, and in the face of the poor and those in need.

Reasons for the Distinction between Church and God
•emphasize God's presence in our daily lives   •appreciate people of other faiths   •retain ability to be critically-minded

Second, identifying God exclusively with the church can hamper one's ability to appreciate the richness of other religious traditions and their ability to mediate that which is ultimate to their participants. Is the Holy Spirit at work within the devout Hindu, Buddhist, Jew, Moslem? Most Catholic theologians today would encourage an affirmative answer.

A third danger is that one might come to worship the church as equivalent to God. It is important to be aware that the church itself is on a journey that is not yet finished. The church is not perfect. It can make mistakes. God is greater than the church, and so it is important that one develop a critical ability to assess whether the church is truly representing the will of God in particular cases.

Importance of the Connection

While it is important to recognize that the church is in one respect the imperfect human *receiver* of what God has revealed to Christians, in another respect the church itself is *part* of that revelation. In other words, Catholics believe that the church is not simply an organization that human beings decided to make up, but rather is part of the divine plan that was instituted by Christ and is sustained by the Holy Spirit.

Lumen Gentium stresses that the church is made up of a human element and a divine element:

> . . . the society structured with hierarchical organs and the Mystical Body of Christ, are not to be considered as two realities, nor are the visible assembly and the spiritual community, nor the earthly church and the church enriched with heavenly things; rather they form one complex reality that coalesces from a divine and a human element. For this reason, by no weak analogy, it is compared to the mystery of the incarnate Word. (LG,8)

Many Catholics today, however, have a hard time seeing the divine element in the church. *Lumen Gentium* teaches clearly that indeed the church that Christ founded subsists within the Catholic church.

Why is this a difficult teaching for some Catholics today? Catholics today are still in a transitional period from a time when the church could hardly be questioned at all to a time when the church is more open to criticism. For now it sometimes seems that the church is being suspiciously questioned about everything. We have yet to achieve a balance. Catholics still take seriously the popular pre-Vatican II belief that the church must be perfect in every way in order to represent God. Only now the tables are turned: Because the church is not perfect in every way, many people feel that it really does not represent God at all.

Alienation from the church among some Catholics is intensified today because of the range of issues on which devout people disagree: from birth control to legalized abortion to pre-marital sex to priestly celibacy to women's ordination to participation in decision making to the question of dissent itself. For many Catholics, the official Catholic positions on these sex, gender, and autonomy issues place the church's very credibility in question. This is compounded by the fact that many Catholics today, perhaps especially the alienated, still operate out of some version of what Avery Dulles called the institution model.

Dulles's *Models of the Church* can help us to realize that recognizing the divine dimension of the church does not necessarily lead one to a narrow institutional view. The church is the Mystical Body of Christ made available for our sanctification; the church is the sacrament that makes Christ explicitly present in our world; the church is the proclamation of the divine word that leads to conversion; the church is the beginning of the kingdom that is experienced whenever oppressions are overcome and human relationships are set right. The church has to do with God, and one who would call oneself Catholic must come to grips with that claim.

After the exciting yet tumultuous decades since Vatican II, many Catholics are coming to realize that a fundamental trust in and loyalty to the church are not incompatible with being critically-minded and working for positive change. The church is to be treasured as a gift from God that makes possible our growth in holiness both individually and socially. God is not limited to the church; for Catholics, however, it is through the church that God comes to us most explicitly and thus helps us be attuned to the presence of the divine in the midst of our everyday lives.

Historically, Protestants have labeled idolatrous the Catholic tendency to associate the church too closely with God. Idolatry is putting something less than God in the place of God. Catholics have at times been guilty of making the church into an idol. I wonder, however, what the opposite of idolatry might be called? How might we label the inability to recognize the divine when God is present? And yet the Protestant critique must be taken seriously. The church's sometimes all-too-human side is not to be ignored.

The community-oriented, sacramental, word-inspired, servant church is supported by certain institutional structures that Catholics have regarded as essential elements. As a Catholic I experience God here, and I trust that in the long run the Holy Spirit will help the leadership of the church be competent and responsible. I personally find myself disagreeing less with current church leaders than many other Catholics that I know; however, disagreement over a few issues or even over a whole range of important issues should not in itself necessarily make a person feel alienated from the church. We Catholics have a lot of issues to work out in the coming years; it will be important to have a charitable, forgiving, and persevering attitude reigning among us as we do, and to believe that God will remain present in our midst.

Church and Eucharist

I most experience the connection of the church with God when I receive communion. At Mass I am aware of being gathered with my fellow Christians to worship God. We have all brought with us the warp and woof of our daily lives to offer at the altar. We are celebrating the depth of meaning that we encounter in the everyday. We are in the presence of Christ, reflecting on our triumphs and our failures, on the love that we give and receive and on the sins that we commit. As I make my way up to the altar I know that Christ is there for me and that as I accept him into my own body Christ has accepted me.

The church in this context is most basically the people assembled at the Eucharist for the praise and glory of God. We are the body of Christ, with Christ present as our head. We are the communion of saints, sharing the same love of God that sustains the people of God throughout the world and including those who have gone before us in death and are now with God. We are the hearers of the Word, who place the will of God above all things. We are the doers of the Word, who carry away with us a sense of mission for bringing about a better world.

Summary

In this chapter we have discussed the importance of seeing the connection between God and the church, as well as the importance of distinguishing between the two. To do one without the other is to miss something essential to the Catholic tradition. Catholics need to find the balance between the "Holy Mother Church" of the 1950s and the contemporary tendency to overlook the divine element in the church.

In the next chapter we will explore the value of myth and symbol as tools for coming to appreciate the reality of church.

FOR FURTHER REFLECTION

1. Have you ever known anyone who seemed to treat the church as if it were God?

2. Why is it important to distinguish between the church and God?

3. In what ways do you experience the church as being linked with God?

4. What does it mean to say that Jesus founded the church? What doesn't it mean?

5. What do you think of when you hear the phrase, "kingdom of God?"

SUGGESTED READINGS

Boff, Leonardo. *Ecclesiogenesis*. Maryknoll, N.Y.: Orbis Books, 1986 [1977]. Chapter 5, pp. 45-60.

Küng, Hans. *The Church*. Garden City, N.Y.: Doubleday, 1967. Part B, pp. 67-144.

Lohfink, Gerhard. *Jesus and Community*. Philadelphia and Mahwah, N.J.: Fortress Press and Paulist Press, 1984.

Ratzinger, Joseph. *The Ratzinger Report*. With Vittorio Messori. San Francisco: Ignatius Press, 1985. Chapter 3, pp. 45-53.

CHAPTER 6

THE SYMBOLIC CHARACTER OF THE CHURCH

A student of mine was having trouble selecting a topic for his term project. In a discussion with him, I discovered that although he had been raised a Catholic and until recently had been very involved in his faith, he now could muster little interest in religion. He explained that in his religion course of the previous semester his teacher had pointed out that the great majority of things he had believed to be true were merely myths. In fact, the student was very upset that he had been lied to about this throughout grade school and high school.

In addition to suggesting to him that perhaps he did not hear all that the teacher had been trying to say on the subject, I recommended that he investigate the topic of the meaning and truth of myths. He agreed readily to this and we worked out a reading list of several articles.

The results were dramatic. The student not only did a good job of reporting back on the readings and relating them to each other, but he had integrated the material well into his own view of things. He talked about the value of myth in structuring a meaningful view of the world and about the new appreciation he had of his own religion when he could interpret it in mythic terms. He had a new sense of attraction to his church community because he felt liberated by his new key of mythic awareness. He recognized that Christianity has historical roots and that these roots are important. He concluded that he still has a good deal of sorting out to do concerning where history ends and where myth begins.

This Chapter

In this chapter we will explore the symbolic and mythic dimensions of religion, religious language, the sacraments, and the church. This chapter draws upon sections 6 and 7 of chapter 1 of *Lumen Gentium*, which offer various images and symbols drawn from Scripture to express the mystery of the church.

Religion as Symbol System

Anthropologists have given us a point of view from which to appreciate religions as systems of symbols. Now famous in scholarly circles is Clifford Geertz's 1968 definition of "religion" as "a system of symbols which act to establish powerful, pervasive, and long-lasting moods and motivations in men, by formulating conceptions of a general order of existence and clothing these conceptions with such an aura of factuality that the moods and motivations seem uniquely realistic."[1] This valuable definition reflects the point of view not of a believing theologian but rather of a social scientist seeking that type of objectivity available to the outside observer. Most believers would think that their beliefs are *true*, rather than settle for saying that the effect of the symbols is so powerful as to clothe them with an aura of factuality.

But the perspective of the social scientist is valuable not just for other scientists but for believers as well. On one level of analysis a religion *is* a system of symbols, and needs to be understood as such. Believers who deny the symbolic content of their religion risk being one-dimensional, literalist, or rejecting of other faiths. Moreover, religious symbols do have a powerful and long-lasting effect upon believers. Although religious persons want to be careful not to ignore the claims to truth made within their own religion, they want also to appreciate how the symbolic nature of their religion allows them to bear deep and forceful meanings with the potential to transform their lives in positive ways.

Joseph Campbell explored the symbolic nature of religion in a six-part public television series hosted by Bill Moyers. This popular and well-received program and its accompanying book were both called *The Power of Myth*. Although Campbell admits that truth claims have their importance, he is not himself personally interested in maintaining the systematic truth claims associated with any particular religion. In fact, he tends to see truth and fact claims as often getting in the way of allowing symbols and myths to do their job. Campbell describes myths as "clues to the spiritual potentialities of the human life." He advises us: "Read myths. They teach you that you can turn inward, and you begin to get the message of the symbols. Read other people's myths, not those of your own religion, because you tend to interpret your own religion in terms of facts—but if you read the other ones, you begin to get the message. Myth helps you to put your mind in touch with the experience of being alive."[2]

Campbell's advice is controversial to say the least. He can be challenged on several points. First, does not the question of the usefulness of a particular faith (not to mention the truth of it) depend upon factors other than simply the question of whether the religion is one's own or not? And is not a person's own religion usually a most suitable context for genuine religious experience? Second, is not the purpose of religion at least as much to draw one outside of oneself as to turn one inward? That is, should not one's faith lead one to develop deeper human relationships and to work for a more just society, not simply the inner experience of being alive? Third, is it not possible to think of fact and myth in ways that are not so dichotomous? That is, Campbell operates as though the two are mutually exclusive, yet in Christianity as well as in some other religions the interrelationship between fact and myth is much more complex.

Campbell's advice is more provocative than precise or accurate. Yet his basic message, that myth puts one's mind in touch with the experience of being alive, is worth savoring. What good is a religion if it does not on some level turn you on? If this were Campbell's only true point, he would still be worth listening to, because the point is that important. Of course, however, the wealth of Campbell's work goes far beyond this single message.

Symbols

What Campbell says about myth can give us a starting point for explaining the meaning of "symbol." A symbol is something that puts one in touch with a reality that would be otherwise out of reach. Money is a good example of a symbol. It is more than a coin or a piece of paper or an account balance. Money is symbolic in that it functionally represents stored and measured economic power. We can distinguish between the economic power and the pieces of paper, yet very few of us would nonchalantly tear up twenty-dollar bills because they are merely paper. Money takes on the reality of that which it represents. It might not have any value at all in a primitive society cut off from the larger world, but for one who participates in that larger world the reality of national currencies is beyond question.

Like other religions, Christianity abounds in symbols. The cross, the

Madonna, the water of baptism, the dove, all are symbolic of various aspects of the Christian faith. Such symbols do not have simply one direct referent, but multiple layers of meaning. The cross represents first and foremost the cross on which Christ died. It also represents, however, the suffering of all people, our own personal suffering, the things in our lives that are difficult to bear, the expectancy that each of us will die some day, and the call to strive for justice and charity no matter where the path leads us. The particular meanings that the cross takes on for people are as varied and as personal as the difficulties people experience in their lives.

The dove is also such a symbol. On one level, it represents the Holy Spirit who descended on Jesus at his baptism. On other levels, the dove represents the inner peace or serenity of one who is filled with the Spirit, the innocence of one who is newly baptized, and the freedom of the Christian's spirit to soar through the heavens. Most Christians do not thoroughly analyze or even consciously reflect upon the various levels of meaning of most symbols that they encounter, yet by living within the tradition within which these symbols take on their meaning, Christians become deeply familiar with the richness of these symbols.

The Symbolic Nature of Sacraments

The seven Catholic sacraments are symbolic in nature. Catholics have traditionally believed that sacraments are effective signs. To say that they are "effective" is to say that they make something happen. To say that they are "signs" is to say that they represent things beyond themselves that are already happening. Baptism is effective in that it makes someone fully part of the Christian community. Yet baptism is a sign of something that is already happening; it would make no sense to baptize a person who was not in a real way being socialized into the community.

The same pattern is true of the sacrament of reconciliation. The sacrament is effective in that through it one receives the forgiveness of one's sins. Yet reconciliation is also a sign in that it celebrates the forgiveness that one is already experiencing from God and from the community.

Catholics strive to achieve a balance between the "effective" nature of sacraments and the "sign" nature of sacraments. To overemphasize the "effective" nature entails the danger of understanding sacraments as presto-chango magic tricks that simply make things happen without reference to real life events (for example, "Of course we have a good marriage—the ceremony was performed properly and legally."). To overemphasize the "sign" nature of sacraments entails the danger of seeing the sacraments as superfluous because they are simply representations of things that are happening well enough anyway ("Why should we bother to get married? What difference does a piece of paper make if we really love each other?"). The Catholic tradition tries to emphasize both dimensions at the same time. Getting married makes a world of difference. The quality of a marriage must be understood as involving much more than a ceremony or a piece of paper.

The Symbolic Nature of Religious Language

Not only are religious traditions filled with many symbols, but the nature of religious language is also symbolic. In a way all language is symbolic, for words are themselves symbols in that they represent realities beyond themselves. The word "table" is not a table, but simply represents a table. Yet when we speak of "symbolic language" we mean something more than this. We are referring to language that goes beyond a simple one-to-one literal correspondence between word and referent.

The language of fiction and poetry is symbolic in this way. Stories and poems can travel simultaneously on various levels of meaning. On one level Albert Camus's *The Plague* is the story of when the bubonic plague hits a city in northern Africa. On another level it is metaphorically a story about World War II and Western civilization. On yet another level it is metaphorically a story about the universal plight of human beings in the face of terrible and seemingly senseless suffering.

Religious language is symbolic. Religious language tries to express dimensions of reality that cannot be expressed in a clear, literal fashion. The particular dimension of reality that religious language tries to express can be called "the ultimate." Religious language deals with the meaning of life, the point of it all, the highest values, God, human relationships, basic life orientations, human growth and development, the deepest levels of self-awareness and self-acceptance.

I know a woman whose role as a pastoral minister often leads her to deal with people in crisis situations, sometimes involving matters of life and death. She shared with me the story of how fifteen years ago her four-year-old daughter suddenly took ill and died. For years she struggled with the question, "Why did God permit this to happen? All things happen for a reason. What meaning did God intend for this to have in my life?" Fifteen years after the event she now says that her experience of suffering has enabled her to enter into the pain of those with whom she ministers. Without the tragic event of her daughter's death she believes she would not be familiar with the depths of meaning that she now needs to navigate on a routine basis in her life's work.

When this woman is telling this story from her life she is using symbolic, religious language. I do not think that she literally believes that God directly intended for her child to die in order to make her a better minister; "God's intention" functions symbolically for her. She knows well that the mysterious ways of God are beyond human comprehension. But she is able to tell a story that grapples with the ultimate meaning of things and why they happen. She is able, through the use of language that is not to be understood in an overly literal fashion, to come to terms with significant life events by relating them to matters of ultimate meaning and purpose. Understood properly her story is a "true" one in that it expresses in a real way her personal integration of her life experiences in terms of her relationship with God and her fruitful life's work.

The Church as Symbol within the Context of the Christian Story

In the Baltimore Catechism, in a definition that hearkened back to the catechisms of the sixteenth century, the church was said to be "the congregation of all baptized persons, united in the same true faith, the same sacrifice, and the same sacraments, under the authority of the Sovereign Pontiff and the bishops in communion with him." This particular definition was aimed more at emphasizing that Protestants and others are not members, than it was at clarifying what the nature of the church is. The defensively institutional nature of the definition is perhaps understandable, because it stems from a time when the institution's very existence was perceived to be gravely threatened. The definition, however, explains little to me about what the church is. If I were not already Catholic, it would say little to inspire me to join it.

Rather than offering a clear definition of the church, the first chapter of *Lumen Gentium* speaks of the church symbolically within the context of the Christian story. The first part of the chapter tells the story of how the church is part of the eternal plan of the Father, how it was inaugurated by the Son, and how it is sustained by the Spirit. When the document focuses on the church itself, it relies upon images drawn from the Scriptures. As *Lumen Gentium* tells us:

In the Old Testament the revelation of the kingdom is often conveyed by means of metaphors. In the same way the inner nature of the church is now made known to us in different images taken either from tending sheep or cultivating the land, from building or even from family life and betrothals. (*LG*, 6)

Some Christians might find the selection of images to be overly passive in what they imply about the role of the members. The church is God's sheepfold, God's tillage, God's building, God's fishing net, Christ's bride. We are thereby sheep, earth, stones, fish, traditional brides. It should be kept in mind, however, that when speaking of the church in a mystical sense, it is appropriate to emphasize that it is, above all, a work of God. The church is a glorious gift from God to us. Later chapters in *Lumen Gentium* highlight more dynamic, community-oriented images, such as the People of God, the Pilgrim Church, and the Communion of Saints.

The final image explored in chapter one of *Lumen Gentium* is that of the Body of Christ. The Body of Christ is itself an active and community-oriented image. It is used in several places in the New Testament, from Jesus' "This is my body," to the famous passages in 1 Corinthians, Colossians, and Ephesians. The Body of Christ has been one of the most important images of the church in the twentieth century. It was used by Pius XII in his 1943 encyclical *Mystici Corporis* as a way of getting beyond more legalistic, bureaucratic, and mundane concepts of church to a concept that connects the church with Christ and makes clear the spiritual character of its nature and mission.

When I think of the church as the Body of Christ, I think of myself as a member of that Body related to other members. Each member has an important role to play. We share an equality in spiritual dignity. We are all interconnected with one another. The joy of others is my joy, their sorrow, my sorrow. We celebrate with one another, and our sharing in the same sacraments symbolizes our partaking in the same love of God. Christ is our head, which means that as human beings we seek first the will of God and the coming of the kingdom in a way that complements our autonomy.

In contrast to the definition of church in the Baltimore Catechism, the Body of Christ is an image that captures my imagination and my spirit. What does this image imply, however, for how I relate with other people who are not explicitly members of the Body of Christ? There are many solutions proposed by contemporary theologians to the problem of religious pluralism. Personally, I interpret the Body of Christ image in a way that does not contradict but, rather, is in harmony with my belief in the interconnectedness and solidarity of all people everywhere. In other words, rather than setting me apart from other human beings, my membership in the Body of Christ functions symbolically to represent my relationship with them.

The Church as Story

Christians believe that God has come to us in the person of Jesus Christ. Catholics as well as many other Christians believe in Christ's ongoing presence in the church. On a fundamental level the story of the church is a story about the meaning of life. The world of meaning in which each of us lives is shaped and to some degree even constituted by stories. As a religious story, the church tells about the ultimate dimensions of life and thus provides an umbrella-like framework within which other levels of the stories of our lives take place.

Of course, the church is more than just a story. The story of the church refers to things that have really happened in the past and that continue to happen. The church is the story of those people who have lived their lives in a world whose meaning takes its structure from the story of Jesus. Jesus is a person who really lived, who died on a cross, who rose from the dead, who was experienced by his followers as God-incarnate on earth. It is difficult if not impossible to draw a sharp line between where "fact" ends and where "story" begins. Story functions to interpret the deeper dimensions of the true meaning of things that have really happened.

Summary

In this chapter we have considered the symbolic nature of religious language, as well as the story dimension of the church. We then examined how *Lumen Gentium* preferred scriptural images and symbols to precise definitions when it came to talking about the church.

The student referred to in the beginning of this chapter had, at first, a difficult time adjusting to the idea that his own religion has dimensions that are mythological. What he now realizes is that "mythological" does not mean "false," and that a life lived without such dimensions would be short on ultimate meaning.

In the next chapter we will examine a basic shift in outlook at Vatican II concerning the relative status of Catholics, both among themselves and with other Christians.

FOR FURTHER REFLECTION

1. What do you think that Joseph Campbell means when he says that "myth helps you to put your mind in touch with the experience of being alive?"

2. Have you ever known anyone whom you thought overly literal-minded about religion? What was that person like?

3. What in your own life did you at one time understand only literally but have now come to appreciate symbolically?

4. Is it possible to be too "symbolic" in one's interpretation of faith without giving enough attention to the literal?

5. In what ways is "symbol" a liberating category for religious persons?

SUGGESTED READINGS

Campbell, Joseph. *The Power of Myth*. With Bill Moyers. Garden City, N.Y.: Doubleday, 1988.

Greeley, Andrew. *The Catholic Myth: The Behavior and Beliefs of American Catholics*. New York: Scribner, 1990.

O'Brien, William J. *Stories to the Dark*. Mahwah, N.J.: Paulist Press, 1977.

Shea, John. *Stories of God*. Chicago: Thomas More Press, 1978.

Tilley, Terrence. *Story Theology*. Wilmington, Del.: Michael Glazier, 1985.

SECTION TWO

THE PEOPLE OF GOD

CHAPTER 7

AN ECUMENICAL OUTLOOK

I know a university student who was raised Catholic but now is alienated from the church. He has come to me a couple of times in order, I believe, to get into a big argument. Inevitably, he raises the point that Catholics hold the ugly belief that anyone who is not Catholic cannot be saved. Apparently, this is the impression he received as a child, and, because he is deeply angry with the church, he has a hard time giving it up. I point out to him that Catholics throughout history have held a wide range of positions on this issue. I show him clear statements in current church documents that contradict his belief. I point out to him that in the early 1950s Father Feeney of Boston was excommunicated for obstinately continuing to preach that no one outside the Catholic church can be saved. So far, however, all of this has been to no avail. He was taught a certain way as a child, and every once in a while he comes across an unfortunate incident of Catholic narrow-mindedness that reinforces his position. For example, he was recently working on a food-relief project when a Catholic refused to donate food to a Protestant-run institution. The student took this as yet another instance of Catholic exclusivity. He claims that history books and official church documents do not reveal the intolerance actually put forth in childhood religious education. Although I hope that this young man will soon let go of his position and realize that the overwhelming majority of Catholics today are not taught such exclusivity, I do have to admit to him that what he says sometimes reminds me of what I was taught in my own religious education in the 1950s.

This Chapter

In this chapter we will examine Catholic attitudes toward the salvation of non-Catholics, concentrating especially on three points from *Lumen Gentium*: how various churches today relate to the church that Christ founded; who can be considered a member of the church; and how all Christians are called to share in the ministry of Christ as priest, prophet, and king. The first point is drawn from section 8 of chapter 1 of *Lumen Gentium*; the next two points are drawn from throughout chapter 2.

Tension Within the Tradition

In the Baltimore Catechism there is a question that reads, "Are all obliged to belong to the Catholic church in order to be saved?" The ominous answer follows: "All are obliged to belong to the Catholic church in order to be saved." This is followed by another question and answer that explains that "those who through their own grave fault do not know that the Catholic Church is the true church or, knowing it, refuse to join it, cannot be saved." Yet another question and answer assures us that those who do not know that the Catholic church is the true church can be saved by making use of the graces that God gives them. In more advanced texts this state of not knowing was called "invincible ignorance." In popular practice it was assumed that those raised as Protestant from birth were in little danger, but those who themselves chose to leave the Catholic church were thought to have much for which to answer.

The traditional Christian adage, "no salvation outside the church," is first attributed to Cyprian, Bishop of Carthage in the third century, during a period of great persecution. His message was addressed to those who were already Christian, advising them that followers of Christ should choose martyrdom over the public denial of their faith. Cyprian himself was martyred for refusing to offer sacrifice to pagan gods.

As hard as Cyprian's words might be, they are a far cry from a sweeping statement that would send to hell people from all over the world who are not members in good standing of the Catholic church. In 1215, at the Fourth Lateran Council, Pope Innocent III declared: "There is but one universal church of the faithful, outside of which no one at all can be saved." In a Bull of 1441, Pope Eugene IV stated even more strongly that the church "firmly believes, professes, and teaches that none of those who are not within the Catholic church, not only Pagans, but Jews, heretics, and schismatics, can ever be partakers of eternal life, but are to go into the eternal fire 'prepared for the devil and his angels' (Matthew 25:41), unless before the close of their lives they shall have entered into that church." It is clear that some medieval popes took "no salvation outside the church" quite literally. A tension can be found throughout the Catholic tradition between positions of openness to people of other faiths and positions that are unequivocally condemnatory of all that is not explicitly Catholic. The position in the Baltimore Catechism, which clearly allows for the salvation of non-Catholics, appears rather mild when compared with the Bull of 1441.

Vatican II made great strides in the direction of ecumenical openness. For the first time in official church writings Protestant congregations were referred to as "churches" rather than merely "sects." Protestants themselves were called our "separated brethren." It was said that "in some real way they are joined with us in the Holy Spirit, for to them too he gives his gifts and graces whereby he is operative among them with his sanctifying power" (*LG*, 15). To say that the Holy Spirit is at work with sanctifying power is to grant a good deal more than salvation through the loophole of invincible ignorance. It is to say that God is at work among them.

The overall stance toward Protestantism taken in *Lumen Gentium* can be explored by examining three points mentioned earlier: the relationship between various churches and the church founded by Christ, the membership of the church, and the sharing of Christians in the threefold ministry of Christ as priest, prophet, and king. Each of these points represents grounds for a new openness in Catholic-Protestant relationships.

The Church of Christ *Subsists In . . .*

In the first draft of what would become *Lumen Gentium,* after a discussion of the church that Christ founded, it was stated that "this church of Christ . . . is the Catholic church." For explicitly ecumenical purposes, the final draft was changed to read:

"this church of Christ...subsists in the Catholic church...although many elements of sanctification and of truth are found outside of its visible structure. These elements, as gifts belonging to the church of Christ, are forces impelling toward catholic unity." (*LG*, 8)

The shift from "is" in the first draft to "subsists in" in the final draft signals a change from presenting the Catholic church as the only true church to a new openness to other churches. That is, in the first draft, the church that Christ founded is identified as the Catholic church, pure and simple. In the final draft, the church of Christ is said to "subsist in" or "dwell within" the Catholic church, but not exclusively so. In other words, although this church of Christ is basically and fundamentally found dwelling in the Catholic church, elements of this church can also be found in Christian churches that are not Catholic. These authentic elements are positive signs of ecumenical progress.

Lumen Gentium still gives a clear priority to the Catholic church insofar as there is a certain fullness or completeness in the way that the church of Christ can be found within it. By implication, Protestant churches are necessarily incomplete to the extent that they disagree with the Catholic tradition on key issues. Many Catholics involved in the ecumenical movement today find this an unsatisfactory position. They would like to see a position more open to the admission of mistakes and even incompleteness on both sides. The following three points may help make a more sympathetic reading of the document possible.

First, one should appreciate how radical and progressive the position of *Lumen Gentium* seemed in 1964. For Catholics who in their youth were taught to question the very salvation of Protestants, the acknowledgment that the Holy Spirit is at work in Protestant churches represented a revolutionary change in attitude.

Second, the Catholic claim—that, although the church may at times make mistakes, there are certain truths so important and certain structures so essential that they represent the very will of God—is not to be taken lightly. From the Catholic point of view, the church has a human side but it is not simply a human institution. It is willed by the Father, founded by Christ, and guided by the Spirit. It is to be expected that on important matters of difference the Catholic church believes itself to be correct. In the same way, those who hold to differing positions believe themselves to be correct.

Third, the position of *Lumen Gentium* is stated against the background of a Catholic tradition that presupposes a distinction between abstract essentials and concrete practice. That is, while *Lumen Gentium* says that in essential beliefs and structures the Catholic church enjoys a certain priority, it does not deny that many Protestant congregations may be doing a better job in practice. In other words, the position in *Lumen Gentium* is simply that the Catholic church is the church that has a complete set of tools. It is presupposed that some Catholic congregations may not be doing a very good job with their tools or are even keeping them locked up in the woodshed; some Protestant congregations may be doing an excellent job with those tools that they have.

As understandable and defensible and even current the position in *Lumen Gentium* might be, the Catholic church has continued to grow in its outlook toward other denominations. In the pre-Vatican II period, ecumenical progress from a Catholic perspective seemed to mean that the other side showed signs of collapsing or surrendering and was going to rejoin the Catholic church to insure its salvation. Instead, many Catholics today hope for continued agreements concerning basic beliefs and sacraments and eventually for a mutual recognition and acceptance of the validity of each others' ministers. There is a willingness on the part of theologians and church leaders to reexamine the Reformation and indeed admit to plenty of mistakes and misunderstandings on both sides. Ecumenical progress is not measured strictly by institutional mergers; rather it is envisioned in such a way that the various denominations can to some degree preserve the integrity of their own identity and traditions.

Who Is Related to the People of God?

English composition textbooks tell us that one way to give emphasis to a particular sentence is to place it at the beginning or end of a paragraph. To place a sentence at the beginning or end of a chapter or of an entire composition is to give it even more emphasis. If you wish to say something but at the same time de-emphasize it, stick it somewhere in the middle.

Somewhere in the middle of chapter two of *Lumen Gentium* the reader is told:

> Basing itself upon Sacred Scripture and Tradition, [the council] teaches that the church, now sojourning on earth as an exile, is necessary for salvation. Christ, present to us in his Body, is the one Mediator and the unique way of salvation. In explicit terms he himself affirmed the necessity of faith and baptism, and thereby affirmed also the necessity of the church, for through baptism as through a door men enter the church. Whosoever, therefore, knowing that the Catholic church was made necessary by Christ, would refuse to enter it or to remain in it, could not be saved. (*LG*,14)

And so *Lumen Gentium* thereby affirms the traditional teaching about no salvation outside the church along with the allowance for invincible ignorance. However, the placement of the passage in the chapter undercuts the traditional force of this position and demands that it be read in the most open way possible. It does this in two ways.

First, in a chapter that includes Catholics, Protestants, people of various faiths, and even secularists, this statement is placed in a section that deals directly with the Catholic faithful. In addressing itself primarily to Catholics, the text hearkens back more to the warning to the faithful made by Cyprian in the third century than it does to the sweeping condemnation made by Pope Eugene IV in his Bull of 1441. In other words, more stress is placed on the idea that those who already accept the Catholic church should not turn away from it, than on the idea that unless non-members are invincibly ignorant they will not be saved.

Second, the statement on salvation outside the church appears in the middle of a chapter that otherwise lays the groundwork for a broad-scale ecumenical understanding. The very first sentence of chapter two reads: "At all times and in every race God has given welcome to whosoever fears him and does what is right"(*LG*, 9). Given that this statement comes first and is used to introduce the very structure of the chapter, it is appropriate to read the necessity of the church for salvation in the light of it rather than vice-versa. In other words, we are to interpret the necessity of the church for salvation in such a way that we keep in mind the prior position that God welcomes at all times and in every race those who fear him and do what is right. The necessity of the church for salvation appears in the chapter because conservative forces rightfully insisted that it is part of the Catholic tradition. Its placement in the document, however, gives it more the status of a qualification than of a basic, grounding position. There is indeed salvation outside the church, although many traditional theologians take instead the route of defining "church" in such a general way that it includes all people of good will and actions.

This is not to say that the document minimizes the role of the church in God's plan of salvation. We are told that God does not simply save people as individuals, but gathers them together as a people. The people of God has historical and continuing roots in the Jews as God's chosen people. Through Christ was formed a new people of God that calls together all people in catholic unity. Catholics are full members, catechumens are joined through their intention, Protestants are linked through the Holy Spirit, and people of various faiths and backgrounds are in some way related. The document explicitly states that salvation is possible for all of these people, although the church retains its mission to preach the gospel to all nations.

Priest, Prophet, King

Another way that *Lumen Gentium* reveals a positive ecumenical outlook is by affirming from a Catholic standpoint several key ideas associated with the most famous of the Protestant Reformers, Martin Luther. A joint commission of Lutheran and Roman Catholic scholars has issued a document, "Martin Luther's Legacy," which includes a discussion of Luther's influence on Vatican II.[1] Some commentators have even joked that Vatican II represents the Catholics finally catching up with the Protestants after four hundred years. A more serious analysis reveals a Catholic church trying to maintain its essential identity as it attempts to formulate some mutually acceptable middle positions on some important matters. In the second chapter of *Lumen Gentium*, two ideas historically associated with Luther stand out: that the church is basically to be thought of as a community of people, and that all Christians participate in the ministry of Christ, the one Mediator. John Dillenberger describes Luther's position:

> As the community of believers, Christians bear each other's burdens and the burdens of the world, as Christ did before them. . . . [Thus] the ministry was no longer understood as a position of *necessary* mediatorship. . . . Rather, in the community of the church, all men were priests to each other, that is, occasions for and messengers of grace and support. This was expressed in the notion of the priesthood of all believers.[2]

Lumen Gentium clearly differs from Luther in its strong reaffirmation of the crucial importance of the structural elements of the church and of the essential distinction between the ordained ministries and the common priesthood of the faithful. The document moves unmistakably in the direction of Luther, however, concerning the church as community and the universal call to share in Christ's ministry.

The existence and placement of chapter 2 of *Lumen Gentium*, on the People of God, reveals a strong emphasis on the church as a community. The first draft of the document contained no chapter on this matter. In the second draft, the people of God was connected with the laity and included as the next to last section in the document. In the final draft, this chapter was placed ahead of the chapter on the hierarchical nature of the church and became second only to the chapter on the mystery of the church and its connection with God. This move can be interpreted as signaling a shift in emphasis from a pyramidal structure of the church with the pope at the top followed by the bishops followed by the priests followed by the religious with the laity at the bottom, to a more circular, inclusive structure of the church formed by all the people of God and served by a hierarchy.

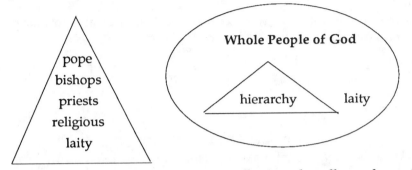

Chapter two of *Lumen Gentium* emphasizes that all members of the People of God share in the threefold ministry of Christ as Priest, Prophet, and King. This notion becomes a major structuring element throughout the rest of the document. For example, chapter three of *Lumen Gentium* tells how the hierarchy shares in this threefold ministry, chapter four discusses the ways in which the laity shares, and chapter six discusses the share of those who have taken religious vows. This concept has roots in the New Testament notion, so important to Luther, that Christ is now the one Mediator who replaces the Old Testament priesthood by forming a priestly people. This priestly people can pray and offer sacrifice to the Father without the need of any mediator other than Christ. This concept also has roots in the writings of several of the church Fathers who expressed that Christ is the fulfillment of the messianic prophecies in that he has taken over the functions of the Priestly books, the Prophetic books, and the Kingly books (a traditional way of categorizing all of the books of the Old Testament).[3]

Each Christian is called, in accordance with one's own state in life, to be the presence of Christ (priest), to bear witness to Christ in one's life (prophet), and to serve in the coming of the kingdom of God (king).

Summary
In this chapter we have investigated how the Catholic church has shifted from a position of casting doubts about the possibility of the salvation of outsiders to a position of ecumenical openness. We focused upon the recognition of the Spirit in Protestant communities, the broad membership of the People of God, and the sharing of all Christians in the threefold ministry of Christ as priest, prophet, and king.

It is my hope that the student discussed in the beginning of this chapter will come to appreciate the ecumenical openness of the positions taken at Vatican II. For my part, I need to appreciate that the churches, Catholic and Protestant, still have a long way to go on these matters.

In the next chapter we will examine the historical background of some of the divisions within Christianity.

FOR FURTHER REFLECTION

1. What is it that might make a person subscribe to a narrow interpretation of "no salvation outside the church"?

2. Have you ever had any personal experience of discrimination among Christian denominations?

3. How did the concept of "the People of God" function in an ecumenical way at Vatican II?

4. Do you think that the concept of the "common priesthood of the faithful" should be taken to mean that in a way every Christian is a priest?

5. What types of experiences might make people grow in their ecumenical awareness?

SUGGESTED READINGS

Rusch, William G. *Ecumenism: A Movement Toward Church Unity.* Philadelphia: Fortress Press, 1985.

Pannenberg, Wolfhart. *The Church.* Philadelphia: Westminster Press, 1983 [1977].

Sullivan, Francis. *The Church We Believe In.* Mahwah, N.J.: Paulist Press, 1988.

CHAPTER 8

DIVERSITY AND DIVISIONS WITHIN CHRISTIANITY

Recently, I gave a talk at a Lutheran church that was addressed to Lutheran-Roman Catholic married couples. I tried to help these couples understand some of the reasons behind the historical divisions between Lutherans and Catholics, as well as the great strides that are being made today in healing such divisions. I thought that I had been extremely sympathetic to both sides in the historical disputes, perhaps especially to the Lutheran side. In the discussion period that followed, however, one woman was upset. "I was raised a Catholic and I married a Lutheran," she said to me. "Now I go to church here (in the Lutheran church), because it doesn't make any difference. Catholic, Lutheran, it's all the same. And now you are saying that there is a difference!"

At first I was taken off guard by her response. Only a few years ago it would have been practically unthinkable to suggest that there were no significant differences between Lutherans and Catholics. Now I had met someone who had shifted to the opposite extreme of feeling hurt by the suggestion that there are some differences, even while emphasizing the need for mutual understanding and acceptance. I think that in her own mind she was justifying her shift in denominations by denying that any differences exist at all.

I replied to her by acknowledging that in the everyday world in which we live it does not seem to make much difference if a person is a Lutheran or a Catholic. Moreover, the Lutheran tradition and the Catholic tradition are extremely similar, especially when compared to the wide range of options both within Christianity and without. I recognized, furthermore, that many of the differences have more to do with theologians and church leaders than with the average Christian. Still, however, some significant historical and theological differences exist. Wars, national boundaries, and individual lives have been impacted by these differences. Even today these differences can be important for people on very deep levels of personal commitment. Ultimately, I argued, healing comes not from ignoring differences but from acknowledging them and working them out.

This Chapter

A good way to begin to understand the current state of affairs is to examine the history of how diverse communities have emerged within Christianity. It would take, of course, many volumes to do justice to this issue. In this chapter, we will look briefly at diversity in the New Testament, the schism between Greek Orthodox and Roman Catholics, and the Protestant Reformation. This material is most related to chapter 2 of *Lumen Gentium* and the Decree on Ecumenism from Vatican II.

Diverse Communities in the New Testament

In *The Churches the Apostles Left Behind,* noted biblical scholar Raymond Brown investigates various communities to whom different books of the New Testament were addressed.[1] Brown argues that each community had a particular identity associated with the apostle or apostolic guide who founded it. As he investigates each community, Brown seeks to understand how it was able to survive after the apostolic guide had departed the scene. In other words, if the founding authority is the original link between the community and Jesus, then what structures or authoritative ideas serve to maintain this community once the founder has left?

Brown finds significant variety in community structure and identity in the seven churches that he investigates. The first three communities discussed have characteristics often associated with Catholicism. In the pastoral epistles (1 Timothy, 2 Timothy, and Titus), for example, the element of survival is the appointment of a bishop in every town. In Colossians/Ephesians (late letters attributed to Paul), it is the ideal concept of the church as the Mystical Body of Christ. In Luke and Acts of the Apostles the continuous element is the Holy Spirit that guides the leaders.

The next three communities Brown discusses are more closely associated with Protestantism. In 1 Peter the guiding factor is the understanding of the church as the new People of God against the background of Israel as God's chosen people. In the Gospel of John the enduring element is the relationship of the individual to Jesus grasped through the image of the Vine and the branches. In the epistles of John it is the Holy Spirit (Paraclete) in the individual that gives authority (though, as Brown shows, this concept tends ultimately to cause great divisions).

Brown ends by discussing a community of ecumenical balance. In the Gospel of Matthew, the element that allows for survival is a stress on authoritative structure balanced by an even greater stress on the compassionate and non-legalistic attitude of Jesus. Brown explains in detail not only how each of these elements functions to provide continuity, but also the strengths and weaknesses of each type of community.

What Structuring Element Replaced the Apostolic Guide?		
Pastoral Epistles	===	bishop in each town
Colossians/Ephesians	===	Mystical Body of Christ
Luke/Acts	===	Spirit guides leaders
1 Peter	===	new People of God
John	===	individual connected with Jesus
Epistles of John	===	Spirit within each individual
Matthew	===	authority not stifling of Jesus

Brown's work is radically ecumenical for several reasons. First, the variety of communities discussed shows that many denominations can find solid grounding for their own church structure within the text of the New Testament. Catholics, mainline Protestants, and Evangelicals can all point to passages that justify their own approaches.

Second, Brown's investigation suggests that no one denomination is currently hearing all of the biblical witness. Each denomination must let itself be challenged by the whole range of biblical testimony. Catholics may tend to underemphasize the importance of the Spirit's presence in each individual; mainline Protestants may not take the need for church unity seriously enough; evangelical Christians may be ignoring the scriptural support for the leadership of bishops.

Third, Brown's analysis of the distortions that arise from argumentative presentations of the faith, whether in New Testament times, the

Reformation, or today, nudges all parties involved in the direction of listening sympathetically and working toward reconciliation. Brown shows how the emergence of two opposing sides causes disputed issues to take center stage and the more important basics of the faith to be pushed aside. For example, Christians in the community addressed by the epistles of John were so intent on defending the divinity and preexistence of Jesus that they had trouble affirming that Jesus was human. Catholics at the time of the Reformation were so intent on discrediting the Reformers that they looked upon Bible reading as suspect. Brown sees a similar thing happening in post-Vatican II rejection of pre-Vatican II Catholicism:

> I...while enthusiastic for what was introduced into Catholicism by Vatican II, see no need for the concomitant losses, e.g., of inner-Catholic loyalty, obedience, and commitment to the church; of dignity in liturgy; of Gregorian chant; of a knowledge of the Latin tradition reaching from Augustine through Thomas to the Middle Ages. To try now to recoup some of those losses while still advancing the gains of Vatican II would be an act of eminent good sense.

Brown's approach represents an irenic spirit that seeks unity, not by avoiding differences, but by avoiding the bitter argumentation that so often results in defensive attitudes and the accompanying temptation to hold others and their ideas in contempt.

Brown does not leave his reader with the impression that all contemporary churches are equally incomplete. He has a distinct preference for churches that follow the model of Matthew's Gospel, in which authoritative structures are essential, yet come in a noticeable second to pastoral sensitivity and loving human relationships. Matthew has traditionally been known as "the church's gospel." Brown does leave his reader, though, with a clear picture of legitimate diversity in the New Testament and of the need for Christians of all stripes to listen closely to each other and to value each others' insights.

Greek Orthodox and Roman Catholic

The types of diversity manifested in the New Testament have existed in various forms throughout the history of Christianity. No time period can be certified as free of dissension from the line preached by official churches. At various times organized movements have arisen that have been labelled heretical, such as Marcionism, Arianism, and Waldensianism. For world Christianity, though, two major divisions stand out from the rest: the schism between the Greek Orthodox and the Roman Catholics of the eleventh century and the Protestant Reformation of the sixteenth.

The Greek-Roman schism was prior to and in a sense deeper than the Protestant Reformation. The former represented a split between the East and the West, whereas the latter was simply a split within Western Christianity. The Greek-Roman schism is the break between the Latin-speaking church, centered in Rome, and the Greek-speaking church, centered in Constantinople (modern-day Istanbul, in Turkey). Although the split took place gradually over a period of centuries, the event to which scholars point most often is the excommunication by a papal legate of Michael Cerularius, Patriarch (head) of the Greek Orthodox church during a Mass in the patriarch's own cathedral in Constantinople in 1054. Cerularius returned the favor by excommunicating the papal legate.

This event was preceded by several hundred years of mutual rivalry and dislike between the two churches. Although Rome's claim to priority was acknowledged somewhat by the Greeks, the nature and extent of this priority was disputed. For example, Roman Catholics held that ecumenical councils had authority because they were accepted by the pope. Greek Orthodox Catholics claimed that ecumenical councils had their own authority, and that papal acceptance simply represented a final confirmation of that authority.

A related theological dispute concerned the Roman addition to the Nicene Creed of a term, *filioque,* indicating that the Holy Spirit proceeded both from the Father and the Son. The Greek original had said only that the Holy Spirit proceeded from the Father. This debate had its own connection with papal authority, for in the Greek version divine authority is mediated more directly by the Spirit through the tradition, whereas in the Roman version the mediation through Christ and the church, and thus through the pope, is more explicit.

Most scholars agree, though, that the real disputes between Constantinople and Rome were more cultural and political than theological. Greek priests were married, bearded, and used leavened bread in the Mass; Roman priests were celibate, clean-shaven, and used unleavened bread. Deeper than this though, was the attitude toward each other. As colorfully expressed by one commentator:

To the Byzantines [Greeks], the Latins, people from dark-age countries, were wild and uncultured savages with huge appetites.

To the Latins, the Greeks were degenerate, effeminate hair-splitters.[2]

After the mutual excommunications in 1054 there was still some openness toward reconciliation, but it did not materialize. In 1204, crusaders from the West were duped into sacking the city of Constantinople by Venetian merchants who had commercial interests.[3] These crusaders established the Latin empire of Constantinople, and imposed Latin liturgy and practices upon unwilling Greek Christians until the crusaders were finally ousted in 1261. Hopes of reconciliation were buried further when Constantinople fell to the Turks in 1453.

At the end of Vatican II, on December 7, 1965, a joint declaration by Pope Paul VI and the Greek Patriarch Athenagoras I was released. Together they expressed regret for offensive words, unfounded accusations, despicable acts, excommunications, and mutual distrust. They also expressed a desire to surmount past differences through repentance and positive concern for common understanding.

Martin Luther and the Protestant Reformation

Scholars can identify many complex causes of the Reformation. Most noticeable among them was the widespread corruption in the church marked by such abuses as rampant superstition, the sale of sacraments, an undereducated clergy, and absentee bishops who made their living through collections. Yet deeper were broad cultural changes, such as the shift from a feudal to a capitalistic social system, bringing with it a rise in nationalism, literacy (because of the printing press), and a new middle class. A church that seemed entrenched in the thought-forms of the Middle Ages came to be disrespected by many people who had new sets of expectations.

Although many organized Christian movements of protest have existed prior to and since Martin Luther, Luther himself symbolizes the heart of the Protestant Reformation. An Augustinian monk who originally intended only internal church reform, and who preferred that his followers be called "Christians," not "Lutherans," Luther, at least at first, did not want to be excommunicated for refusing to back down on the charges that he laid at the doorstep of the church and of the papacy. "Here stand I; I can do no other," he told his accusers.

Initially, Luther became upset over the manner in which the sale of indulgences was conducted to raise money for the building of St. Peter's in Rome. His famous "95 Theses" of 1517 are concerned entirely with this issue. Indulgences are remissions of punishment due for sins, usually in recognition of good works, pilgrimage, or prayer. Luther objected to indulgences being sold for money, being applied to punishment in purgatory, and being "plenary," meaning that all punishment whatsoever would be remitted. Luther held that the authority of the pope to bind or loose from specific penalties was limited to canonical penalties in this life. The "95 Theses" were widely distributed throughout Europe. The next few years were filled with various threats, engagements, disputes, and debates between Luther and representatives of Rome.

In 1520, Luther wrote three works now known as the "Reformation treatises" that contain his full-blown theology of reform. His attacks on the papacy and the current state of the church escalated enormously. Luther saw the Catholic church and the papacy as human inventions that were falsely claiming divine power. In this they represented not God but the Devil. Luther called for a recognition that all Christians have the power proper to priests and bishops of baptizing, forgiving, and consecrating. It is appropriate that certain people be granted the office to do these things, but they differ only in function, not in essence, from other Christians. Luther condemned the "worldly and ostentatious style" of the pope. He called for the abolition of forced celibacy among clerics, endowed Masses for the dead, chapels intended as places of pilgrimage for the raising of money, church licenses, papal bulls, and begging, as well as indulgences. He argued that Christians are saved by faith alone, not by their works; that Scripture alone is the word of God, not the decisions of human beings; that the church should humbly pick up its cross, not proclaim its own glory.

That same year, 1520, a papal bull was issued that condemned Luther's writings and gave him sixty days to recant. At the Imperial Diet of Worms in 1521 Luther stated unequivocally that he would not withdraw his positions because he found nothing in reason or Scripture to convince him to do so. At that the Reformation was fully underway. Luther spent the remaining years of his life working for church reform. Among other things, he tried to make the basics of the Christian faith available to the people by translating the Scriptures into German and by writing the first catechism in history.[4]

Until recent years, it was difficult to find a balanced treatment of the Reformation. Protestants and Catholics have both been grossly unfair and one-sided in their portrayals of the characters and events of the time. Each side can point proudly to instances of true outreach and attempts at compromise. Each side can also find plenty of examples of its own pride, arrogance, stubbornness, and narrow-mindedness.

Over the last four hundred years hundreds of Protestant denominations have emerged. All share in having some distance from the papacy. Some, such as Episcopalians and Lutherans, maintain an apostolic succession of bishops. Others, such as Methodists and Presbyterians, place democratic authority in the people who form the congregations. Yet others, such as Baptists and Pentecostals, grant final authority to the individual who interprets Scripture by the Holy Spirit within.

Summary

In order to gain some perspective on the divisions that exist within Christianity today, we have reviewed briefly the diversity in the New Testament, the Greek-Roman schism, and the Protestant Reformation.

There are no easy answers for people, whether Protestant or Catholic, about these issues. About all I can offer is an ecumenical perspective that acknowledges two sides of the story as we try to work out a reconciliation that will respect our diversity as it brings about real unity.

In the next chapter we will examine some of the progress being made in the ecumenical movement today.

FOR FURTHER REFLECTION

1. Which of the many issues that have divided Christians strike you as most significant?

2. Which of the many issues that have divided Christians strike you as most insignificant?

3. How might Raymond Brown's study of diversity in the New Testament be useful for ecumenical dialogue today?

4. For both the Greek-Roman schism and the Protestant Reformation, can you distinguish between issues that are "religious" and issues that are more "cultural?"

5. How does the picture of Luther in this chapter fit with what you have heard previously?

SUGGESTED READINGS

Brown, Raymond. *The Churches the Apostles Left Behind.* Mahwah, N.J. : Paulist Press, 1984.

Chadwick, Owen. *The Reformation*. Volume three of *The Pelican History of the Church*. New York: Penguin Books, 1964.

Comby, Jean. *How to Read Church History*. New York: Crossroad, 1985.

Dillenberger, John, ed. *Martin Luther: Selections from His Writings*. Garden City, N.Y.: Doubleday, 1961.

CHAPTER 9

ECUMENICAL PROGRESS

Two friends of mine are Protestant women who come to Mass at my parish every Sunday. Terry is Methodist; Brenda is Episcopalian. Both are married to Catholic men. Both have several children being raised Catholic. Both participate in various church functions and socials. Both remain vocally and proudly Protestant. Neither is officially permitted to receive communion in the Catholic church unless she becomes Catholic.

Terry goes to communion every Sunday. She does not think that the pope and the bishops should exclude her from the communion to which the rest of her family is invited. She feels that by raising her children Catholic and by having her family attend Catholic Mass each Sunday she is already making great concessions. Should not the Catholic church also make concessions? Would it be better for her to attend a different church from the rest of her family? Terry feels no compunction to obey what she perceives to be pointless rules that human beings have r) business making up in the first place.

Bre..da does not go to communion. She considers this a sign of her lack of agreement with certain teachings of the Catholic church. Her father had been a Catholic, and he left specifically because of his disagreements. In particular, Brenda feels that papal authority is overblown, that many Catholic beliefs about Mary are not justified by the Scriptures, and that Catholic rituals and prayers tend often to be superstitious. She is by no means hostile to the Catholic church, but she likes to draw her lines clearly. Her not receiving communion is a powerful symbol for her of how her Protestant identity continues even though she attends Catholic Mass for the sake of her family.

Lack of intercommunion stands as the great symbol of divisions that remain among Christians. The Catholic church is clear in its official policy that only full-fledged Catholics are to receive communion, barring exceptional circumstances when dispensations are granted, such as a wedding, an explicitly ecumenical service, or an occasion of great need. This policy is widely violated, particularly when interfaith marriages are concerned. Many theologians and lay Catholics today are pressing the leadership of the church to allow intercommunion on a broad scale. Church leaders, supported by other theologians and lay Catholics, argue that such a move would be dangerously premature.

Intercommunion stands as a great symbol of ecumenical progress. "One bread, one Body," goes the scripturally-based hymn, with "body" referring both to the Eucharist and to the church itself. Jesus is portrayed in John 17:21 as praying to the Father that his followers may be one. In Ephesians 4:3–6, the advice is given: "Make every effort to preserve the unity which has the Spirit as its origin and peace as its binding force. There is but one body and one Spirit, just as there is but one hope given all of you by your call. There is one Lord, one faith, one baptism, one God and Father of all, who is over all, and works through all, and is in all." The unity of the church is part and parcel of the teachings of the church Fathers and the early creeds: "We believe in one, holy, catholic, and apostolic church." Divisions among Christians are thereby a great scandal, and have been experienced as such even by those who have created them, though each party has usually blamed the scandal on the other side.

This Chapter

In this chapter we will investigate some of the progress being made in contemporary Christian ecumenism. We look first at an ecumenical proposal made by Catholic theologians, followed by a brief overview of ecumenical dialogues, and finally a document of the World Council of Churches that is intended to foster church unity. As with the last two chapters, this chapter corresponds with chapter 2 of _Lumen Gentium_ and with the Decree on Ecumenism.

The Eight Theses

Heinrich Fries and Karl Rahner, two noted Catholic theologians, collaborated on a book called _The Unity of the Churches: An Actual Possibility_.[1] They call for intercommunion and pulpit sharing among "the large

Christian churches." Such churches would then be identified as "Partner churches." Fries and Rahner claim that now is the time for such a move because "more has been achieved ecumenically in the last three decades than in previous centuries." The events they are referring to are Vatican II and the publication of various official documents that have been hammered out jointly by Orthodox and Catholics, Anglicans and Catholics, and Lutherans and Catholics on such topics as ministry, Eucharist, and salvation. The following is a simplification of the eight theses that they propose and explain in their book:

1. Partner churches will accept Scripture and early Creeds.
2. Partner churches will not reject decisively what is binding dogma in another partner church; no dogma will be imposed on any partner beyond Thesis 1.
3. Regional partner churches can maintain their existing structures side by side in the same territory as other regional partners.
4. Partner churches all acknowledge the Petrine ministry of the pope as sign of church unity; the pope will agree to exercise his highest teaching authority only in conjunction with general councils representing the whole church.
5. All partner churches will have bishops at the head of larger subdivisions, though the method of election may vary.
6. Partner churches live in mutual fraternal exchange with each other so that the experience of each can become effective in the other.
7. Partner churches will from now on conduct ordinations with prayer and the laying on of hands.
8. There is pulpit and altar fellowship between the individual partner churches.

Fries and Rahner express impatience over the reluctance of church leaders to execute bolder ecumenical measures. However, Cardinal Joseph Ratzinger, head of the Congregation for the Doctrine of the Faith, strongly disagrees with their proposal.[2] His main objection is that intercommunion should require a real unity of faith that does not as yet exist. Ratzinger holds that the unity that now exists in part is welcome but not enough. He cites the difficulties and disagreements still remaining over such matters as transubstantiation and the sacrificial character of the Mass even in those joint documents on the Eucharist that have been issued. Beyond that, Ratzinger points to differences concerning the relationship among Scripture, Tradition, and church authority as well as the meaning of the act of faith itself.

It is this last point that Ratzinger sees at the root of differences between Catholics and Christians of the Reformation. Ratzinger explains that Luther's faith involved an encounter of the individual with God; the faith of a Catholic involves acceptance of what God has done for us as a people in a way that continues through the church. Luther's radical personalism carries over to all of the other matters of dispute. Ratzinger holds that it would be better to explore these fundamental issues of truth more deeply than to engage in the "forced march towards unity" proposed by Fries and Rahner.

The difficulty of this issue can be seen further in the somewhat contrary positions taken by Catholic theologian Avery Dulles and Lutheran theologian Wolfhart Pannenberg.[3] Each uses at the base of his argument the concept that the Eucharist is both a sign of unity and a cause of unity. Each engages in a quite similar discussion of the issues at hand. In the end, though, Dulles, while in favor of easing overly stringent restrictions for occasional intercommunion, argues strongly against an excessive laxity in eucharistic sharing. He holds that anything more than occasional intercommunion would be premature because it may foster indifference and would likely inhibit the drive to continue to forge more and more substantial agreements. Neither side would feel as motivated as they do now to be reformed by listening closely to the other. When "eucharistic promiscuity" takes place, the effectiveness of the sacrament as signifying a real church unity is diminished.

On the other hand, Pannenberg holds that such progress has been made so far in ecumenical agreements that the Eucharist can function in general as a cause of unity. In other words, he believes that general intercommunion should be permitted because it would give new impetus to mutual understanding and reform. The Eucharist could function in a sense as a present sign of the future unity for which Christians hope. He feels that the present restrictions do not represent the inviting attitude of Jesus.

Current disagreements about intercommunion, therefore, involve differences of judgment concerning how important remaining divergences are, and how, in a practical way, the Eucharist should function in bringing about deeper unity.

Quests for Theological Agreement
In the last few decades the Catholic church has worked jointly with many other denominations to try to resolve some of the theological

differences of the past.[4] After Vatican II, Paul VI established the Secretariat for Promoting Christian Unity. This office has co-sponsored dialogues that have linked Catholics with Orthodox, Anglicans, Lutherans, Reformed, Methodists, Disciples of Christ, Baptists, Pentecostals, and some Evangelicals.

A few of these dialogues have had notable success in issuing joint statements that point to substantial agreement over many issues that have divided Christians in the past. Lutheran-Catholic dialogues have produced joint statements on the relation of Scripture to church, the importance of Martin Luther, and the meaning of justification (salvation). Current talks focus further on justification, ecclesiology, and sacrament. Orthodox-Catholic dialogues have produced joint statements on the relationship of church, Eucharist, and Trinity, and the relationship of faith, sacraments, and church unity. The Anglican-Roman Catholic International Commission has issued joint documents on Eucharist, ministry, and authority, as well as a recent (1987) statement, "Salvation and the Church," which announced that "we believe that our two communions are agreed on the essential aspects of the doctrine of salvation and on the church's role within it."

The official response of the Catholic church has been positive and encouraging on the one hand, while being hesitant and critical on the other. The documents are produced by commissions co-sponsored by the Vatican, but their conclusions have the status in the Catholic church of committee reports that need the approval of the Congregation of the Doctrine of the Faith (CDF), headed by Cardinal Joseph Ratzinger. The CDF tries to sound encouraging by acknowledging the real progress that has been made, but the majority of the comments are analyses of the difficulties that are still present, and reminders that real unity will require a lot more. For example, concerning the documents of the Anglican-Roman Catholic International Commission, the CDF has noted remaining problems over the Eucharist, the papacy, Mary, the sacraments, the church, and human freedom and merit.[5] Specifically in regard to the 1987 document, the CDF writes that "The criticisms which have been expressed do not in any way deny that [the commission has] been partially successful. But one cannot affirm that full and substantial agreement on the essential aspects of this doctrine has been achieved, primarily because of deficiencies concerning the role of the church in salvation."

Much ecumenical progress is currently being made on the grassroots level through interfaith marriages and through shared liturgies, Scripture studies, and social action projects. Many who feel the scandal of division also feel that the time to move is now. Raymond Brown has issued the warning:

> If in the next two decades the churches do not seize the opportunity, if a union between two major churches does not take place as a sign of what may be possible, and if consequently Christianity enters the third millennium much more divided than it entered the second millennium, is it not possible, and even likely, that the opportunity will never come again? Almost by definition the Spirit surprises, but at times the surprise may be that the Spirit lets God's people pay the price of its failures.[6]

In contrast, Cardinal Ratzinger sounds a bit like former President Reagan in the early days of his administration when he argued against nuclear arms agreements that were worked out too quickly without making the other side give up as many concessions as could be squeezed from them. Reagan seems to have gained from his caution insofar as he was able to attain much more satisfactory agreements later on. Whether or not such strategy will prove appropriate in the ecumenical movement is difficult to foresee.

Baptism, Eucharist and Ministry

The World Council of Churches has served as a force for unity among Christians since its creation in 1948. Many national councils and international conferences preceded it. Because of theological difficulties that would be involved, the Roman Catholic church is not officially a member, but Catholics are appointed by the Vatican to participate and vote in their own names.

In 1982 the World Council of Churches issued a document entitled *Baptism, Eucharist and Ministry*, abbreviated as BEM and also known as the Lima document. Twelve participants, a full ten percent of the 120 members of the Faith and Order commission that produced the statement, were Roman Catholics. This document attempted to make a strong theological statement about the three issues named in the title to which virtually all Christians could give assent. The most difficult part of this endeavor was to avoid being so general that it would not really say anything. BEM was sent out to various Christian churches throughout the world who were asked to respond by saying to what extent they were able to endorse the positions of the document. They were also asked for suggestions for the ongoing work of the commission. The official responses fill six volumes.[7]

Baptism, Eucharist and Ministry is remarkable for its ability to say substantial things about its topics while remaining sensitive to different approaches. Baptism is described as a sign of new life, a participation in the death and resurrection of Christ, a conversion that entails cleansing of sin, an incorporation into the Body of Christ, and a sign of the kingdom of God. The document tries to use traditional terms in laying out sensitive positions on disputed matters of the past, such as whether infants should be baptized, whether rebaptism should be practiced, and whether confirmation is necessarily a separate sacrament.

Eucharist is described as a communion with Christ involving forgiveness of sin and the pledge of eternal life, as a memorial of the risen Christ, as a sign of community and unity, as a call to justice, and as the meal of the kingdom. Sensitive positions are put forth on such disputed issues as the nature of the Mass as a sacrifice, the real presence, and the manner of celebration.

Ministry is described first and foremost as a call given to all Christians. It is further affirmed that there is a need for people who are continually and publicly responsible—hence, for ordained ministers. Ordained ministry is rooted in Jesus' calling of the twelve. Ministers have a special though not exclusive responsibility to build community through word and sacrament. The document attempts to lay out sensitive positions on questions of the meaning of apostolic succession, the need for an episcopate, and the ordination of women.

Of the 185 official responses to BEM received by early 1990, the overwhelming majority have affirmed in a positive way that they are able to recognize in the document the Christian faith as they understand it. Almost all of the responses then give particular criticisms from their own point of view. Many of the less structured churches complain about what they perceive as a high church bias; some of the more traditionally structured churches wonder about no mention of the papacy. Many commentators make note that the document avoids strong stands on the most controversial issues. All in all, though, the reception of the document has been tremendously positive. One reaction to the responses has been the commissioning of a new study in ecclesiology.[8]

The official Catholic response from the Congregation for the Doctrine of the Faith was, as expected, both encouraging and hesitant.[9] It will be good if BEM receives wide affirmation, said the Congregation, but such agreement should be recognized as a stage along the way and not as representing a full consensus. The CDF was impressed with the theological depth in relating the topics to Father, Son, and Spirit and with the general positive understanding put forth on each issue. The document, however, "falls short at certain points," particularly in its understanding of sacrament, apostolic tradition, and decisive authority. The CDF points to the need for more understanding of the Roman Catholic perspective in ecclesiology. Such an understanding will be the topic of many of the following chapters.

Summary

In this chapter we have looked at proposals for Christian unity, cautions about moving too fast, and agreements among various Christian denominations.

Divisions among Christians remain a scandal. Given that the causes of these divisions are not just theological but are more deeply practical and cultural, the healing that needs to come will not be accomplished simply through theological dialogues. We need to continue to live, talk, play, work, and worship together. Christians of all types need an attitude of humility and repentance, as well as the fortitude to not simply give in on essential matters. Like the kingdom of God itself, Christian unity remains not simply the work of human beings but the work of God.

Now that we have set out an ecumenical framework for this book, we will proceed in the next chapter to consider the particular authoritative structures of the Catholic church.

FOR FURTHER REFLECTION

1. Given the information in this chapter, are you more inclined to be for or against widespread intercommunion at this time?

2. How should married couples of different denominations respond to current policies against intercommunion?

3. What faith or denomination other than your own do you find most attractive? What is it about that faith or denomination that attracts you?

4. What do you find most attractive about your own denomination (or worldview)?

5. How important (or unimportant) is the ecumenical movement to you personally?

SUGGESTED READINGS

Fries, Heinrich, and Karl Rahner. *The Unity of the Churches: An Actual Possibility*. Philadelphia: Fortress Press, 1985 [1983].

Lawler, Michael. *Ecumenical Marriage and Remarriage: Gifts and Challenges to the Churches*. Mystic, Conn.: Twenty-Third Publications, 1990.

Ratzinger, Joseph. *Church, Ecumenism, and Politics*. New York: Crossroad, 1988.

Thurian, Max, ed. *Churches Respond to BEM*. Geneva: World Council of Churches, 1986– . 6 vols. to date.

World Council of Churches. *Baptism, Eucharist and Ministry*. Geneva: WCC, 1982.

Section Three

The Hierarchical Structure of the Church

CHAPTER 10

BISHOPS AND THE POPE

A few years ago I began a class on the episcopacy by asking my students what they thought a bishop is. After a pause, a student raised her hand and said that a bishop is someone who is higher than a priest. The rest of the students nodded their heads; the explanation had captured their own ideas well.

As a teacher I have various ways of talking about bishops. I can speak about the history of the development of their office, of their place in the structure of the church, and of the nature and extent of their powers and authority. Through the course of my theological studies, however, I had forgotten the common sense experience of the ordinary Catholic without specialized training. A bishop is someone who is higher than a priest. Why didn't I think of that?

It is important for us to remember this perspective as we explore the episcopacy in a more structured and theoretical fashion. Bishops function symbolically for Catholics as people who are "up the ladder" of power, authority, and prestige. They are the leaders of the church; many people function in various types of leadership roles, but it is the bishops, taken together with the pope, the bishop of Rome, who have the official capacity to lead and the final say in matters that affect the church as a whole.

This Chapter
In this chapter we will discuss the collegial power of the bishops, their role in the church, papal primacy and infallibility, recent controversies, and the current stress on humility and service. This material corresponds with chapter 3 of *Lumen Gentium.* Also relevant is Vatican II's Decree on the Pastoral Office of Bishops in the Church. Following the organization of *Lumen Gentium,* I have intentionally put off any in-

depth exploration of the structure of the Catholic church until we could appreciate it within the more general context of the mystery of the church and our relations with other Christians. It is my hope that we are now ready.

Power to the Bishops

Clarifying the role of the bishops was a priority item on the agenda of Vatican II. Vatican I had declared the primacy and infallibility of the pope, but that council had not been able to complete its work on bishops, because the Franco-Prussian War forced it to adjourn abruptly. This is one reason why the understanding of papal power tended to be exaggerated among Catholics: There was no understanding of episcopal power to balance the relationship. Vatican II needed to set the relationship right.

While strongly reaffirming the Vatican I teaching about papal primacy and infallibility, *Lumen Gentium* introduced the concept of collegiality. The bishops form a stable group or college. This college of bishops is continuous with the twelve apostles whom Jesus sent out to preach the gospel. This continuity is known as apostolic succession. The pope is a brother bishop who functions within this college as its head. The papacy finds its heritage in Peter, whom Jesus chose to be the head of the apostles. There are current theological debates about whether the office of the papacy must always be considered in conjunction with the college or can also, in some sense, function independently. Interpreters of *Lumen Gentium* agree, though, that the document emphasizes both the apostolic authority of the bishops and the primacy of the pope.

"Collegiality" functions today with two meanings. In its strict sense, the term refers to the sharing of authority among bishops and pope as detailed in *Lumen Gentium*. In its broader sense, "collegiality" refers to a general movement within the church toward more sharing of authority on all levels.

The manner in which the bishops of the U.S. have written their pastoral letters on peace and on economic justice in recent years reflects this second meaning of "collegiality." The bishops form a writing committee that interviews many experts. A first draft is then widely distributed in dioceses and universities to solicit the feedback of the Catholic faithful as well as other interested persons. A second draft is written in response to the suggestions and criticisms. This second draft is then distributed as the first draft was. After another revision the letter is presented for the bishops' final approval. Many U.S. Catholics think that the collegial spirit reflected in this process should become a model for how authority might operate throughout the church as a whole.

Collegiality differs from both monarchy and democracy. An absolute monarch may seek advice but is not bound in any way to take it. In representative democracy, the voice of the people is the final word, and any representative who does not reflect the will of the majority may be voted out of office. In Catholic collegiality, the head of a college or authoritative body must take ultimate responsibility for decisions that are made, but is expected to act in a consultative manner so that what is expressed is not a personal opinion but the faith of the church. When a leader is said not to have acted in a collegial manner, the implication is that other peoples' opinions were not considered seriously.

Bishop as Priest, Prophet, King

Lumen Gentium's chapter on the People of God proclaimed that all Christians participate in the threefold ministry of Jesus as Priest, Prophet, and King. The particular way that bishops participate in this ministry is by sanctifying, teaching, and governing. As Jesus instituted the Eucharist in memory of his life, death, and resurrection, so the bishop takes the place of Christ in the diocese and is charged with administering the Eucharist and the other sacraments. As Jesus taught in parables and preached the coming of the kingdom, so the bishop is charged with teaching and the preaching of the gospel. As Jesus led the disciples and formed a community that continues even in the present time, so the bishop is charged with the official leadership of the diocese.

Ministry of the Bishop	
• Priest ——>	sanctify, give sacraments
• Prophet ——>	teach, preach the gospel
• King ——>	govern, lead

Taken together with the pope as their head, the college of bishops has authority over the whole of the Catholic church. When the bishops are referred to specifically in regard to their teaching authority, again taken together with the pope, they are known as the magisterium. The magisterium, then, is the authority exercised by those responsible for the official teaching of the church. Its highest forms of expression are *ex cathedra* papal statements and the formal definitions of ecumenical councils. Magisterial teaching is also found when there is fundamental agreement of the bishops even when not gathered in council, in the teachings of synods that are representative of the bishops, and in documents issued by Vatican offices that receive approval by the pope.

Taken individually, the bishop is the head of a diocese. (An archbishop is the head of an archdiocese, which serves as a center for the dioceses in its general area.) No individual bishop (other than the pope) has authority over the church as a whole or over any diocese other than his own. The bishop does, though, have complete authority over his own diocese. This authority is proper to his office as a successor of the apostles, and so the bishop is not simply the vicar of the pope.

Power to the Pope

Papal primacy means that the pope, by virtue of his office, is the head of the church. Throughout much of the church's history there has been controversy over whether an ecumenical council representing all of the bishops might not constitute the highest church authority. In Roman Catholicism, this matter has been settled decisively in favor of the pope. The passages in Scripture in which Jesus chooses Peter to be the head of the twelve apostles, as well as the long and complex tradition of the leadership of the bishop of Rome, provide the underpinnings for this position. One of the main purposes of the office of the papacy is to function as a source of unity for all Christians; it is unfortunately ironic that for many Protestants the papacy is a great stumbling block to unity.

Contemporary theologians disagree about the extent of the pope's constitutional obligation to consult other bishops and the faithful as a whole when making decisions, but *Lumen Gentium* is clear that the pope is not simply a dictator who has no restraints on his authority. Take, for example, the doctrine of papal infallibility. To say that the pope is infallible does not mean that the pope as an individual person can never make a mistake. Infallibility refers only to the pope's official capacity to define a teaching as true such that it is considered as being settled beyond question for the Catholic faithful. Yves Congar has referred to the popular tendency to include more and more ordinary papal teaching within the category of infallible truth as "creeping infallibility." Actually very few teachings have been formally defined as infallible by a pope.

The church's gift of infallibility functions as a tool to be used when the beliefs of the faithful need special support or when false beliefs are endangering the basic teaching of the church. Who is to decide about crucial questions that may threaten the church's very unity? Catholics say it is the pope who has the official authority, grounded in Scripture, to decide such issues. This is what infallibility is basically about.

When *Lumen Gentium* emphasizes that infallible definitions of the pope are true because the pope says so, and not because of the approval of others, the point is that the office of the papacy constitutes the highest authority in the Catholic church. If the pope by church law needed the approval of others, then those others would constitute a higher authority. This does not mean, though, that the approval of others is completely disregarded.

Francis Sullivan, an expert on structures of authority in the church, offers an explanation of this in his book *Magisterium*.[1] Suppose that the pope came out tomorrow with a pronouncement about the faith that he claimed to be infallible but which the majority of Catholics around the world rejected. Is *Lumen Gentium* claiming that the pope must be right and that those who disagree should get in line? Sullivan argues that that is one of two possibilities.

The first possibility is that the pope is right and that the majority of Christians need to change their belief to be in accordance with him. Sullivan gives the example that it took about fifty years for the teaching of Nicaea that Jesus is "one in being with the Father" to gain general acceptance by the faithful as a way of combatting the Arian heresy that denied the full divinity of Christ. So, if one accepts today the authority of Nicaea, one should also accept the possibility that church leadership might be right and the majority might be wrong.

The second possibility discussed by Sullivan is that the pope might be wrong, not because he needs the approval of others, but because there may have been some deficiency in the process through which the pope arrived at his decision. There are several conditions that function as limitations on the official ability of the pope to define a matter infallibly. The pope must be speaking *ex cathedra*, that is, in his capacity as the official head of the church. He must not be openly in heresy or in schism; he must be of sound mind and free of coercion. He must be defining a matter of faith and morals that is necessary for salvation, and so it must either be part of divine revelation or a teaching necessary to explain and defend divine revelation. Sullivan discusses how these conditions require that the pope consult the faith of the church, though they do not specify precisely *how* the pope must do this. It could be possible, then, that if the faithful on a large scale rejected a teaching that a pope had proclaimed as infallible, the process might be reviewed to see if the pope is not a heretic, insane, being forced, or inadequately consulting the faith of the church. When a teaching is determined to be true, though, it is technically defined as such by the pope, not needing the rubber stamp of the faithful as if they constituted a higher authority.

Lumen Gentium fights against exaggerated notions of papal infallibility not only by stating its limitations but also by placing it within the context of the infallibility of the church as a whole. Infallibility, the capacity to define essential matters as certainly true, belongs, first of all, to the church. It is manifested in different ways in the pope, the bishops, and in all the faithful. Hence, *Lumen Gentium* tells of how the bishops teach infallibly when "they are in agreement on one position as to be definitively held"(*LG*, 25). This is especially clear when the bishops are gathered in an ecumenical council. The document also says that "the entire body of the faithful, anointed as they are by the Holy One, cannot err in matters of the faith"(*LG*, 12). This property of the people of God is called the *sensus fidei* or "sense of the faith."

Infallibility is an important characteristic of the church as well as a useful tool that helps the church maintain the integrity of its most basic teachings. It is also, however, a source of confusion for Catholics and non-Catholics alike. Many Catholic theologians who agree wholeheartedly with the doctrine of infallibility wish that it had been called something different. To people in our culture, "infallible" seems to imply arrogance. Nobody is infallible, we are told. Ironically, the technical doctrine of papal infallibility does not at all mean that the pope is personally infallible; in fact it functions as much to define the limitations of his office as it does to grant him a special ability. Infallibility is related to the Catholic belief that the church is indefectible insofar as the Holy Spirit will not ultimately mislead us. Infallibility does not guarantee that the church will never make mistakes. Rather, it assures us that the Holy Spirit will not let us down on matters that are essential for our very identity.

Two Recent Controversies

The bishop's authority in his own diocese became a publicized issue in October 1986 in the case of Raymond Hunthausen, the archbishop of Seattle. His case illustrates well the complexities that often come into play in church politics. Hunthausen had come under fire from the Vatican for his liberal stands on a number of issues, including allowing liturgical irregularities such as general absolution without individual confession when there was a shortage of priests, first communion before first confession, and a Mass in the cathedral for the national convention of the gay Catholic group, Dignity.[2] The archbishop was also known for his personal refusal to pay taxes in protest against nuclear weapons, though the Vatican claimed that that was not a reason for its action.

The Vatican's response to the situation was to appoint an auxiliary bishop, Donald Wuerl, who was given charge of the areas of liturgy, moral teaching on sex-related issues, priestly formation and discipline, and the archdiocesan tribunal that handles annulments. What is exemplary for our point here is that Hunthausen could have contested the pope's order that he give up the authority in those areas that are proper to his office. Hunthausen chose not to contest this decision out of deference to the pope, but it remained his choice as long as he remained archbishop of Seattle. Of course if the pope had so chosen, he could have transferred Hunthausen to the South Pole. The tension was between the bishop's authority in his own diocese and his duty to submit to the authority of the pope; Hunthausen recognized the latter as the more important. After protests by the people of Seattle and negotiations between several American bishops and Rome, Hunthausen's full authority was restored in June 1987.

Another controversy that exemplifies the political intricacies of church structure took place in January 1989 when 163 German-speaking theologians issued the Cologne Declaration. The signers included such well known figures as Bernard Häring, Heinrich Fries, Hans Küng, Johann Baptist Metz, and Edward Schillebeeckx. The theologians complained that in places such as Cologne and Salzburg, the pope had been appointing bishops in a manner that disregarded centuries-old traditions of dioceses putting forth several candidates, of whom the pope would confirm one. Instead, the pope had been "unilaterally filling vacant sees around the world, without regard for the recommendations of the local church and without respect for their established right."[3] In the same document the theologians also complained about the denial of permission to teach on officially Catholic faculties to theologians whose positions on issues such as birth control differed from the Vatican, and about attempts in general to exaggerate the authority of the pope. For our purposes, what this incident highlights is both the primacy of the pope and the expectation that the pope should act in a collegial manner. Although Vatican II clarified many points concerning the relationship between pope and bishops, there are still many issues that are yet to be decided. What precisely is required of a pope in order to say that he has acted collegially?

Humility and Service
Amid the centuries-old arguments over who has how much authority, there has been a distinct movement stemming from Vatican II toward taking more seriously than ever the connection in the church

between leadership and service. Jesus said that the one who would be the greatest should be as the least. He washed the feet of the disciples at the Last Supper. He said that he came not to be served but to serve. He gave his life so that others might live. *Lumen Gentium* says that "Just as Christ carried out the work of redemption in poverty and persecution, so the church is called to follow the same route that it might communicate the fruits of salvation"(*LG*, 8). Specifically of the bishops, the document says that in the use of their power they need to remember "that one who is greater should become as the lesser and one who is the chief become as the servant."

In the early centuries of the church, bishops actually functioned as pastoral ministers who provided spiritual leadership for their particular church. Through the growth of the church as a huge and complicated organization bishops gradually became more administrators than actual ministers. A bishop today can be more easily compared to the CEO of a large corporation than to a priest working directly with the people. For that matter, some priests today complain that they themselves entered the priesthood to work with people and yet now function more as administrators.

In recent years the pope and the bishops have moved in the direction of a more simple lifestyle. The pope is installed rather than crowned; kissing his ring is optional; he is no longer carried into ceremonies by four seat-bearers. John Paul II has a habit of kissing the ground when he steps off the plane in any country that he visits. This basic direction can be observed in general in the lifestyle of bishops. Bishops who ride the bus to work are by far the exception, but so are bishops who present themselves as if they were royalty. Treating church leaders as royalty has noble roots in a religion that has symbolized the kingship of Christ through such treatment. The spirit of the Reformation, however, to which Catholics have been listening seriously of late, highlights the danger in such symbolism of putting human beings in the place of God. Without denying that bishops have never ceased to play a tremendous pastoral role in the diocese, one can acknowledge that bishops today often go to extraordinary lengths to move beyond administrative roles and minister directly with their people. A notable example is Cardinal John O'Connor of New York who works extensively with persons with AIDS.

The role of the bishop is fraught with a difficult mixture of raw power and Christian service. In the words of St. Augustine as quoted in *Lumen Gentium*:

What I am for you terrifies me; what I am with you consoles me. For you I am a bishop; but with you I am a Christian. The former is a duty; the latter a grace. The former is a danger; the latter, salvation. (LG, 32)

Bishops are fellow human beings and fellow Christians. Their office presents the danger that they might become out of touch with the people. Yet through that office, which bishops are called to fill in a spirit of humility, they provide the authoritative and continuous structure that links current Catholic belief and practice with the ministry of Jesus Christ.

Summary
In this chapter we have examined collegiality and the authority of bishops, papal primacy and infallibility, some recent controversies that illustrate some of the intricacies of internal church politics, and the new emphasis on humility and service. The experience of the ordinary Catholic is that a bishop is someone higher than a priest. A more systematic overview shows that bishops are the leaders of the Catholic church who succeed the apostles and who are responsible for sanctifying, teaching, and governing.

In the next chapter we will focus on the priesthood.

FOR FURTHER REFLECTION

1. What are your own personal images of the Catholic hierarchy today?

2. Would you prefer for the Catholic church to be more collegial or more democratic?

3. How do you think that most people understand the concept of papal infallibility? How does the popular understanding relate with the information in this chapter?

4. Do you tend to experience disputes within the Catholic hierarchy more as the natural working out of kinks within a huge organization or as an annoying blight upon the good news of Christ?

5. Do you find it personally important that many bishops seem to be pursuing more simple lifestyles?

SUGGESTED READINGS

Hebblethwaite, Peter. *In the Vatican*. Bethesda, Md: Adler and Adler, 1986.

Heft, James. *John XXII and Papal Teaching Authority*. Lewiston, N.Y.: Edwin Mellen Press, 1986.

Miller, J. Michael. *What Are They Saying About Papal Primacy?* Mahwah, N.J.: Paulist Press, 1983.

Reese, Thomas J. *Archbishop: Inside the Power Structure of the American Catholic Church*. San Francisco: Harper & Row, 1989.

CHAPTER 11

ORDAINED PRIESTHOOD

I remember a difficulty I had during my first week in graduate school at Catholic University in Washington, D.C. in the late 1970s. My professors, many of whom were priests, expected to be called by their first names. At that time I could hardly call a priest anything but "Father" without choking a bit, but I quickly got over this hesitancy.

The issue of names came up later in that first week when I addressed a fellow graduate student who was a priest from my native Philadelphia by his first name. He replied testily, "Didn't they teach you in your Catholic education to address a priest as 'Father?'" Embarrassed, I mumbled an apology. Standing with us, though, were two other priests, one of whom took up my cause. He argued that whereas the average Catholic in a parish situation should address a priest formally, in our situation as fellow students we should all be peers. The third priest agreed. The priest from Philadelphia was irritably silent. The issue remained unsettled. Whenever I saw the priest from Philadelphia after that I would greet him as "Father," but my voice would strain awkwardly. We never really had any conversations after that.

In the years prior to Vatican II there could be no doubt that priests were regarded as far above lay people. Although the life of the average priest was never easy, priests were well-educated academically, and trained in virtue. More than that, they were responsible for making Christ present in the community through the Eucharist. In my youth, my Catholic family and Catholic school taught me in no uncertain terms that the priesthood was the highest vocation to which a young man could be called. Many of the best and the brightest among male Catholic youth aspired to be a priest.

For many reasons, the status of priests in the Catholic community shifted after Vatican II. To call this shift a "drop" would not be quite accurate. Those wedded to the prior vision of the source of a priest's respectability might perceive the shift as a drop, but a closer reading of both Vatican II and contemporary Catholic culture reveals a more complex situation. Clearly, though, there has been a sharp decline in the number of men who enter the seminary.

This Chapter
In this chapter we will discuss first a current problem with the image of the priesthood, then the meaning of the priesthood as put forth by Vatican II, and finally the current shortage of priests as well as proposed solutions. This material draws upon section 28 of chapter 3 of *Lumen Gentium*. Two other documents of Vatican II are also relevant here: the Decree of the Training of Priests and the Decree on the Ministry and Life of Priests. A related question, the ordination of women, is addressed in chapter 27 of this book.

Image Problems
Lawrence Cunningham, a contemporary theologian, has said of the post-Vatican II period that "There was once a very clear vision of what Catholicism was and what it wanted; today we grope for that vision again, but have not yet articulated what it is."[1] This has perhaps been especially true of the priesthood. In the 1950s Catholics knew what a priest was: the distributor of the sacraments, the consecrator of the hosts, the spiritual advisor who represented the church, a holy man who had dedicated his life to God. A priest was Bing Crosby in *The Bells of St. Mary's.*

In the post-Vatican II period priests have suffered an image problem. Whether due to the perception of celibacy as weird in an age of sexual license, the exodus of large numbers of men in the late 1960s and early 1970s, the exaggerated publicity given to the rare cases of pedophilia, the association of the priesthood with the exclusion of women, the speculation about a large percentage of priests being gay, or just the general depiction of priests in films and television as naive, corrupt, or sex-starved, the image of the priest is just not the same as it used to be.

I would like to think that the perspective of the future will classify this image problem as a by-product of a temporary transitional period during which one meaning of priesthood was lost and had not yet been replaced by the fuller meaning of priesthood articulated at Vatican II. Already there are signs: The *Father Murphy* of the 1980s had much more dignity than the gullible Father Mulcahey of the early M*A*S*H episodes. (Even Father Mulcahey became a more subtle and sophisticated character as the series progressed.) Films such as *The Mission* and *Romero* clearly portray the priesthood and the episcopacy as reflecting a dignity that has little to do with social status but is connected, instead, with service to the poor. Some priests have commented to me that they now feel liberated from the mystique of the past and are more able to relate with their fellow Christians in a truly pastoral manner.

Vatican II helped to unsettle the traditional concept of priesthood in a couple of ways. First, so much emphasis is given to the bishops in *Lumen Gentium* that priests are characterized mainly as "bishop's helpers" who have little identity of their own. Although Vatican II issued an entire document that recognized the importance of priests, the Decree on the Ministry and Life of Priests, the fullness of this teaching has yet to affect the church at large.

Second, Vatican II tended to relativize the priesthood by placing it within a context that emphasized the ministry of all Christians through their participation in the priesthood of Christ. *Lumen Gentium* insisted that the ordained priesthood is essentially different from the common priesthood of the faithful, but the precise nature of that essential difference has not yet been clearly spelled out. What remains is that the role of the ordained priest is seen as much more analogous to that of the laity than in the past.

The Meaning of Priesthood at Vatican II

In a masterful work, theologian Kenan Osborne has traced the history of the Catholic priesthood up through the teaching put forth at Vatican II.[2] Osborne finds in the Vatican II documents a coherent and profound vision capable both of reviving current appreciation of the priesthood and of furthering ecumenical progress. Osborne sees the concept of the priest in the Counter-Reformation period (the four hundred years between the Council of Trent and Vatican II) being taken over and transformed within a much broader view. This broader view emerges from Vatican II's integration of new scriptural and historical perspectives available through scholarly studies. Osborne is careful to insist that the new vision does not contradict the old, but rather subsumes it within a fuller understanding.

Within this careful framework, however, Osborne is clear about the limitations of the Counter-Reformation concept of priesthood. Its main limitation is in linking the very definition of "priest" almost exclusively with the power to consecrate the Eucharist. Osborne characterizes this definition as narrow and one-sided. It provided the underpinning for a concept of priesthood that was overly separate, personal, and other-worldly. The priest was set apart from other people. He was thought to personally possess the priestly character and power derived from ordination, rather than to exercise an office that belongs first of all to the church community. The role of the priest was to pray the Divine Office and distribute the sacraments, not to become caught up in the transitory, vain things of this world.

Osborne cites several significant developments in the meaning of the priesthood in the documents of Vatican II. Vatican II rooted the ministry of the priest in the ministry of Jesus as prophet, priest, and king, not just in the power to consecrate the Eucharist. Thus, there was a new stress placed upon the duty of the priest to preach the gospel. There was a corresponding stress on the service role of the priest as a community leader. The priest's role in presiding at liturgy remains strong, but is situated within the context of the prophetic and kingly roles. The priesthood is presented in a way that is more related to other ministries in the church and thereby less separate. It is more connected with church structure, and thereby less personal or individual. It is more connected with community involvement and thereby less other-worldly.

Whereas in the pre-Vatican II church the priest would "say Mass" or even "read Mass" to the congregation, today the priest leads the congregation in celebrating the Mass. The priest presides over the congregation, each member of which participates in a real way. *Lumen Gentium* speaks of how the laity bring with them to the Mass the spiritual sacrifices of their everyday life, which "are most fittingly offered in the celebration of the Eucharist. Thus, as those everywhere who adore in holy activity, the laity consecrate the world itself to God" (*LG*, 34). The traditional emphasis on the real presence of Christ in the consecrated bread and wine is complemented by a contemporary focus on the presence of Christ throughout the eucharistic assembly. In the celebration of the Mass there is a new stress on the common priesthood of the faithful, the importance of the community, the spiritual value of everyday life, the preaching of the Word, and the connection between the Eucharist and social justice. The image of the priest has been shifting accordingly.

This shift in meaning is partly what was symbolized by moving the altar away from the wall and having the priest face the people. The priest today symbolizes less a mediator between the people and God and more a representative of a priestly people who experience Christ present among them.

In more practical terms, the Vatican II concept of the priesthood is more connected with the ministry of Jesus, more connected with the people of the church, more connected with a scripturally-based spirituality, and more connected with community issues of justice. It is to be hoped that the current state of affairs represents the transitional period that accompanies any major shift in vision. A renewed vision of the priesthood may help to attract more candidates.

The Shortage of Priests

Dean Hoge, a Protestant sociologist at the Catholic University of America, has studied both the current shortage of priests and possible solutions to the shortage problem.[3] A great rise in the number of priests retiring is accompanied by a sharp decline in the number of men entering the seminary. As Hoge shows, some church leaders view the shortage as representing a crisis of faith, so that the ultimate solution is Christian renewal. Hoge himself takes a different view: The problem is really more of an institutional one that calls for intelligent decisions in the face of sweeping social change. Although Hoge may lack appreciation for the way that Catholics refuse to separate completely institutional issues from faith issues, the statistics and options that he offers merit serious consideration.

Hoge offers eleven options for response under four basic categories. He uses statistical analysis to determine the potential impact for each option. Some of the options, such as married priests or the ordination of women, would pose theological difficulties. Hoge wants only to offer sociological information. His options are as follows:

Hoge's Options for Addressing the Priest Shortage
Type A: Reduce the Need for Priests
1. Combine or restructure parishes, or reeducate Catholics to have lower expectations of priestly services.

Type B: Get More Priests, with Existing Eligibility Criteria
2. Reassign or redistribute existing priests to get better utilization for parish leadership.
3. Get more parish priests from religious orders.
4. Get priests from foreign nations.
5. Recruit more seminarians.

Type C: Get More Priests, with Broadened Eligibility Criteria
6. Ordain married as well as celibate men.
7. Ordain women.
8. Institute a term of service for the priesthood, or institute an honorable discharge.
9. Utilize some resigned priests as sacramental ministers.

Type D: Expand the Diaconate and Lay Ministries
10. Expand and develop the permanent diaconate.
11. Expand and develop lay ministries.

Hoge argues that to do nothing is actually to opt for number 11, the expansion of lay ministries. This Type D option is what is already happening. According to Hoge's findings, this is also the only option within existing constraints that will have a high impact on the problem.

The other Type D option, the expansion of the diaconate, is also already happening, but it is not projected to have a high impact on the problem. For centuries prior to Vatican II, the diaconate was only a temporary stage in the ordination of a priest. Vatican II had recommended that the permanent diaconate, which had been one of the ministerial offices in the early church, should be restored and opened to married men. The permanent diaconate reinstitutes the traditional threefold division of ordained ministry into the offices of bishop, priest, and deacon, as had been established by the middle of the second century. Many parishes today have one or more deacons who assist in preaching the gospel and being of service in various ways in the parish. Hoge argues that the diaconate as it now exists is too part-time, limited in scope, unclearly defined, and lacking in recognizable status to offset the shortage of priests in any major way.

Hoge argues statistically that none of the Type A or Type B options are likely to have a major effect. This is because the larger causes of the priest shortage involve shifts in cultural values concerning career choices, marriage, sex, and styles of authority. The church has little control over these shifts. The only options that will have a high or medium impact are Type C, all of which would involve serious changes in current church policies.

Of the Type C options, the utilization of resigned priests would itself have a low impact. Allowing for a limited time of service would have a medium impact, but would involve abandoning the traditional Catholic understanding of the permanent sacramental character of the priesthood as a lifelong vocation. According to Hoge's statistical projections, ordaining women would have a limited numerical impact, at least at first. There are many reasons given today both for and against ordaining women, but this option too would require letting go of a long tradition in the Catholic church.

The option that would have the most significant numerical impact on the priest shortage and require relatively the least change in church tradition is the ordination of married men. Hoge found that if celibacy were made optional the enrollment in the seminaries would likely increase fourfold. Although celibacy itself has a long tradition in the Roman Catholic church, it is recognized as being a matter of church discipline and not an essential condition of the gospel message.

Hoge's viewpoint is strictly sociological. He himself is clear that he does not intend to settle theological or doctrinal matters. He wants to provide information and perspective that will help church leaders make decisions. He wants to address institutional matters, not faith matters.

As Phillip Murnion has pointed out, however, the Catholic style of faith does not allow for a complete separation of institutional matters and matters of belief.[4] For Catholics, the institution of the church and the substance of the faith are intimately related. Hoge himself agrees that any solutions need to be examined, not just for statistical probability, but for whether they can be harmonized with Catholic outlooks.

There are many arguments in favor of retaining celibacy as a requirement for priesthood. Although it is usually admitted that celibacy is a church rule that can change, some argue that it is a good rule that should remain in effect. Most defenders of the celibacy requirement reason along lines similar to the following: Since Catholic tradition holds that Jesus himself was celibate and since the priesthood is a special way of following Jesus, such a sacrifice is appropriate. Some passages in Scripture can be interpreted as lending support to this appropriateness. Celibacy functions as a sign of total dedication to bringing about the kingdom of God. Celibacy enables the priest to operate free of the obligations that come from a family. For the parish priest, one's first love is God and one's family is one's parish. Celibacy functions further as a witness that sexual activity, though beautiful and important, is not the absolute necessity it is held to be in our culture. To change the celibacy requirement would be simply to give in to a culture that really needs to be challenged by this witness.

There are also many arguments in favor of dropping celibacy as a requirement. Here are some of the more common ones.

Statistics show that many Catholics are already open to the idea.

Some of the cultural changes concerning the value of sex have been good ones; it is no longer necessary to cut a priest off from sexual intercourse in order to see him as "pure." Although celibacy can indeed function as a sign of the kingdom and a witness to sexual responsibility, that is no reason against making it optional rather than required of all. Although it might be true that Jesus never married, many of the apostles were married. In order to follow Jesus should one need to have a beard or be an experienced carpenter? Also, might not married priests be more pastorally sensitive to the needs of married couples and families? Moreover, is it not possible to have a total love commitment to God and to one's spouse at the same time? What is the conflict between loving God and loving a woman? Finally, does not the obligation of the church to provide ministers for the people in this time of shortage outweigh its preference for required celibacy?

This is a difficult issue with strong arguments on both sides. Inevitably, a debate about an issue such as this will lead people to examine their deeper presuppositions about God, tradition, culture, and the church.

A Blessing in Disguise?

Hoge cites some lay people who see the priest shortage as an opportunity to get more involved and to bring about needed changes in the structure of parish life. Such people would see it as a worse problem if the priesthood were to continue as a spiritually elite corps who tend to be out of touch with the problems and desires of the average person. Hoge offers statistics testifying to the willingness of Catholics to be more active. I have even heard it said that the Holy Spirit is causing the priest shortage in order to get the laity more involved.

Not everyone thinks that way. Most Catholics wish that there were more priests. It can be argued that an increase in the number of priests today would not necessarily detract from the quantity or quality of opportunities for lay people who want to get involved in church activities. More important, it would free up those lay people who recognize their Christian mission as being within the world. Most Catholics whom I know who have school-age children dread the moment when they will be asked to serve on one more committee or undertake one more ministry. As Hoge notes, Catholics want priests not only for presiding at the Eucharist but for baptisms, marriages, and preaching. For Catholics there is something special and even sacred about the priesthood. No matter how much the meaning or role of the priest changes in our time, we should not allow its sacredness to fade away any more than it already has. Any changes in church policy need to be accompanied by a renewed valuing of the priesthood by Catholics and, I would hope, a renewed encouragement of vocations by parents, teachers, lay people, and priests themselves.

Summary

In this chapter we have examined current concern over the shortage of priests against the background of shifting images and understandings of the priesthood. It seems as though the priesthood is in a difficult transitional period when one vision is fading while another has not quite yet taken its place. In this way, what is happening to the priesthood symbolizes what is happening to the church itself.

In the next chapter we will examine the relationship between the official teaching of the church and the beliefs of Catholics.

FOR FURTHER REFLECTION

1. In what ways have you been aware of the shifting image of the priesthood?

2. Do you think that as Vatican II becomes more understood, the priesthood may gain a renewed appreciation?

3. Which of Dean Hoge's options for addressing the priest shortage do you most favor? Which do you least favor?

4. Do you think that the celibacy requirement should be changed?

5. Is the priest shortage necessarily a bad thing?

SUGGESTED READINGS

Hoge, Dean R. *The Future of Catholic Leadership: Responses to the Priest Shortage.* Kansas City: Sheed & Ward, 1987.

Osborne, Kenan. *Priesthood: A History of Ordained Ministry in the Roman Catholic Church.* Mahwah, N.J.: Paulist Press, 1988.

CHAPTER 12

LEVELS OF TEACHING, LEVELS OF ASSENT

A t the end of a course on Catholicism I ask my students to write about the two or three most important things that they have learned. Their answers vary greatly overall, but each semester one particular issue is mentioned most frequently by far: Students report that they were pleased and even relieved to find out that it is O.K. to remain Catholic while disagreeing with some of the church's official teaching.

As I write this, I have an urge to gather together in the gymnasium all of the students whom I have taught over the last few years and holler, "That isn't exactly what I said!" But, as I think about it, I did not ask them to repeat back what I said; rather, I asked them to report about what they had learned. I respect and even basically agree with what they learned; I only hope that they do not remember that point apart from the many necessary qualifications that we cover in class.

This Chapter
In this chapter we will consider the importance of beliefs, the relative ranking of beliefs, and matters of assent and disagreement. In *Lumen Gentium*, the sections most relevant to these matters are section 25 in chapter 3 and section 37 in chapter 4. Also of relevance is Vatican II's Declaration on Religious Liberty.

Beliefs Are Crucial
Our pluralistic society has a tendency to down play the importance

of religious beliefs. We want to affirm the rights and dignity of every human being regardless of one's religious affiliation. We want to say that it really doesn't matter what one believes; one has the same constitutional rights as everyone else.

The tendency to minimize the importance of belief has carried over even to religions themselves. Sometimes it is done out of deference to other world religions. Sometimes it is done in reaction against past tendencies to overemphasize the role of belief to the neglect of other elements of religion such as prayer, religious experience, or social transformation. Orthopraxy (right doing), we are told, is more basic than orthodoxy (right belief).

It is possible, however, to combine an affirmation of human rights, other faiths, and religious experience with the recognition of the crucial role that beliefs play in the life of the individual and the community. As the theologian Bernard Lonergan has pointed out, beliefs shape the very world in which a person lives.[1] Social institutions and human cultures have sets of meanings at their very core. These meanings can be detected as presuppositions and formulated as beliefs. For example, the judicial system of the United States rests upon a set of beliefs about the meaning and importance of justice. The institutions of marriage and the family rest upon a set of beliefs about how men and women should relate with each other in regard to sex and children.

Religious beliefs shape one's understanding of the meaning and purpose of life. They are part of the very world in which you live. When you wake up in the morning, into what kind of world do you awaken? What do you perceive? Is it a world created by an all-powerful and all-loving God who has a good purpose in mind? Or do you awaken into an absurd world that yields no ultimate meaning no matter how much we long for answers? Do you awaken into a world that, though fallen in sin, has been redeemed by Christ? Or is it a world in which the false, nasty belief in sin has covered over the true innocence of human beings? Do you awaken into a world in which the Spirit is guiding us to relate with each other more fully and deeply as human beings? Or is it a world in which each of us needs to look out for number one because if we don't nobody else will? What do we believe about the ultimate nature of reality and the purpose of our lives?

The dichotomies offered in the preceding paragraph are not the only choices we have. My religion is not the only one in the world. Even secular worldviews can offer alternative meaning without preaching despair. I do not wish to suggest that people's civil rights, dignity, or freedom should be determined according to their religious beliefs. I only want to emphasize that what you believe is absolutely crucial to who you are as a person and to what sense your life will make.

Some Beliefs More Central Than Others

Vatican II's Decree on Ecumenism called for partners in interfaith dialogue to "remember that in Catholic doctrine there exists an order or 'hierarchy' of truths, since they vary in their relation to the foundation of the Christian faith" (section 12). In other words, Catholics recognize that some beliefs are more central than others to the core of the Christian faith. When engaging in ecumenical dialogue, it is often appropriate to put disagreements on less central matters to the side in order to affirm agreements on more basic points. For example, when Catholics dialogue with Lutherans, it may be desirable to dwell first on areas of agreement, such as the utter gratuity of salvation through Christ, without always concentrating on such disputed points as the role of human merit.

At present there is no sure way systematically spelled out to determine a ranking of beliefs in a hierarchy of truths. Perhaps some guidance can be drawn from Bernard Lonergan, who speaks about the "original message" of Christianity. All other teachings are "doctrines about this doctrine."[2] For a reference to this original message, Lonergan cites 1 Corinthians 15:3ff, in which Paul says "I handed on to you first of all what I myself received, that Christ died for our sins in accordance with the Scriptures; that he was buried and, in accordance with the Scriptures, rose on the third day." Paul goes on to list many witnesses to the resurrected Christ, and concludes, "...this is what we preach and this is what you believed." The core of the Christian message is the good news that through the risen Christ, who fulfills the expectations of the Old Testament, we find salvation from sin.

The hierarchy of truths would then be determined by assessing how close to this basic core any particular belief is. That in itself is far from an easy task. One of the arguments in favor of strong authoritative leadership in the church is the almost endless variety of interpretations one might give to the original message and its implications. Who is to say which interpretations fall within an acceptable range? Who is to say which beliefs are crucial and which are less central?

The official Catholic position is that the magisterium of the church has the power to define the meaning and importance of matters of faith and morals. The position articulated at Vatican II in the Decree on Revelation is that the gospel message is expressed through Scripture and Tradition. The magisterium of the church does not have authority over

Scripture or Tradition, but it does have authority over human interpretations of Scripture and Tradition. At the present time, though, there exists no systematic presentation of the hierarchy of truths.

In my opinion, the belief that Jesus is one in being with the Father is central; the belief in the intercession of the saints is important but not as central. The belief that adultery is wrong is central; the belief that artificial birth control is always immoral is not as central. The belief that the Holy Spirit guides the church is central; the belief in the infallibility of the pope is not as central. It is unfortunate when a not-so-central issue receives attention disproportionate to its worth and thereby takes attention away from more central matters. This is not to suggest that beliefs that are not central are thereby necessarily less true; it is to suggest, rather, that such issues do not have to be made pressing concerns in ecumenical dialogue.

What Must Catholics Believe?

The basics of the Christian story are to be found in the Apostles Creed and also in the more technical Nicene Creed. Catholics are expected to accept the faith witness of the Bible, the three persons in one God, the decisions of the ecumenical councils, the teachings of the pope and the bishops, and the sacraments as instruments of grace.

In recent years, some theologians have attempted (amid controversy) to apply the idea of a "hierarchy of truths" beyond ecumenical dialogue to internal matters of Catholic belief. What beliefs must be accepted if one is to consider oneself a Catholic?

Theologian Monika Hellwig, drawing upon the work of Yves Congar, distinguishes between capital "T" Tradition and small "t" tradition.[3] On the one hand, Tradition refers to those things that are an essential part of the Catholic faith; if Tradition changed, the very faith would be altered. On the other hand, tradition refers to those things that may be important but are not essential. For example, the Catholic belief in Christ's presence in the Eucharist is part of Tradition; the rule that the priest giving communion must place the host directly on the tongue was a tradition that could and has been changed.

This distinction between Tradition and tradition is helpful, but it does not by itself settle all matters. Catholics still can disagree about whether a particular issue is Tradition or a tradition. The church's official position that it does not have the authority to ordain women is based on the judgment that an all-male priesthood is a Tradition established by Christ himself. Many Catholics who favor the ordination of women argue that the all-male priesthood is a tradition related to an ancient, patriarchal culture and not something essential to the gospel.

Also, when we ask questions about which beliefs are crucial, we should not forget that many believers have different understandings of the same beliefs. What one Catholic accepts when believing in the doctrine of the Assumption may be very different from what another Catholic accepts. One Catholic may recite the Creed and believe everything quite literally; another might recite the Creed and understand just about everything symbolically; yet another might have a very nuanced understanding of how myth and history interrelate, and understand the Creed accordingly. While it is not necessary for all Catholics to understand every belief in exactly the same way, Catholics can only share the same faith when there is some uniformity. The question of doctrinal pluralism, like that of the hierarchy of truths, is one that is not currently clarified, and one that should receive more attention in the future.

Assent Deeper Than Dissent

John Paul II spoke out against dissent in the church when he visited the United States in the fall of 1987. Noting that many Catholics have not accepted certain church teachings, "notably sexual and conjugal morality, divorce and remarriage, and abortion," the pope said: "It is sometimes claimed that dissent from the magisterium is totally compatible with being a good Catholic and poses no obstacle to the reception of the sacraments. This is a grave error." Later, when talking with a group of bishops about theological freedom, the pope said that the bishops "should seek to show the inacceptability of dissent and confrontation as a policy method in the area of church teaching." In the same talk, he said, "Dissent remains what it is: dissent. As such it may not be proposed or received on an equal footing with the church's teaching."

Guidelines for legitimate dissent among theologians were in existence long before Vatican II. Since Vatican II, Catholic theologians and Catholic textbooks have clarified conditions when an ordinary believer's dissent from official teaching is legitimate. Even bishops' conferences and individual bishops have issued documents that discuss when dissent is legitimate and when it is irresponsible. Is the pope, then, flatly contradicting and retracting what has become ordinary church teaching about dissent over the last few decades?

It is possible that this is what he intends. I have a memory, although I find no written record of it, of seeing John Paul II on television saying, "Dissent, no. Assent, yes." Such sloganeering, however, is meant to communicate with crowds on an immediate level, and does not always represent a careful or complete position. I wish to offer an alternative interpretation of what the pope is saying.

As I see it, the pope is not necessarily trying to say in a technical way that no disagreement can ever be legitimate; rather, he is launching a full-scale attack against an attitude that promotes dissent as normal and that places dissent on the same level as the acceptance of fundamental beliefs. The pope is stomping on what has come to be called "pick-and-choose Catholicism" or "salad bar Catholicism": the attitude that Catholics are free to select some beliefs and reject others without giving most serious attention to church teaching. He is saying that behaviors such as sex outside marriage, remarriage without annulment, and abortion are grave matters that are not just questions of personal conscience. He is saying that these things are sinful, and that Catholics are not free simply to pick and choose in all cases what they will personally consider to be right and wrong. Some Catholics today would argue that each of these issues is too complex to make any sweeping judgments. It is with this attitude that the pope is taking issue. In a sense, this is another form of the question of what counts as Tradition and what counts as tradition.

The pope is also saying that believers must not put dissent on the same level as acceptance. Acceptance is much more basic; it is a matter of faith. The believer's yes is prior to and deeper than the believer's no.

It is a mistake to think that the believer starts out with a mind like a blank sheet and then goes about selecting and rejecting various pieces of the Catholic faith. In a basic sense a Catholic is one who embraces the whole of the Catholic faith. A Catholic accepts the Christian message through the Scriptures, the Creed, the sacraments, and church teachings. Any talk of disagreement or dissent should take place only after this context has been established.

Responsible and Irresponsible Disagreement

I wonder what associations the pope links with the term "dissent." Perhaps he thinks of a full-scale revolution in which bishops and priests are sent to the guillotine. It would not be the first time in church history that such would happen. The word "dissent" carries undesirable connotations for our situation today. I would prefer to talk about "disagreement" with church teachings.

In the Catholic church today, disagreement is a reality that is unlikely to go away. Some theologians argue that disagreement is part of a healthy process by which the church changes. Not all disagreement, though, is legitimate. There is a need to distinguish between responsible and irresponsible disagreement.

Francis Sullivan explains that Catholics are expected to give basic assent to church teaching. One cannot disagree with those teachings that are held to be infallible if one wishes to remain Catholic. But if a Catholic approaches a non-infallible teaching with an attitude of openness, tries to conform one's mind and will, and still after a period of struggle cannot wholeheartedly assent to the teaching, the result is a disagreement that is probably both responsible and legitimate.

Sullivan points out that in the original draft of Vatican II's Declaration on Religious Liberty a sentence read, "In the formation of their consciences, the Christian faithful ought carefully to attend to the sacred and certain doctrine of the church." During council debate of the document, it was proposed that the wording be changed from "ought carefully to attend to" to "ought to form their consciences according to." The committee in charge of the document rejected the proposed change on the grounds that it was excessively restrictive.[4] The original statement stands as is in the final document (section 14). This example illustrates that although the council calls Catholics to be predisposed to assent to church teachings, there is also a recognition that Catholics have some personal responsibility in the formation of their consciences. Catholics are not robots programmed by the Vatican.

I have tried to formulate some strict ground rules for disagreement with church teaching that conform with official outlooks. From that point of view, responsible and legitimate disagreement requires the Catholic to:

1. have an open attitude, including a predisposition to give religious submission of mind and will to official church teaching;
2. not challenge the very ability of the church to teach authoritatively;
3. investigate the matter in question to a reasonable degree, including the reasoning behind the church's teaching;
4. continue to be open-minded and willing to be challenged again periodically by the church's position;
5. not scandalize others by encouraging them to disagree as well.

These ground rules can be useful for stating various issues to be considered when asking when disagreement is responsible. They are not sufficiently precise, however, for judging whether any particular disagreement is itself responsible. Most disagreement among U. S. Catholics would not strictly measure up to these ground rules, and yet I would personally be hesitant simply to label it irresponsible.

For example, there are some Catholics who disagree with church teaching about artificial birth control who would meet these criteria. There are also some who have closed-minded attitudes and who would clearly be irresponsible. The majority of American Catholics who disagree with church teaching about artificial birth control, however, probably neither meet the criteria listed above nor could be facilely dismissed as irresponsible.

Some Catholics have found Natural Family Planning methods to have more to offer than artificial means of birth control; a large majority of Catholics, however, do not share this point of view. The historical impact of this issue in American Catholicism makes disagreement too complex a matter to be judged by any pre-set criteria. Birth control was the first issue subject to massive disagreement by the laity. It stands today as a symbol that much remains to be worked out concerning the manner in which the church should teach and the manner in which believers are to respond. Most Catholics who disagree do so because a teaching both interferes with their lifestyles and does not make any sense to them. It is too simple to just label their disagreement irresponsible. On a deep level there is a communication problem going on here, with each side needing to listen more closely and speak more sensitively to the other.

Summary

In this chapter we have explored the importance of belief, the hierarchy of truths, the relation between assent and dissent, and some ground rules for responsible disagreement. So many of my Catholic students seem to be relieved when they hear that disagreement can be legitimate; I cannot help but worry about the range of beliefs, attitudes, and behaviors that they may be wanting to justify through rationalization. I would be even more worried, however, if my students would not take seriously their responsibility to think for themselves.

In the next chapter we will investigate the changing status of lay people in the church.

FOR FURTHER REFLECTION
1. Which Catholic church teachings give you the most trouble?
2. Do you think that problems over controversial issues can get in

the way of a person's basic beliefs?

3. Are you inclined to think that most issues in dispute in the Catholic church today are capital "T" Tradition or small "t" tradition?

4. How would you distinguish between "responsible disagreement" and "pick-and-choose Catholicism?"

5. Do you think that Catholics tend to be more responsible or irresponsible in their disagreements?

SUGGESTED READINGS

Curran, Charles. *Faithful Dissent*. Kansas City: Sheed & Ward, 1986.

Drane, James. *Authority and Institution: A Study in Church Crisis*. Milwaukee: Bruce Publishing, 1969.

Marthaler, Berard. *The Creed*. Mystic, Conn.: Twenty-Third Publications, 1992 [1987].

Orsy, Ladislas. *The Church: Teaching and Learning*. Wilmington, Del.: Michael Glazier, 1987.

Sullivan, Francis. *Magisterium*. Mahwah, N.J.: Paulist Press, 1983.

SECTION FOUR

THE LAITY

CHAPTER 13

LAY PEOPLE

A lcoholics Anonymous consists of an extensive network of groups of various sizes spread throughout the world. If you want to contact A.A., you can call the number listed in virtually any phone book. There is another way, though, to contact the organization: Talk to any member. Any and every member of A.A. is a representative of the group. Members think of themselves as the hand of A.A. Whenever and wherever someone needs help, A.A. members take responsibility. If you are talking with a member, you are talking with A.A.

This has generally not been the case with lay people in the Catholic church. (A lay person is defined in *Lumen Gentium* as any Catholic who has not been ordained or taken religious vows.) If you want to talk with someone who represents the Catholic church, you will probably be told to make an appointment with a priest. A bishop represents a higher level, and of course the pope represents the highest level. Catholic lay people do not usually regard themselves as representing "the church."

This is not to say that A.A. does not have its own growing centralized structures of organization. The point of comparison is simply that members of A.A. think of themselves as representing the group such that they themselves can share with the newcomer about the basics of staying sober one day at a time. Most Catholics have not traditionally thought of themselves in an analogous way about being able to share the basics of Christian living.

This Chapter

The need for and the willingness of the laity to take personal responsibility for the church is changing. In this chapter we will discuss four interconnected issues: the laity's relation to church, their spiritual dignity, their sharing in the ministry of Christ, and the particular ways in which they are called to live a Christian life. These issues are drawn from chapter 4 of *Lumen Gentium*.

We Are the Church

Daniel Pilarczyk, Archbishop of Cincinnati, has written that the church is basically an organization of lay people who are served by a hierarchy. This revolutionary definition reverses the centuries-old Catholic tendency to think of the church most basically as a hierarchical institution in which bishops, priests, and religious were the real members of the club and the laity were there as sheep to be led and tended. To this day, when most Catholics think of "the church," they image the pope and the bishops in Rome making up rules and regulations for the preservation of Catholic teaching. It is still the rare Catholic who has appropriated the spirit of Vatican II that leads one to say, "We are the church!"

I can remember hearing another bishop say that his main disappointment in the implementation of Vatican II has been that the laity have not yet begun to think of themselves as the church. "You are the church!" was his message. The church is not just over in Rome. The church is the People of God. The church is comprised of each one of us who is a member.

Thinking of the church as a lay organization carries forward the thrust of Vatican II, which stressed the equality in spiritual dignity of all who are baptized, the common priesthood of the faithful, and the importance of Christian involvement in the everyday world of human affairs. At the same time, such thinking does not in any way have to be anti-institutional or anti-hierarchical; a confident lay-centered church can arrive at a renewed appreciation of the hierarchy that serves it.

Equality in Spiritual Dignity

Clericalism is the practice of granting too much influence and power to the clergy. To say that pre-Vatican II Catholicism tended to be clericalistic is to utter an obvious truth; it should not be forgotten, however, that many pre-Vatican II priests as well as lay people fought hard against these clericalistic tendencies. It should also be remembered that the current overreaction against the clericalism of the past may be a contributing factor in the shortage of priests.

As a practical issue in the Catholic church, clericalism has most often been thought of as placing priests and religious so high up on pedestals that one forgets that they are just as human as the rest of us are. There is, however, another way to think of the problem: Clericalism can be the result of not recognizing the importance and dignity of lay people. In other words, instead of thinking of priests as too high and needing to be dragged down, it is better to think of lay people as being too low and needing to have more recognition.

This is the approach taken in *Lumen Gentium* when it says:

> ...the chosen People of God is one: "one Lord, one faith, one baptism"; sharing a common dignity as members from their regeneration in Christ; having the same filial grace and the same vocation to perfection; possessing in common one salvation, one hope and one undivided charity. (*LG*, 32)

The document is emphasizing that in a most fundamental spiritual sense the members of the church are equal. By virtue of one's baptism, one is a full member of the church with a full share in God's grace insofar as one perseveres in love. When it comes to faith, spiritual dignity, grace, salvation, hope, and love, each member is invited to share fully. There are no second-class Catholics. There is no hierarchy when it comes to being called to holiness.

Becoming a priest or a brother or a sister may play a crucial role in the life of an individual and in the life of the church as a whole. It changes one's status in relation to the hierarchical structures of the church. But it does not change one's status in relation to one's basic membership or one's most fundamental relationship with God. Every member of the church is called to a life of holiness:

> ...all are called to sanctity and have received an equal privilege of faith through the justice of God. And if by the will of Christ some are made teachers, pastors and dispensers of mysteries on behalf of others, yet all share a true equality with regard to the dignity and to the activity common to all the faithful for the building up of the Body of Christ. (*LG*, 32)

Lay people, vowed religious, and ordained clergy are called to collaborate in carrying out the mission of the church. They are not to get hung up in worrying about who is holier.

This strong assertion of the equality in spiritual dignity among members of the church raises some critical questions for Catholics today. If we are all equal, why cannot lay people preside at the eucharistic celebration? Why are lay people not permitted to preach without special permission? Why does it seem that in many places lay people do not experience great respect from the hierarchy? It seems as though, à la George Orwell's *Animal Farm*, some people are more equal than other people.

One way of responding to these issues is to point out that saying people are equal in spiritual dignity is not the same as saying they are equal in everything. It is true that no one can claim entitlement or privilege for themselves over others in regard to the grace of God. But this does not mean that everyone is equal in talents and abilities, intelligence and wit, social status and rank, or compassion and understanding. The church has hierarchical structures that specify offices and functions, but this does not detract from its assertion of the spiritual equality of its members.

An alternative response to the charge of real inequalities still existing in the church is to point out that Vatican II took place so recently in the history of the church that its full implications are still being worked out. Many changes loom on the horizon.

I take both of these responses very seriously. Not everyone is equal in everything. Many new things are yet to come.

Another challenge to the claim of the spiritual equality of members is the question of the relative status of non-members. Is the church implying that non-Catholics and non-Christians are spiritually second-class? This is a difficult issue that arises in many places in this book. In this context I wish to say only that the matter of spiritual equality was dealt with at Vatican II as an internal question, and that there was no intention of implying anything derogatory about people of other faiths.

Lay People as Priests, Prophets, and Kings

We have seen how *Lumen Gentium* declares that all members of the church participate in the threefold ministry of Christ as priest, prophet, and king. We have seen further how the document specifies that the particular way that the bishops and priests participate is through sanctifying, teaching, and leading. *Lumen Gentium* also spells out the specific ways in which the laity are called to participate in Christ's threefold ministry.

Ministry of the Lay Person		
Priest	——>	bring holiness to the world
Prophet	——>	let Gospel shine through daily life
King	——>	work toward the kingdom

Lay people carry out Christ's *priestly* function through their sacrifice and holiness as they live their lives in the world:

For all their works, prayers, and apostolic endeavors, their ordinary married and family life, their daily occupations, their physical and mental relaxation, if carried out in the Spirit, and even the hardships of life, if patiently borne—all these become "spiritual sacrifices acceptable to God through Jesus Christ." Together with the offering of the Lord's body, they are most fittingly offered in the celebration of the Eucharist. Thus, as those everywhere who adore in holy activity, the laity consecrate the world itself to God. (*LG*, 34)

In other words, lay persons act as priests insofar as they offer their very lives to God. In practical terms, this can mean that the lay person makes God present in the world by striving to live a holy life.

Lumen Gentium depicts the *prophetic* function of the laity as the promise that "the power of the Gospel might shine forth in their daily social and family life" (*LG*, 35). The laity are to give witness to their faith by the way that they live. The *kingly* function of the laity is expressed in *Lumen Gentium* as the call to spread the kingdom of God throughout the world. The laity are to work to bring the world in the direction of "truth and life...holiness and grace...justice, peace, and love" (*LG*, 36). Again, it is through the manner in which the lay person lives life that the mission of Christ is carried to the world.

Spheres of Lay Activity

Lumen Gentium does not shut lay people out from all ministry within the church. The laity "carry out for their own part the mission of the whole Christian people in the church and in the world" (*LG*, 31). Indeed, the document says that "the laity can also be called in various ways to a more direct form of cooperation in the apostolate of the Hierarchy....Further, they have the capacity to assume from the Hierarchy certain ecclesiastical functions, which are to be performed for a spiritual purpose" (*LG*, 33). And so, since Vatican II, there has been a virtual explosion of lay ministries within the church.

The main thrust of *Lumen Gentium*, however, emphasizes that the special function of the laity is precisely their role in the world. The document states that "What specifically characterizes the laity is their secular nature....the laity, by their very vocation, seek the kingdom of God by engaging in temporal affairs and by ordering them according to the plan of God" (*LG*, 31). Three worldly spheres of lay activity are stressed in *Lumen Gentium:* family, work, and social transformation. It is through their family life, their work, and their striving for a better human world that lay people find their most basic call to live as followers of Christ.

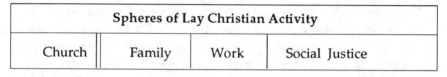

Spheres of Lay Christian Activity			
Church	Family	Work	Social Justice

One upshot of this delineation of spheres of activity has been Pope John Paul II's insistence that priests and religious not hold political office. As he sees it, such worldly activity is properly the role of lay people. Those who officially represent the church should preach high ideals, but should not become overly identified with particular nations, political parties, or ideological platforms. This division of labor is intended to allow lay people motivated by their Christian consciences to become deeply and passionately involved in the ambiguities of human affairs, without being perceived as acting as representatives of official Catholic policies.

The pope has reinforced this division of labor in a 1989 document on the laity. He warns lay people against "the temptation of being so strongly interested in church services and tasks that some fail to become engaged in their responsibilities in the professional, social, cultural, and political world."[1] As the pope sees it, it is the general calling of lay people to work for the transformation of the world and the coming of the kingdom through their family and work life and their political involvements. Otherwise, lay people might fall prey to a second temptation, that of "legitimizing the unwarranted separation of the Gospel's acceptance from the actual living of the Gospel in various situations in the world."[2] Lay people are not to use the church as a place to hide from the world but as a source of faith and holiness for tackling life's challenges.

Summary

In this chapter we have examined the shift in the role of the laity signaled by the documents of Vatican II. In particular, we have focused on sharing in the threefold ministry of Christ, being equal in spiritual dignity, and being called to action in the spheres of family, work, and social justice.

This new focus on the laity is part of a broadened understanding of the mission of the church to the world. One cannot understand "church" just by concentrating on matters of internal structure and authority. What it means to live as a Christian in the world is as much a part of the church as what it means to be a bishop.

"We are the church!" is the new cry of the laity. It is the cry of the joy of a new birth. It is the cry of the pain and the resignation of a new responsibility. It is hard for me to envision the ordinary lay Catholic assuming the kind of personal ownership for the church that a recovering alcoholic assumes for A.A. But if I stretch my imagination…

In the next chapter we will study various ways that Catholics are using to revitalize lay participation in the life of the church.

FOR FURTHER REFLECTION

1. Have you had any experience of lay Catholics displaying a sense of "ownership" in the church?

2. Do you yourself tend on an everyday basis to regard lay people as equal in spiritual dignity with ordained ministers?

3. Should "equality in spiritual dignity" mean that all roles in the church should be open to everyone, or do you agree that different people can play different roles and still share a fundamental equality?

4. Some Catholics do not like the pope's emphasis that the laity's primary mission is in the world, *not* in the church. What do you think?

5. Do you think it is common for people to make a mental division between their religious life in church and their everyday life in the world? If so, how might such a split be healed?

SUGGESTED READINGS

Congar, Yves. *Lay People in the Church*. Westminster, Md.: Newman Press, 1957 [1956].

Faivre, Alexander. *The Emergence of the Laity in the Early Church*. Mahwah, N.J.: Paulist Press, 1990 [1984].

John Paul II. *Christifideles Laici* (The Vocation and Mission of the Lay Faithful in the Church and in the World). Washington, D.C.: United States Catholic Conference, 1989.

Parent, Rémi. *A Church of the Baptized: Overcoming the Tension Between the Clergy and the Laity*. Mahwah, N.J.: Paulist Press, 1989 [1987].

CHAPTER 14

TOOLS FOR CHURCH RENEWAL

S everal years ago a young woman, thirteen years old, used to deliver the newspaper to my door. She was tall and slender, and tended to stand a bit hunched over looking down at the ground. She mumbled when she spoke, and I often had to ask her to repeat what she said. She baby-sat my children a couple of times, and so we got to know a little bit about each other. She knew that I was a Catholic teacher of religion. I knew that she had been brought up Catholic but was now a non-churchgoer from a family of alienated Catholics.

There came a point when she became much more talkative. She started asking me many questions about the Bible. She began to share with me about her home life and her father's drinking problem.

What had brought about this openness in her was the experience of going to a new church. A friend of hers in junior high had invited her to the services at a Pentecostal church. She got into the habit of going regularly and then her mother started to attend. She and her mother went to three-hour services twice a week, and also volunteered several hours cleaning the church.

The people in her new church interpreted the Bible literally, word for word. They told the young woman that she should not cut her hair, because the Bible says that a woman's hair is her glory. They told her not to go swimming at public pools, because the Bible says that she should dress modestly. They told her that people who weren't born again could not be saved, because the Bible says that unless a man be born again of water and the Spirit he will not enter God's kingdom. She still continued to cut her hair and to swim and to believe in the salvation of non-Christians. Her pastor said that was all right for now. He told her that when she was ready she would accept these teachings by the conviction of the Holy Spirit within her, not because anyone told her to do it.

The young woman looked to me for the reassurance that she did not have to interpret the Bible that way at all. She told me that she still believed the Catholic way, but that there was something about this church that she knew was right for her.

And there was. This young woman had found a group of people who were willing to reach out and love her until she could love herself. They told her that she was a creature of God, and that God didn't make junk. They welcomed her, got to know her, got her talking about her life, and helped her to turn her life around. The transformation that they generated in her was near miraculous. She was visibly changed. She stood up straighter. She dressed better. She had more confidence. She spoke up so that she could be understood the first time. She talked about the real issues in her life and expressed her deepest feelings and beliefs. She stood up to her father and confronted him about his drinking and his need to get help.

My overwhelming reaction to her experience is a positive one. I thank God for the people in that Pentecostal church and for the grace that worked through them. I maintain some sharply different beliefs about interpreting the Bible, but I am also left with a twinge of jealousy for their church's Spirit. Sometimes I wonder: Why isn't my church more like that? Why isn't my church more of a welcoming community?

This Chapter

In recent years the Catholic church has been consciously moving in the direction of building dynamic faith communities. There already exists a growing sense of participation whereby the laity are assuming more personal ownership for the parish. In this chapter we will discuss three developments that are functioning as tools for the renewal of the Catholic church: lay ministries, the Rite of Christian Initiation for Adults, and Renew, a program for community formation in the parish.

This chapter reflects on developments relevant to the shift in status of the laity discussed in chapter 4 of *Lumen Gentium*. It is also related to the discussion of the development of local faith communities in Vatican II's Decree on the Church's Missionary Activity.

Tools for Church Renewal		
lay ministries	——>	empower people to serve
adult initiation	——>	initiates into community
Renew	——>	builds small faith groups

Lay Ministries

In recent years, Catholic parishes have experienced a virtual explosion of lay ministries. The pope has called for a clarification of terms in this area. The term "ministry" has come to be used in a broad sense to mean any work that one does as a Christian. Not only has the lay eucharistic distributor been called a "minister," but also the teacher, the counselor, and the nurse. The term has even been extended by some to include the baker and the plumber, as long as they are conscious of serving God and community through their work. In a document on the laity, the pope has asked that an end be put to this confusing usage by restricting the terms "minister" and "ministry" to services performed explicitly in connection with the church. At the same time, he calls for the laity to have as their main focus the church's mission to the world through family, work, and social transformation. The laity are to beware of the danger of being too focused on the church's internal matters.

Even when using "ministry" in its restrictive sense as a church-related service, the recent growth in lay ministry has been enormous. This is true both of professional, trained, salaried lay ministers and those who perform volunteer service. The shortage of priests and religious and the new sense of participation among lay people has made such a development inevitable.

Many Catholic parishes today employ lay people as professional ministers. Pastoral associates and pastoral administrators work alongside priests in running entire parishes, performing virtually every service short of celebrating the Eucharist and hearing confessions. In priestless parishes, the pastoral administrator simply runs the parish. Directors of religious education are responsible for adult education programming and classes for youth who do not attend Catholic schools. Youth ministers run comprehensive programs for adolescents.

The lay people who fill these positions often have either an academic degree in theology or pastoral ministry or have completed an extensive program for lay ministry training in their diocese. The need for such people is still growing, both within and beyond the parish. Lay Catholics today serve as ministers in Catholic high schools, colleges, hospitals, dioceses, and social service organizations.

Even larger than the growth of professional lay ministries in the Catholic church is the expansion of the services performed by nonprofessional ministers. Since Vatican II virtually every parish has developed a council of members who evaluate the state of the parish and advise the pastor on any major decisions. In addition to the council are various committees or commissions, each of which is responsible for a particular ministry. Most parishes have a worship commission, an education commission, and a finance commission. In my parish we have a visitation committee that visits the sick, a bereavement committee that ministers to families when a loved one has died, a welcoming committee that smooths the entry of newcomers into the parish, a peace and justice committee that addresses social issues and holds letter-writing campaigns, an evangelization team that tries to spread the gospel within the parish and to reach out to the unchurched, a parish outreach that runs programs for shelter and food and literacy training, and many, many other forms of volunteer involvement of lay persons in ministry.

Lay ministries function as a tool for church renewal because they get the people to claim ownership of the spiritual life of the parish. The main role of the priest, the pastoral associate, and the director of religious education is to train, facilitate, coordinate, and empower the people of the parish to form a vibrant faith community. The professionals cannot simply do it for them. The Catholic laity are being treated as adults who need to take responsibility for their own spiritual growth.

Rite of Christian Initiation for Adults

Another tool for church renewal is the Rite of Christian Initiation of Adults.

Catholic theology concerning baptism focused on infants for over a thousand years prior to Vatican II. Infants constituted the great majority of people being baptized. Numerically this remains true, but, since the council, the theological focus of baptism has been on adults. In other words, when we think of what baptism means, we should think first of what it means to initiate an adult into a faith community. Baptism involves more than pouring water on a head and saying some words; it involves a complex process of socialization through which a person becomes truly part of a community that is struggling to live the life of grace.

Preparation for adult baptism prior to Vatican II centered around "convert classes" in which those who wished to become Catholic would learn the basic beliefs taught by the church. Often the text was the same catechism used by children. The focus was on information: what Catholics believe about God, grace, church, sacraments, and commandments. If the prospective convert could demonstrate an understanding of the faith commensurate with personal ability, he or she was deemed ready to be baptized. The brief baptismal ceremony would most often take place in a room separate from the main church at a time when only a few friends or relatives might be present.

The Rite of Christian Initiation of Adults restores the basic sacramental process used by the church in the third through the fifth centuries. It can last anywhere from one to three years. The focus is on formation rather than information; that is, the main concern is one's growth as a member of the church community more than the understanding of Catholic beliefs. This is not say that beliefs are not important, even crucial; it is only to say that beliefs do not take priority over the even more important element of experiencing life as a committed Christian within the context of a spirited faith community.

Preparation for baptism centers around meetings of small groups that include those who wish to be baptized, those already baptized who wish to become Catholic, sponsors, and an adult initiation team. Typically these groups meet twice a week: one evening, and then again on Sunday after the liturgy of the Word. Catechumens, as those who are being initiated are called, participate in the liturgy of the Word, but then are dismissed after the homily to attend their meeting. The pre-baptismal period is in a sense a time of anticipation for the full Eucharist. This period highlights for the catechumens, as well as for full-fledged Catholics, what a privilege it is to participate in and receive the Eucharist.

The meetings are times not only to learn about Catholic beliefs but also to pray, to read Scriptures, to share experiences, to commune with each other, to establish relationships, and to grow in faith. It is a time for becoming Catholic together. One of the beautiful dimensions of adult initiation is the underlying philosophy that both what it takes to *become* a Christian and what it takes to *remain* a Christian involve basically the same process of growth in faith. The newcomer can offer as much to the old-hand as vice-versa. It is not as though Catholics are saying "we've got it" and we're going to let the catechumens get it also. It is more that we are saying we are growing in faith and we ask the catechumens to join with us in our journey. We do not assume that we are necessarily further along than the initiates when it comes to the most basic issues of relationship with God and spiritual maturity. Many sponsors claim that their own encounter with the Rite of Christian Initiation of Adults gave them an experience of the Catholic faith on a level that they never knew existed.

Catechumens who are preparing for baptism at Easter are enrolled in the book of election during a Mass on the first Sunday of Lent. Lent begins a more intense period of preparation. The catechumens are baptized during the Easter Vigil on Holy Saturday night. They also receive the sacraments of confirmation and communion. These three sacraments are known as the sacraments of initiation; they had been administered together in early centuries of the church. Those who had been baptized previously receive confirmation and communion only. Over the next few weeks the newly initiated group will continue to meet in order to reflect more deeply on the meaning of receiving the sacraments and becoming full-fledged Catholics.

What makes adult initiation a tool for church renewal is the way that it thrusts the parish in the direction of community formation. Once a parish begins celebrating the rites for initiating adults into a dynamic faith community, that parish feels more than a little pressure to become a dynamic faith community. The initiation group itself—inquirers, catechumens, elect, the newly baptized, sponsors, catechists—functions as a model that draws the whole parish to participate in some way. Sponsors and other parishioners represent the presence of the parish within the group itself. Parishioners and catechumens get to know each other through events in the normal course of life in the parish. Parishioners witness the catechumens leaving Mass after the homily. Parishioners participate in the liturgies when the catechumens are elected and when they receive the sacraments of initiation. The process of initiation calls upon all Catholics to reflect more deeply upon what it means to be a Christian. The congregation's renewal of baptismal vows at Easter takes on a new depth. The Rite of Christian Initiation of Adults can generate a contagious Spirit that catches fire throughout the parish.

Renew

Renew is the most popular of several programs designed to aid Catholic parishes in the process of community formation. The basic program lasts two and a half years, but the effects are intended to take permanent root. Although the program has many components that involve the whole parish, such as prayers, liturgies, social celebrations, and take-home Scripture materials, the heart of Renew is the formation of small faith-sharing groups.

When my parish underwent the Renew process, over fifty percent of the members joined a small faith-sharing group. We were told by the diocesan coordinators that this was an unusually high number. I myself became part of such a group. When the program ended after two and a half years, all of the groups chose to continue meeting. Now, three years later, my group still meets for two periods during each year, each period involving one meeting a week for six weeks. Other groups have similar schedules.

In these groups we learn to share about the events in our lives within the context of a discussion about our faith. We get to know each other well and to develop a high level of trust. The group gives us a source of support to help cope with our personal struggles. It gives us the assurance that we are not alone in our quest to make sense of a crazy world and of a God whose ways are hard to understand. It gives us the challenge to make our faith a reality in our daily lives.

Renew is a tool for church renewal because it provides Catholics with a way to participate in a meaningful faith community. Like lay ministry and the Rite of Christian Initiation of Adults, it gets people involved on a deeper level of experiencing what it means to be a follower of Christ. They all have a ripple effect. The entire parish feels the impact.

Summary

In this chapter we have examined several means that the Catholic church is using to build community: lay ministries, adult initiation, and Renew.

Catholic parishes in general still have a long way to go in becoming lively communities of people who empower each other to live as disciples of Christ. We have a long way to go in becoming attractive communities that readily draw people in and make them feel welcomed. At the same time, though, we have come a long way, we are setting our goals clearly, and we have in place many effective tools. Has the day finally arrived when I can say to the young woman who used to deliver my newspaper that not only are we offering a wide array of true beliefs, but that we also have something that is right for her?

In the next chapter we will examine the spiritual dimensions of one of the main spheres of lay activity: the world of work.

FOR FURTHER REFLECTION

1. Do you know any stories of people who have been changed through their experience within a church community?

2. Can you think of an example to illustrate the difference between treating lay people as children and treating them as adults who have responsibility for their own spiritual life?

3. Do you personally feel as comfortable being ministered to by lay people as you do by ordained priests?

4. Have you ever experienced a "dead" Catholic parish or other church community? What ever might make such a community come to life?

5. Will it take more than the rites of initiation and Renew to revitalize Catholic parishes?

SUGGESTED READINGS

Brennan, Patrick J. *Re-Imagining the Parish: Base Communities, Adulthood, and Family Consciousness.* New York: Crossroad, 1990.

Dolan, Jay P., et al. *Transforming Parish Ministry: The Changing Roles of Catholic Clergy, Laity, and Women Religious.* New York: Crossroad, 1990.

Dunning, James B. *New Wines, New Wineskins: Exploring the RCIA.* Chicago: W.H. Sadlier, 1981.

Hater, Robert J. *The Ministry Explosion: A New Awareness of Every Christian's Call to Minister.* Dubuque, Ia.: William C. Brown, 1979.

CHAPTER 15

A Spirituality of Work

A first-year student in an introductory course that I teach came to see me. He was about nineteen years old. He told me that he had decided to major in Ecological Science. I asked him what had made him decide that. He replied that his brother had told him that there were good jobs open at the Environmental Protection Agency that paid a decent salary. He thought that given present trends there would be a secure future in such work.

I asked him if there were any other reasons for his choice. He thought for a second and said yes, there was. He had always wanted to be a policeman. Law enforcement attracted him. When he watched cop shows on television he felt that was what he wanted to be. The type of work he would go into at the E.P.A. would allow him to combine law enforcement with a technical skill. He could have a well-paying job and still do something that would allow him to be himself.

I asked if there were any other reasons for his choice. He said that there were none that occurred to him immediately. I asked him if he had any personal concern for the environment or for the impact of environmental deterioration on human society. He replied that he had never thought of that, but that he was not against considering it.

Some people might feel tempted to interpret this young man's response as a depressing sign of an age when students are interested in making money and doing what they like without any broader social commitment. If this young man had been a graduating senior, his response would represent a real problem; for an entering student, however, he had many positive things to say. In fact, measured against the three main purposes of work talked about by Pope John Paul II and discussed later in this chapter, his response indicates that he exhibits the first two and is open to the third.

This Chapter

As discussed in an earlier chapter, the main spheres of lay Christian activity outlined in *Lumen Gentium* are work, family, and social transformation. In this chapter we will consider the place of a person's work in living a Christian life; that is, we will explore a spirituality of work. In doing so, we will draw heavily upon themes from John Paul II's 1981 encyclical on work, *Laborem Exercens*.[1]

Three Purposes of Work

I remember a snobbish position I held when I was in college in the early 1970s, which, as an era, was still part of the 1960s—Viet Nam, rock music, sexual freedom, and cultural revolution. I thought that to be a real human being a person had to major in a subject like English, Philosophy, or Social Work. I tended to look down on students who majored in business or technical areas as people who had copped out by joining the corrupt military-industrial establishment. I divided the world into two kinds of people: those who cared about life and love and peace and brotherhood and those who wanted to make a living.

I have learned a lot since those days. I no longer divide the world into two kinds of people. Nor do I pit making a living against social commitment. What I have come to realize is that the world is crying for socially committed people to go into business and technical areas. We do not need a world populated solely by English teachers and social workers. What we need, rather, are business people, English teachers, technicians, and social workers who care about the world beyond themselves and are committed to a vision of a more just society.

I have found John Paul II's thinking about the three purposes of work to be helpful in this regard. He does not say that it is a sin to want to make a decent living. He does not say that it is selfish to be concerned about self-fulfillment. Rather, he offers a vision in which these concerns are balanced by concern for others.

Pope John Paul II's Three Purposes of Work
make a living
self-expression/fulfillment
social contribution

The first purpose of work is to earn enough money to support oneself and one's family. This should not be an exclusive or an overriding concern, but it holds an important place. The second purpose is to find self-expression and fulfillment. Work is what most of us do for a large percentage of our waking life. What we do is an expression of who we are. The third purpose is to contribute to the larger society. We work not simply for ourselves but for the good of others. We draw upon our talents and strengths to provide services for those who need them.

What I find important about these three purposes is that they are not pitted against each other. They can co-exist in harmony. John Paul II suggests that all three are very important, and that the absence of one or more of these purposes can indicate a problem in the meaning of work for that person.

These purposes may seem idealistic when applied to the real world. I have known many people who hate their jobs. I have known many for whom work is nothing more than a way to make a living. I have known people who are embarrassed by the work that they do because of its low social status. I have known people who think not at all of the service that they provide, but rather resent their customers and try to get by with doing as little as possible. For many people, work is anything but fun. Instead of being a means of self-fulfillment and an avenue of social contribution, it is a prison from which to seek escape during off-hours.

John Paul II is not unaware of the ambiguity of work. In *Laborem Exercens*, he says:

> Human life is built up every day from work, from work it derives its specific dignity, but at the same time work contains the unceasing measure of human toil and suffering and also the harm and injustice which penetrate deeply into social life....(section 1)

In the face of this ambiguity of work, it is important to examine other dimensions of what the pope offers for considering work's meaning.

The Dignity of Work

What gives work its dignity? In addressing this question, John Paul II distinguishes between the subjective and objective dimensions of work. Work in the objective sense refers to the various technologies by which human beings manipulate the world for the fulfillment of human needs. The pope mentions agriculture, industry, service industries, and research as examples of fields of economic activity in the objective sense. That is, work in the objective sense refers to the type of work that is done.

Work in the subjective sense refers to the activity of the worker in a way that is independent from the particular type of work being done. That is, whenever work is being accomplished, it involves a human being, made in the image of God, called to self-realization, performing certain tasks and activities. This is true no matter what the types of activities are. Work in the subjective sense thus refers to the fact that no matter what the particular task, the one doing the work is a human being.

John Paul II draws two points from this distinction that are important in discussing a spirituality of work. First of all, he declares that, by his definition, virtually all people are workers. Whether one is a housewife, a student, a bricklayer, an artist, a manager, an investment broker, an owner, or a professor, one is a worker. One performs tasks that are both expressive of self and in the service of others. The pope devotes a subsection to explaining how disabled people are also to be considered workers and given opportunities to contribute.

I have noticed in my own neighborhood a tension between mothers who work and mothers who stay home to raise their children. Each group has a way of resenting and looking down at the other. Each group also seems to be somewhat aware of the ridiculousness of this and tries to overcome it. By the pope's definition, both groups are made up of workers. Getting paid a salary is not what differentiates a worker from a non-worker. At least on that point the mothers should be united.

The idea that all people are workers also has implications in the economic and social spheres. Although there may be different classes economically and socially, in the subjective sense we are all workers. Capital investment is only an instrument; work has to do with people. Work must be recognized as being at the service of human beings, because people are more important than things. Labor takes priority over capital. In saying this, though, John Paul II does not pit the laborers over against the capitalists; rather he calls for the realization that all stand ultimately on the same side as workers. John Paul II thus subverts the notion of classes when it comes to the value of the human person. Rich people are not better than poor people or working class people; everyone is a worker called to self-expression and social contribution.

A second point that John Paul II draws from his distinction between the objective and subjective dimensions of work is that work takes its dignity primarily from the subjective dimension. That is, what gives work its dignity is not the type of work being done but that the one doing it is a person. By this measure, there is nothing less dignified about being a migrant farmer, a sanitation worker, or a car wash laborer than about being a doctor, an engineer, or a manager. In *Laborem Exercens*, the pope is very clear about this point and its connection with the notion of class:

> . . . the basis for determining the value of human work is not primarily the kind of work being done, but the fact that the one who is doing it is a person. The sources of the dignity of work are to be sought in the subjective dimension, not in the objective one.
>
> Such a concept practically does away with the very basis of the ancient differentiation of people into classes according to the kind of work done. This does not mean that from the objective point of view human work cannot and must not be rated and qualified in any way. It only means that the primary basis of the value of human work is human beings themselves, who are its subject. (section 6)

The pope is not saying that all workers should receive exactly the same salary; he is not saying that objectively speaking there should be no classes. He is saying, rather, that the basic human dignity connected with work does not derive from its social status.

The pope's positions have many practical implications. Everyone is a worker. All workers should keep in mind that work is in the service of human beings. All workers have a basic dignity that does not derive from the type of work being done. All workers have rights, including the right to just wages and benefits and the right to form unions for defending vital interests. Ultimately, workers should share as much as possible in the decision making and ownership of the firms for which they work. These practical points have been emphasized in recent Catholic social teaching.

The real world seems a long way from the vision offered by the pope. Could it really be true that we could experience each other as equal in spiritual dignity in a way that is independent of our social status? The British Catholic author G.K. Chesterton describes this ability as one of the distinguishing characteristics of St. Francis of Assisi:

> St. Francis...honoured all men; that is, he not only loved but respected them all. What gave him this extraordinary personal power was this; that from the Pope to the beggar, from the sultan of Syria in his pavilion to the ragged robbers crawling out of the woods, there was never a man who looked into those brown

burning eyes without being certain that Francis Bernadone was really interested in *him*; in his own inner individual life from the cradle to the grave; that he himself was being valued and taken seriously...he treated the whole mob of men as a mob of kings.[2]

For most of us, such an ability is a long way off.

The Cross and the Resurrection

We are still left with the ambiguity of work. John Paul II returns to this issue in the final section of *Laborem Exercens*. On the one hand, work is a sharing in the creative activity of God. God is still actively at work in the world, and when we work we participate in our limited way in this creativity. Jesus himself is a working man, a carpenter, who is familiar with the world of work and who frequently refers to workers in his parables and other teachings.

On the other hand, though, work is toil and suffering, pain and sweat. What meaning does this have?

The pope refers us to the cross of Christ. Jesus' work of redemption involved a great deal of pain and suffering. Through our work we share in the cross of Christ and even in his work of redemption: "One shows oneself a true disciple of Christ by carrying the cross in one's turn every day in the activity one is called upon to perform" (section 27).

The pope also reminds us that the cross leads to the resurrection. The work that we do contributes to bringing about a new earth that awaits its final redemption through the coming of the kingdom of God. The positive results of our work should reinforce our ultimate hopes by revealing a "glimmer of new life."

In other words, in this final section the pope uses religious language to remind us that work is one of the main ways that Christians participate in the mystery of Christ. The suffering involved in work is not explained away, but rather is placed in the context of this mystery. We do not know the answer to the why of our pain, but we can look at the cross and believe that, through the suffering Christ, this too will ultimately make some sense.

Work and Leisure

In *Laborem Exercens* the pope mentions that both work and rest involve a sharing in the creativity of God. When Genesis says that God rested on the seventh day, we are to interpret this as a comment on the appropriateness and even holiness of rest.

This is an important point to consider in a society that has witnessed a rise in workaholism. A workaholic is a person who compulsively seeks escape through work. Usually what the workaholic is seeking to escape is low self-esteem, inadequate human relationships, and a truncated spiritual life. Workaholism can build social status and bank accounts as it destroys the lives of individuals and families.

Jesus was not a workaholic. Jesus did not ask for the sick and possessed to be lined up so that he could labor from dawn to dusk healing and casting out demons. Jesus is portrayed in the Scriptures as often seeking out time for prayer and rest.

Rest and leisure are as important as work. The development and enjoyment of human relationships is as much a part of our purpose on earth as any external social contribution we might make. John Paul II says that the rhythm of work and leisure "must leave room for human beings to prepare themselves, by becoming more and more what in the will of God they ought to be, for the 'rest' that the Lord reserves for his servants and friends" (section 25).

Summary

In this chapter we have discussed various dimensions of a spirituality of work: the purposes of work, the source of its dignity, the meaning of toil and accomplishment, and the need to balance labor and leisure.

I still think that the young man who told me of his decision to major in Ecological Science is off to a good start. He sees a way to make a living. He is attracted to an occupation that will allow him to express himself. He is not closed to the idea that his work will enable him to make a needed social contribution.

How will he see himself in relation to other workers? From what source will he derive a sense of his own dignity in work? How will he interpret the pain and toil that inevitably go along with work? Will he become lost in his work, or will he maintain a strong sense of human relationships and of a personal spirituality?

In the next chapter we will discuss basic shifts in how Catholics image and relate with God.

FOR FURTHER REFLECTION

1. Have your own experiences of work been more positive or negative in regard to fostering good human relationships?

2. Are students these days too focused on making money?

3. Do you think that it is common for young people to take social contribution into account in career decisions?

4. Is workaholism truly a major problem, or is it just a trendy way of talking about people who simply work too much?

5. Does it sound far-fetched to suggest that everyday people relate their work with Christ's death and resurrection?

SUGGESTED READINGS

Baum, Gregory. *The Priority of Labor: A Commentary on Laborem Exercens.* Mahwah, N.J.: Paulist Press, 1982.

Holland, Joe. *Creative Communion: Toward a Spirituality of Work.* Mahwah, N.J.: Paulist Press, 1989.

Gillett, Richard W. *The Human Enterprise: A Christian Perspective on Work.* Kansas City: Leaven Press, 1985.

John Paul II. *Laborem Exercens* (On Human Work). Washington, D.C.: United States Catholic Conference, 1981.

Oates, Wayne E. *Confessions of a Workaholic: The Facts about Work Addiction.* Nashville: Abingdon Press, 1971.

SECTION FIVE

THE UNIVERSAL CALL TO HOLINESS

CHAPTER 16

CHRISTIAN SPIRITUALITY

W hen I was an altar boy in the early 1960s my nickname was "Shaky" because when I held the glass cruets of water and wine for the priest at the altar they could be heard clinking all the way in the back of the church. I was deathly afraid of God. I lived by what I now think of as a "musical chairs" spirituality. In a musical chairs spirituality the great focus is on what will happen to you when you die. That is, when the music of life stops, will there be a place open for you in heaven?

The fear of hell, the belief that it was not so difficult to go to hell, the trap of mortal sin: These specters haunted my consciousness when I was a child. I did not learn about these things at home. I learned about them in my Catholic grade school.

I also learned many wonderful things about religion in that school. I learned about the importance of loving God and neighbor. I learned about receiving Jesus in the Eucharist and the other sacraments. I learned how to tell basic right from wrong. I learned the value of sacrifice and discipline.

Nor etheless, the fear of God and of hell that pervaded my youth went l.nd in hand with my understanding of what it meant to live a Christian life. Being a Christian involved more than just loving God and neighbor. It involved getting yourself ready for the day of judgment. In fact, it was as though a whole system was set up according to which God would judge your eternal state of being.

Basically, it went like this:

If you die in a state of grace, you go to heaven. If you die out of a state of grace, you go to hell. If you die with a lot of venial sins but still in the state of grace, you will spend much time in purgatory, but that is all right because you will still end up making it into heaven.

What determines whether you are in a state of grace or not is, first of all, whether or not you are baptized. Unbaptized people such as infants or those from cultures foreign to Christianity will go to limbo rather than hell. For Catholic school students, however, baptism is a must. Once baptism puts you in a state of grace, you need to maintain it by keeping the commandments and not committing any mortal (very serious) sins. Venial (less serious) sins would put a mark on your soul, but they would not put you totally out of a state of grace. You know a sin is mortal if it is 1) a seriously wrong thought, word, or deed, 2) you have given sufficient reflection before committing it, and 3) you chose to do it with no one forcing you. If you commit a mortal sin, you are no longer in a state of grace and are thereby a candidate for hell if you should die.

If you are in a state of mortal sin, then you need to have your mortal sins forgiven. The best way to have mortal sins forgiven is by telling them to the priest in confession and receiving absolution. If you cannot make it to confession immediately, you should say an act of contrition (a prayer asking God to forgive you) and strive to have true sorrow for your sins. Perfect contrition, which is sorrow out of love of God and revulsion at having offended God, wipes out mortal sin immediately with or without confession, though one is still obliged to go to confession when one is able. Imperfect contrition, or sorrow out of a fear of punishment, is sufficient for the forgiveness of mortal sin in the context of the sacrament of confession. Once your mortal sins are forgiven you are back in a state of grace.

This system provided the underlying philosophy for our textbook, the Baltimore Catechism, throughout grade school. This textbook contained many beautiful teachings about the meaning of life, such as God creating us because of love, the commandment to love God and neighbor, the virtues, the gifts and fruits of the Holy Spirit, the spiritual and corporal works of mercy, the beatitudes, and many other treasures that genuinely inspired me then and that continue to enrich my life. I still also believe that some notion of hell and the possibility of throwing one's gift of life away for all eternity remain meaningful and in some sense true. To this day I believe that, if you take away the overly systematic and impersonal nature of the system, it can function as a way of opening up truth about the meaning of life. As I remember it, though, the quality of these teachings was hampered by the strong focus on hell and the overly mechanical ways one could use to judge where one stood in relation to God and eternity.

A distorting element of my early spirituality was thus a near obsession with staying in a state of grace. This was accompanied by the belief that it was easy to commit a mortal sin and not even be aware of it. I also believed that probably many people went to hell. I thought of God as one who, as a punishment for original sin, had made the world a place from which only the lucky few would be saved. God was a stingy and angry God who needed to be appeased.

Is this really an accurate picture of how I thought about God in those days? Probably not. The stingy, angry God and the loving, generous God were all mixed up together in my mind. Did the grade school teach me these fearful images of God? Yes and no. These ideas were in the air, but I am sure I latched onto them in relation to my own already established fears and insecurities. Whether it was me or the school, though, much of my spirituality as a child was based on a mechanical system implemented by an angry God who struck fear in the very depths of my soul.

This Chapter

The fifth chapter of *Lumen Gentium* speaks of the universal call to holiness in the church. When I was a child holiness was a thing for priests and sisters and brothers and saints to worry about, not something for regular people. Vatican II called for more than that. Vatican II stressed that all Christians are called to live a holy life.

The topic of this chapter is Christian spirituality. It addresses the issue of what it means to live a holy life. This topic is at the heart of understanding the church. Prior to Vatican II, official Catholic theology dealt with the topic of church too impersonally and without reference to love and holiness. It was as though "church" had to do only with things like organizational structures and appropriate procedures. Love and holiness were important topics, but they were dealt with in separate treatises on grace and sacraments. Vatican II changed that segmented approach to theology by making the chapter on holiness the centerpiece of one of the two main documents on the church. The church is holy, marked with a holiness that comes from Christ himself. Anyone who is a member of the church is called to follow Christ by striving to lead a holy life.

The rest of this chapter will explore some contrasts between the spirituality I lived as a child and some things that I have learned since then.

Personal and Ongoing

Spirituality deals with our faith-journey through rich, multi-layered territories. There are no foolproof systems that can guarantee our growth. Systems can function as useful maps, but it should be remembered that the map is not the territory. The territory has too much depth and too many dimensions to be captured by any one map. There is always more to the mystery of God and the mystery of life than we can realize in any one system.

The God of Christians is personal, not mechanical. God does not operate with a big scoreboard in the sky to decide by numbers whether you will go to heaven or to hell. Christian doctrines about sin put us in touch with the reality of the negative side of our shared human situation, of our individual inclinations, and of the tremendous and terrible choice that we face: Will we ultimately embrace God and life or will we reject them? Sin is a reality; the reality, however, has to do most basically with our relationship with God and with other human beings. When the level of personal relationship remains primary, the system is put in its place as a useful but partial tool that aids us in understanding.

For example, what do I take as evidence that offers me hope for my salvation? My first inclination is not to think hard about whether I have committed any mortal sins. Rather, I am inclined to think first about my ongoing commitment to God and others. This includes my prayer life, my commitment to my family, my involvement in deep human relationships, my disposition toward honesty, my concern for social and environmental improvements, and my faith in a loving God who accepts me even though I just listed all of these positive qualities about myself without mentioning any of my deep and many faults. In other words, when I think about my salvation I think first about personal relationships. Thinking in terms of a system of sin and grace can help me assess such relationships, but should not become more important than the relationships themselves.

My understanding of the sacraments, like my understanding of God, has also become less mechanical and more personal. Sacraments are not just rituals that dispense grace; rather, sacraments key into and celebrate the religious dimensions that we experience in the context of our lives. Baptism celebrates entry into the faith community. Confirmation celebrates conscious embracing of the faith. Eucharist celebrates ongoing personal unity with Christ, with other Christians, and with the entire human family. Reconciliation celebrates forgiveness received from God and from others. Anointing of the Sick celebrates the healing love of God and community. Marriage celebrates the ongoing covenant of married love. Holy orders celebrates the reality of sacramental leadership. Sacraments give grace, but they do so in conjunction with the meaning that we experience at the depth of our lives as we relate with God and with others.

Spirituality, then, has to do with an ongoing process in the midst of our lives. It is not something to be confined to the day of judgment. Lay people live their spirituality not only in church but in the context of their family, their work, and their efforts toward social transformation.

Love and Fear

I am not of the trendy school of thought that says that all fear is bad. The Scriptures in several places tell us that "Fear of the Lord is the beginning of wisdom." Yet it says in 1 John 4:18 that "perfect love drives out fear." I think that fear has its place in this world, where we do not as yet know perfect love. Thomas Aquinas taught that there are different types of fear. The fear of punishment will not remain with the blessed in heaven. But the fear of offending God and others, which is a healthy fear, will remain.[1]

Just as fear of physical harm can keep us alert to possible dangers, so fear of offending God can aid us in our spiritual journey. The Protestant theologian Rudolf Otto has described the fundamental religious experience as being that of the "holy," an overpowering mystery that elicits dread, awe, majesty, urgency, and fascination.[2] God is not a familiar pal whose back we feel free to smack. God is one who holds our attention, one whose enormity and otherness can make us quake in our boots. Watch out for God. God will change you. If you encounter God, your life will never be the same.

My teachers in grade school did me a favor by introducing me to this God. And I must say that if I knew that I was going to meet God in the next five minutes, I would be more than a little awestruck. A problem arises not when someone is taught a basic, healthy fear of God, but when fear becomes ingrained as the primary means of relating to God.

It is possible for fear to become the ruling emotion in a person's life. There are people who live by what they fear others will think. Such is the case with the speaker in T.S. Eliot's poem, "The Love Song of J. Alfred Prufrock," whose introverted life is ruled by his insecurities:

Shall I part my hair behind?
Do I dare to eat a peach?
I will wear white flannel trousers
And walk along the beach.
I can hear the mermaids singing each to each.
I do not think that they will sing to me.

There are other ways to live a life ruled by fear. Some people live with the fear that they are worthless and that, therefore, they will not really try to communicate who they are to others. Some live with the fear of loneliness or abandonment, and so they remain in relationships in which they are abused. Some live with the fear that they will not be successful, and so they lie and cheat and deceive others for money. Alcoholics and compulsive gamblers live in such fear that they often cannot admit to themselves that they have a problem. Some people live with a deep-seated fear of God.

Fear has many companions. Anger, resentment, self-pity, jealousy, self-righteousness, and ingratitude can often be found associating with fear. A life of fear is a terrible way to go.

The Christian God, the Father about whom Jesus taught, is a God not of fear but of love and forgiveness. The Christian God calms our fears. Jesus taught about a God who loves and accepts us. This is not a God who wants to make sure that a large enough quota of people go to hell. God numbers and treasures the very hair on our heads. God is like the father of the prodigal son; he hurries out to forgive his son before he even reaches his home (Luke 15:11–32). God so loved the world that he gave his only begotten Son that the world might be saved through him (John 3:16–17).

And yet this God challenges us to grow. Jesus never said to his disciples: "Don't change a thing. I love you just the way you are." God is not a rubber stamp; God is one who calls us to stretch and at times to groan. I think of a saying I saw on a poster recently: "Just because I love you unconditionally does not mean that I have given up all hope for your improvement."

Faith, hope, and love are the Christian remedies against fear and its companions. Faith gives us the trust that opens us to a worldview based on the goodness of God. Hope enables us to take the risks of honesty and humility in reaching out to others for help and support. Love opens us up to care for others in a way that takes us out of our own problems and heals us. Paul says that "There are in the end three things that last: faith, hope, and love, and the greatest of these is love" (1 Corinthians 13:13).

In the church today the need to grow in one's individual faith journey is balanced by the need to work for peace, justice, and ecological wholeness. In these issues, too, we are called to be motivated out of love rather than fear. As Catholic theologian Daniel Maguire puts it:

> One thing that hasn't changed in our understanding of sin is our concept of God's love and mercy. God doesn't want us to be weighed down with an overblown sense of our own failure or responsibility or guilt. That would only immobilize us and keep us from the task at hand. Our call to help transform and liberate the world...is an opportunity to participate in the creative work of God. We are not alone. The risen Lord and his Spirit are with us, thirsting for justice in our midst. That is good news—and cause for joyful service![3]

Summary

In this chapter I have described something of my own personal journey from a spirituality based in fear to one more grounded in faith, hope, love, and social commitment. The more I think about what I said in the beginning of this chapter about my own education, however, the more I wonder whether I was really being accurate. Few things are harder to interpret than one's own life story. In the midst of all the negativities from my grade school, I retain clear memories of how much was taught to me about the love of God.

Having focused in this chapter on God the Father, we will consider, respectively, Jesus and the Holy Spirit in the next two chapters.

FOR FURTHER REFLECTION

1. Have you ever been taught to fear God?
2. Do you believe that some people go to hell?
3. What is it that can move a person from fear to love?
4. In what ways has your own religious education focused on your life-journey and on the quality of your relationships?
5. How do you think religious education in Catholic schools today most differs from that of the 1950s?

SUGGESTED READINGS

Au, Wilkie. *By Way of the Heart: Towards a Holistic Christian Spirituality*. Mahwah, N.J.: Paulist Press, 1989.

Brennan, Patrick J. *Spirituality for an Anxious Age*. Chicago: Thomas More Press, 1985.

Conn, Joann Wolski. *Spirituality and Personal Maturity*. Mahwah, N.J.: Paulist Press, 1989.

Merton, Thomas. *Seeds of Contemplation*. Norfolk, Conn.: New Directions, 1949.

Merton, Thomas. *New Seeds of Contemplation*. New York: New Directions, 1961.

Nouwen, Henri. *Making All Things New: An Invitation to the Spiritual Life*. San Francisco: Harper & Row, 1981.

Phillips, J.B. *Your God Is Too Small*. New York: Macmillan, 1953.

CHAPTER 17

BREAKING THE CYCLE

M y wife and I have four boys. The two older ones often seem locked in conflict. They will be playing together fine one minute, but then in the next minute things degenerate into "he took my seat," "stop making that noise," "yes I did," "no you didn't," "I don't want to play with you," "you're the biggest creep I ever met," "why do I have to have you for a brother?"

It happened again yesterday. The two older boys were playing a basketball game called HORSE. The eight-year-old made his shot, and then, just for fun, tossed up a quick practice shot that he missed. The six-year-old did not see the first shot but did see the missed practice shot, which he thought should count. The younger one called the older one a name. The older one hit him with the ball. The younger one ran into the house screaming.

It took me a while to get the two of them to speak calmly enough to help us figure out what had happened. Even when they both understood that there was just a big mix-up, each still proceeded to defend his own position vehemently and to say nasty things about the other.

It was clear that the argument between these two went far beyond the precipitating incident. There are extremely deep and complex issues that underlie this type of sibling rivalry. As Jacob was born with his hand on Esau's foot, so any two brothers close in age find themselves engaged in an ardent contest. Does an eighteen-month old baby really have room in his heart for a competitor? Will a newborn grow to love the idea that someone comes before him in rank, privilege, and opportunity?

I separated the two boys and briefly gave comfort to the six-year-old. Then I went in to have a talk with the eight-year-old. Without his brother around he was like a different kid. He got over his anger and was willing to talk. We talked in general about what kind of family we want to have: a family where everybody gets along, where no one has to be afraid of another, where we love and forgive one another. He agreed. Then we talked about his relationship with the six-year-old. I invoked a phrase that has been a useful catchword in our ongoing discussions: I asked, "who is going to *break the cycle?*"

My son understood what I meant. He and his brother are locked in a conflict with such complex roots in the distant past that it never was either of their faults. They were born into rivalry. It is a no-win situation as long as each simply defends himself. One of them has to break the cycle of conflict by dropping his defenses and reaching out to the other. Somebody has to be willing to start a new cycle of forgiveness and love.

The six-year-old went over to a friend's house to play. The eight-year-old read a book, practiced his piano, and watched part of a ball game. Later that evening we all went swimming as a family and the boys got along fine. All was well—until the next conflict.

This Chapter

In this chapter, we will consider the mission of Jesus against the background of human conflict. After a discussion of the meaning of original sin, we will examine Jesus' teachings about the kingdom of God. This material is related to chapter 5 of *Lumen Gentium.*

A Global Cycle

Human society on a global scale can be compared to the relationship between my boys. There are so many conflicts of class, sex, race, nation, and creed, with such complex roots so deep in the past that no one could ever dream of sorting it all out. We are all born into this world of continual conflict for which we are not ourselves initially responsible, but which we inherit and which conditions the very fabric of our lives. Many people benefit from institutions and social systems that have unfairness built into them. Many who are disadvantaged are socialized into having traits that work against them. As we live our lives, we inevitably become collaborators in structures that help to cause human misery.

This profound truth is part of what Catholic doctrine is trying to get at in its teaching about original sin. The effects of sins of the past are structured into the world in which we are born. As we grow, we internalize these structures. They become part of us. Eventually they help to lead us to make our own sinful choices.

An obvious example is racial prejudice. If one is born into a family and a neighborhood that manifests deep racial prejudice, at what point does one become responsible for being prejudiced oneself? This is a difficult issue to sort out. What makes this issue even more difficult is that there are many sinful structures that we do not recognize as such because we buy into them so deeply. Some socially "successful" people do not recognize any problems whatsoever in our social and economic structures and just think that if everyone would be like them the world would be a perfect place. Some disadvantaged people think that it is perfectly all right to "beat the system" (cheat) because they never had a fair chance.

The world is basically good, and human society represents a tremendous achievement. But the world is also plagued by hunger, poverty, lack of medical treatment, war, and wide-scale ecological destruction. The first world points its finger at the second and third worlds. The second and third worlds point their fingers at the first world. Nuclear armaments remain poised as international terrorism grows. Who is going to break the cycle?

I do not wish to propose any vague idealistic or utopian solutions to the complex problems of the world. My Catholic faith calls me not to be a silly dreamer, but rather to have a realistic hope that collaboration with our loving God can move us in the right direction. But who is going to break the cycle?

There are many profound ways of interpreting Jesus. I think that one useful way to see Jesus is as one who came to break the cycle.[1] He lit up the path and showed us the way. The path is the journey toward the kingdom of God. The way to follow the path is through self-sacrificing love. In this chapter we will concentrate on Jesus' teaching about the kingdom.

A Kingdom of Love

When I shared with my eldest son a vision of what our family might be like, I was doing on a very small scale what Jesus was doing when he taught about the kingdom of God and what the human family might be like. Jesus' teaching, of course, was much more powerful and mysterious. As he is depicted in the gospels, Jesus does not matter-of-factly offer a clear vision with a few well-defined values; rather, he teaches through proclamation, parable, confrontation, healing, and example.[2]

The coming of the kingdom of God is the central focus of all of the teaching of Jesus. In the Gospel of Mark, which most scholars think is the earliest of the gospels, the first thing Jesus says is "This is the time of fulfillment. The reign of God is at hand. Reform your lives and believe in the gospel" (Mark 1:15). The kingdom of God is breaking in; it is right within our grasp; it is inside us. What opens us up to the kingdom is our willingness and effort to change our lives.

Jesus stressed that we must remain ready for the coming of the kingdom. He told stories about servants who were unprepared for the return of the master, and about virgins who were unprepared to keep their lights burning when the bridegroom would arrive. He said, "Be constantly on the watch! Stay awake! You do not know when the appointed time will come" (Mark 13:33).

The Lord's Prayer is a prayer about the coming of the kingdom:

Thy kingdom come
Thy will be done
On earth as it is in heaven.

One might paraphrase this by saying that the kingdom of God exists wherever and whenever the will of God is being done. Jesus exemplifies this by his prayer in the Garden of Gethsemani, as he contemplates his impending death: "Abba (O Father), you have the power to do all things. Take this cup away from me. But let it be as you would have it, not as I" (Mark 14:36). Just as Jesus brings about the entry of the kingdom by his obedience to the will of his Father, he calls us to the kingdom through our own seeking and doing of the will of God.

The will of God is, above all, that we love one another. When queried as to which commandment was the greatest, Jesus replied:

You shall love the Lord your God
with your whole heart,
with your whole soul,
and with all your mind.
This is the greatest and first commandment. The second is like it:
You shall love your neighbor as yourself. (Matthew 22:37–39)

When Jesus gave his farewell discourse to his disciples at the Last Supper, he said:

As the Father has loved me,
so I have loved you.

Live on in my love.
You will live in my love
if you keep my commandments,
even as I have kept my Father's commandments,
and live in his love.
All this I tell you
that my joy may be yours
and your joy may be complete.
This is my commandment: love one another
as I have loved you. (John 15:9–12)

There is an irony in the commandment to love one another. We tend to think of commandments as stern obligations. To be ordered to love one another is the best commandment we could hope for; it is what we really want for ourselves.

Blest Are the Poor

Loving one another entails a special concern for the poor and the socially disenfranchised. Jesus reached out to those whom others found unacceptable. He had dinner at the house of Zacchaeus, a much-disliked tax collector (Luke 19:1–10). He told stories about how the beggars the cripples, and the lame were the ones to be invited to the banquet (Luke 14:12–24). He broke custom by socializing with the Samaritan woman at the well, and even made one of the hated Samaritans the hero of the parable about the man who helps a Jew in trouble after many respectable Jews pass him by (Luke 10:25–36). Jesus reaches out to include in his family all those who share his love and his vision, and not necessarily just those related to him by blood or nationality. When told that his mother and brothers were outside, he replied, "Who are my mother and my brothers?" And gazing around him at those seated in the circle he continued, "These are my mother and my brothers. Whoever does the will of God is brother and sister and mother to me" (Mark 3:33–35).

Jesus teaches that we should not be selective or exclusive in whom we love. In the radical Sermon on the Mount, Jesus says:

My command to you is: love your enemies, pray for your persecutors. This will prove that you are sons of your heavenly Father, for his sun rises on the bad and the good, he rains on the just and the unjust. If you love those who love you, what merit is there in that? Do not tax collectors do as much? (Matthew 5:44–46)

The Sermon on the Mount is filled with provocative, challenging teachings that show that no one can perfectly live up to the law. We should thereby relate with others humbly out of a sense of our own weaknesses and failings. We are not to sit in judgment on others; otherwise, we ourselves might be liable to judgment.

The New Testament records Jesus as emphasizing the danger that material riches pose to entry into the kingdom. He says, "I assure you, only with great difficulty will a rich man enter into the kingdom of God. I repeat what I said: it is easier for a camel to pass through a needle's eye than for a rich man to enter the kingdom of God" (Matthew 19:23–24). Yet Jesus adds that although such would be impossible for human beings, with God all things are possible. In the beatitudes, Jesus proclaims, "How blest are the poor in spirit; the reign of God is theirs" (Matthew 5:3). In Luke he says even more bluntly, "Blest are you poor," without the additional "in spirit" (Luke 6:20).

More so than the other gospel writers, Luke portrays Jesus as admonishing the rich, which has led scholars to speculate that issues of wealth and poverty were of pressing concern to the community Luke was addressing. Luke's Jesus tells of a foolish rich man who wanted to store more and more of his earthly harvest, not realizing that he was to die that very night and that he could not take it with him (Luke 12:16–21). It is in Luke that Jesus says that the poor and the crippled are invited to the banquet; that no servant can serve two masters, God and money; that the rich man who cared not for Lazarus in his poverty will have a parched tongue in hell; that the higher choice for the rich young man is to leave his wealth behind to follow Christ; that the poor widow with her mite gives more than the rich because she has given out of her need; and that the one who would be the greatest should be as a servant.

Other gospel stories seem to soften or at least to contextualize Jesus' warnings to the rich. In John's Gospel, for example, when Judas complains that the expensive oil for anointing Jesus should have been sold and the money given to the poor, Jesus responds, "The poor you will always have with you. But me you will not always have" (John 12:8). No matter how we might interpret or contextualize them, however, Jesus' warnings are too well recorded to simply ignore.

Stories of the Kingdom
The evidence in the New Testament is that Jesus taught mainly through parables. Parables are compressed stories bursting with meaning. By now you will not be surprised to learn that the parables of Jesus are stories about the kingdom of God.

The parables tend to have similar characteristics. Most of them draw their materials from ordinary, everyday events. They thereby set up a certain set of expectations as to how things should go. Then they pull the rug out from under this set of expectations. They thus reorient the hearer on a new level of understanding.

Characteristics of the Parables
Concern the kingdom of God
Draw materials from the everyday
Set up common expectations
Thwart those expectations
Reorient the hearer
Open to multiple interpretations

The parables of Jesus are usually not translatable into only one meaning. They can be legitimately interpreted as having multiple meanings on many levels. They are not intended to communicate some clear piece of information about the kingdom of God; rather, they are intended to have an impact upon the consciousness of the hearer. They give one a feel for what the kingdom of God is like that would be difficult to express without simply repeating the same story.

Take the following parable as an example:

The reign of God is like the case of the owner of an estate who went out at dawn to hire workingmen for his vineyard. After reaching an agreement with them for the usual daily wage, he sent them out to his vineyard. He came out about midmorning and saw other men standing about the marketplace without work, so he said to them, "You too go along to my vineyard and I will pay you whatever is fair." At that they went away. He came out again around noon and midafternoon and did the same. Finally, going out in late afternoon, he found still others standing around. To these he said, "Why have you been standing here idle all day?" "No one has hired us," they told him. He said, "You go to the vineyard too." When evening came the owner of the vineyard said to his foreman, "Call the workmen and give them their pay, but begin with the last group and end with the first." When those hired late in the afternoon came up they received a full day's pay, and when the first group appeared they supposed they would get more; yet they received the same daily wage. Thereupon they complained to the owner, "This last group did only an hour's work, but you have put them on the same basis as us who have worked a full day in the scorching heat." "My friend," he said to one in reply, "I do you no injustice. You agreed on the usual wage, did you not? Take your pay and go home. I intend to give this man who was hired last the same pay as you. I am free to do as I please with my money, am I not? Or are you envious because I am generous?" Thus the last shall be first and the first shall be last. (Matthew 20:1–16)

We know that this parable is about the kingdom of God because, like so many other parables, it begins, "The reign of God is like...." It draws its materials from the ordinary event of hiring laborers to work in a vineyard. We have a certain expectation: People who work longer should receive more pay. That expectation is thwarted by the owner who claims that his generosity toward some does not make him unjust toward others. What does this have to do with the kingdom of God?

Instead of trying to offer one single interpretation, I will share a few of the many interpretations that students have related to me in class. First of all is the traditional "death-bed conversion" interpretation that stresses that even though one has lived a bad life one can still be saved if one repents. Another interpretation is that God's justice is not our justice, and that we simply cannot understand why things in this life often do not seem fair. Yet another interpretation focuses on the theme that in the kingdom the first shall be last and the last first. Still another interpretation is that those who have just begun to live their life on a spiritual basis can be just as close to God as those who have been trying for years; seniority does not count for much when it comes to holiness.

The most important thing about a parable is not how you interpret it but how it strikes you. The multiple meanings are like tiny bombs that go off in a series of synchronized explosions. When you have been hit, you know that you are that much closer to being open to the coming of the kingdom.

Following Jesus

Jesus' teaching of the kingdom offers us an inkling of what things could be like if we human beings would drop our defenses, reach out to each other in love, and together seek out the will of our loving God. *Lumen Gentium* speaks of "a kingdom of truth and life, a kingdom of holiness and grace, a kingdom of justice, love, and peace" (*LG*, 36). The church itself is not fully the kingdom, but is the seed of the kingdom

(*LG*, 5). The church is not without imperfections, but strives to be a model community in which love is truly the first and final word. The church also works as a leaven in the world, pointing the world in the direction of the kingdom (*Gaudium et Spes*, 40).

Christians believe that Jesus, through his life, death, and resurrection, broke the cycle of sin and hate and rationalization that holds us back from being prepared for the kingdom to come. He dropped his defenses, taught the truth, acted out of self-sacrificing love, and was put to death as an innocent man. Christians have traditionally interpreted the resurrection as God's final seal of approval of the path that Jesus walked. Jesus' life and death were vindicated by his rising from the dead.

One way of understanding the fifth chapter of *Lumen Gentium's* universal call to holiness is to see it as a mandate for all Christians to follow Christ in breaking the cycle of sin. Jesus taught us to love even our enemies and to do good to those who hate us. He broke the cycle of sin by living a life based on love. *Lumen Gentium* says that in order for love to grow, "each of the faithful must willingly hear the Word of God and accept his will, and must complete what God has begun by their own actions with the help of God's grace" (*LG*, 42). To follow Jesus is to break the cycle of sin by making love the basis of one's life: "It is the love of God and the love of one's neighbor which points out the true disciple of Christ" (*LG*, 42).

Summary

In this chapter we have examined the teaching of Jesus. We concentrated on Jesus' proclamation of the kingdom, his special concern for the poor, and his parables. Through his words and deeds, Jesus taught people how to break the cycle of sin.

The cycle of sin has deep and unrecoverable origins. Its roots are personal, but it has branched out in social, economic, and political spheres. As I said earlier, I try not to be wildly utopian or idealistic in my expectations of what we can make this world to be. And yet I also do not wish to underestimate the tremendous and far-reaching impact it can have when even one human being truly repents, forgives others, and seeks to bring about the kingdom of God. Perhaps some day even my own children may stop fighting.

Having studied spirituality in relation to the Father and Jesus, in the next chapter we will turn our attention to the Holy Spirit.

FOR FURTHER REFLECTION

1. How can a person come to know the will of God?

2. What is your own understanding of original sin?

3. How might Jesus' warnings to the rich apply to today?

4. Saying that Jesus "broke the cycle" of sin through his life based on love is one interpretation of his mission. How does this interpretation compare with other interpretations with which you are familiar?

5. What images come to mind for you when you think about the kingdom of God?

SUGGESTED READINGS

Chilton, Bruce, ed. *The Kingdom of God in the Teaching of Jesus.* Philadelphia: Fortress Press, 1984.

Crossan, John Dominic. *In Parables: The Challenge of the Historical Jesus.* New York: Harper & Row, 1973.

Hamm, Dennis. *The Beatitudes in Context.* Wilmington, Del.: Michael Glazier, 1990.

Perrin, Norman. *The Resurrection According to Matthew, Mark, and Luke.* Philadelphia: Fortress Press, 1967.

Young, Brad. *Jesus and His Jewish Parables.* Mahwah, N.J.: Paulist Press, 1989.

CHAPTER 18

A JOB DESCRIPTION
FOR THE HOLY SPIRIT

S ome Catholics who do not like Vatican II tell the story of when Pope John XXIII died and went to heaven. Peter brought him through the gates and began introducing him to various personages. When the pope was introduced to the Holy Spirit, the Spirit appeared momentarily puzzled and then, after a flash of recognition, looked slightly embarrassed. The Spirit said, "Oh, yes, yes, that's right. You know, I did receive the invitation you sent me to that council, but I'm sorry, I just couldn't make it."

This story illustrates more than just the vicious humor that Catholics can revert to when they feel their faith has been threatened or diminished. It also illustrates more than the deep feelings of resentment that some Catholics harbored toward the council. What this story most reveals is the Catholic belief that it is the abiding presence of the Holy Spirit that guides the church on the proper path. If someone thinks the church is straying from the path, the absence of the Spirit can be cited as the reason.

Catholics, like most other Christians, believe in three persons in one God. The church is not based solely on a belief in God the Father, nor is it based solely on the teachings of Jesus. The church finds its origins also in the encounter with the resurrected Christ and in the experience of being filled with the Holy Spirit on Pentecost. It is the Spirit who transforms the lives of individuals, who inspires people in praise of God, who guides leaders in making intelligent decisions, and who accompanies the church in its journey toward truth and holiness. The Spirit is also the presence of God to be encountered through the people and events of the world.

Catholics today experience the resurrected Christ and the reception of the Spirit in a way that is, perhaps, not so unlike the experience of the original apostles. Our encounter is a *mediated* one; that is, we do not encounter Christ directly through personal appearances, but through people and events in our lives. The encounter with Christ is represented for Catholics above all through Christ's real presence in the Eucharist. The Eucharist points also to the places that we meet Christ in the everyday: in prayer, in loving relationships, in growth experiences, and especially in the face of the poor and the suffering and anyone who is in need. The transformation we experience through our encounter with Christ fills us with the Holy Spirit.

Such language is, of course, highly symbolic. Religious language must be symbolic because it "packages" for us things that we otherwise would not be able to understand. To say that it is symbolic is not in any way to say that it is not true; it is to indicate, though, that the truth of the language can only be grasped by those for whom the language is meaningful. In the case of religious language, this usually means those who structure the meaning of their lives according to that particular religion. In an academic setting, however, it can include anyone willing to try thinking analogously in terms of that religion.

For example, a secular student who takes my course on the church might not believe in Christianity or the Holy Spirit; that student, however, can relate to this language as a way of talking about human openness and transformation. Most Christians believe that this language is more than just a way of labeling; it is, rather, a key to entering into a tradition that communicates to us the very revelation of the three-personed God. Both types of students, however, can recognize the symbolic nature of the language as it tries to put us in touch with the meaning of life.

This Chapter

I raise these points because in my classroom experience I have found many students, both Christian and non-Christian, to be thoroughly confused by the concept of the Holy Spirit. To address this confusion, I have formulated a job description for this least familiar person of the Trinity.

Some job descriptions have the purpose of letting an employee know what is expected of him or her; that is not my purpose here. Another common function of a job description is to communicate to others what it is that a person does. I have seen this happen in a parish. Parish council members sometimes wonder what it is that particular employees such as a pastoral associate or a director of religious education do. The job descriptions provide this information. In this chapter, I will furnish a job description that attempts to reflect the various functions attributed by Catholics to the Holy Spirit. This material relates to chapter 5 of *Lumen Gentium*.

Summary Job Description—Holy Spirit
Be the presence of God working through people.

Former Work Experience
- Participated in the creation of the world. (God's breath, sometimes symbolically identified as the Holy Spirit, is involved in the creation of the universe and particularly in the creation of human beings, when "God blew into his nostrils the breath of life" [Genesis 2:7].)
- Has spoken through the Prophets (as recited in the Creed).
- Inspired the entire Bible.
- Was the one through whom Mary conceived Jesus (Matthew 1:18; Luke 1:35).
- Descended upon Jesus at his baptism (Mark 1:9–11).
- Was the one whom Jesus promised to send to his disciples (John 15:15–16:15).
- Participated in the resurrection of Jesus (Romans 1:4).
- Empowered the disciples on Pentecost to spread the gospel in continuance of the saving mission of Christ (Acts 2:1–4).
- Has worked in the lives of Christians to bring forth the fruits of holiness (Gal 5:22).
- Has guided the major decisions made by church councils. (When the apostles choose a replacement for Judas, they invoke the guidance of the Spirit (Acts 1:16). When later they meet in council in Jerusalem to settle a dispute between Peter and Paul, they announce their conclusion as "the decision of the Holy Spirit and not of us" (Acts 15:28). Even such a crucial decision as which books to include in the Bible was made at an early council. According to Catholic belief, then, the Holy Spirit has guided not only major decisions, but also the evolution of the tools and authoritative structures by which decisions are to be made. These include the councils, the Scriptures, the Tradition, the threefold office of bishop, priest, and deacon, and the papacy.)
- Has functioned as the source of holiness and renewed life throughout the history of the church (*LG*, 4).

Current Task: Transform the Lives of Individuals

The Holy Spirit has the job of transforming the lives of those who open themselves to God. Many theologians today speak of such life transformation in terms of "conversion." Conversion refers not just to deciding to become religious or to changing denominations, but to a lifelong process of growth in faith. Bernard Lonergan has distinguished three types of conversion: religious, moral, and intellectual.[1] In Lonergan's perspective, each type of conversion is rooted in the work of the Holy Spirit, for religious conversion is the most basic type from which the others flow.

Religious conversion is an other-worldly falling-in-love with God. It involves getting in touch with the love of the Holy Spirit that floods our hearts even prior to our being aware of it (Romans 5:5). In other words, Lonergan believes that every human being is filled at the core with the love of God through the Holy Spirit. To be religiously converted is to open ourselves to this love. Lonergan also draws upon Ezekiel 36:26 to describe religious conversion: It is what happens when God rips out our heart of stone and replaces it with a heart of flesh. Many people can point to select moments in their lives when religious conversion took place; many cannot. All who are religiously converted, however, are engaged in a lifelong journey of growth.

Moral conversion refers to the process by which a person stops making decisions solely according to self-interest and seeks instead to do what is truly good. We grow through various stages of motivation for being good, from compulsion, to social acceptance, to principles, to the need to be an authentic person who acts out of love for God and others.

In Lonergan's analysis, intellectual conversion is very technical. It involves getting in touch with the process by which one knows things, thereby becoming adept at sorting out various levels of consciousness and various dimensions of reality. For our purposes, intellectual conversion can refer to the gradual process by which one grows in an appreciation of the complexity and multidimensionality of reality, including its transcendent dimensions. That is, the intellectually converted person is one who neither confuses religious language with scientific description nor reduces everything religious to the level of the material. The intellectually converted person has a grasp of how symbolic language can function to put one in touch with the deeper dimensions of human existence.

That the Holy Spirit will transform the lives of individuals who follow Christ is central to the teaching of Paul in the New Testament. The way that Paul spoke of such transformation has been codified in the tradition as the gifts and fruits of the Holy Spirit. Instead of a life based on fear, resentment, and self-pity, the follower of Christ displays "love, joy, peace, patient endurance, kindness, generosity, faith, mildness, and chastity" (Galatians 5:22–23). Other traditional gifts and fruits of the Spirit found in Paul include self-control, wisdom, ability to make good decisions (counsel), piety, moral courage, and fear of the Lord. These characteristics are not so much things sought for themselves; they are more the qualities that people find themselves possessing as they struggle to follow Christ.

Current Task: Inspire Groups in Prayer and in Decisions

In Alcoholics Anonymous there is a belief in a "group conscience." Individuals are free to express whatever opinions they want to at meetings, no matter how profound or how ridiculous. The recovering alcoholics trust that the group itself will be guided by a higher power such that the overall message of the meeting will express the will of a loving God (though not all alcoholics use the term, "God"). What an individual says is simply a personal opinion; what comes through the group is a power greater than any one individual and that draws upon the experience, strength, and hope of all who are present.

Catholics have traditionally believed that one of the jobs of the Holy Spirit is to act as a kind of "group conscience" when Christians are gathered in prayer or engaged in decision making. This belief is reflected in the following traditional prayer:

Come, Holy Spirit
Fill the hearts of your faithful
And enkindle in them the fire of your love.
Send forth your Spirit
And they will be created
And you will renew the face of the earth.

Many Catholics today believe that the Holy Spirit is currently engaged in a broad-scale renewal of the Catholic church through small groups. Liberation theologians in Latin America point to the workings of the Spirit through base Christian communities that engage in both the reading of Scripture and in political activity. Those involved in the charismatic renewal point to signs of the Spirit in healing, prophecy, and speaking in tongues. Groups of women activists, the Cursillo movement, various prayer groups, Renew groups, parish councils, and other parish committees, all point to the activity of the Spirit in their midst.

Current Task: Guide the Church as a Whole

Catholics have traditionally believed that the church is *indefectible;* that is, that the Holy Spirit will protect the church from straying from the true path. Indefectibility is based in part on the Catholic interpretation of Matthew 16:18, when Jesus says, "And so I say to you, you are Peter, and upon this rock I will build my church, and the gates of the netherworld shall not prevail against it." "Peter" means "rock" in Aramaic, and so Jesus is portrayed as using a pun in communicating his guarantee of the church's steadfastness through all of time. This line is often read in conjunction with John 16:13: "But when he comes, the Spirit of truth, he will guide you to all truth."

Indefectibility should not be read as a guarantee that the church will never make a mistake or have to reverse itself on a teaching. History offers too many examples to the contrary. It means, rather, that the church is to be relied upon as the continuation of Christ's saving presence and work on earth. The church might make some mistakes (as in the rejection of Galileo's theories) or engage in horrendous activities (the mass slaughter of Jews and Moslems during some of the crusades), but in its most important teachings and in its sacramental ministry it continues to be guided by the Holy Spirit. In a basic sense, the Catholic can trust the church and its teachings.

On an institutional level, the Holy Spirit is believed to have some influence in the election of popes, the selection of bishops, the decrees of councils, and, in general, all teaching, leadership, and sacramental ministry. If Jesus promised that the Spirit would be with us, we can expect to experience that presence in these areas. Current disputes about how bishops are selected involve debates about where the voice of the Spirit can most clearly be heard.

From a Catholic perspective, the most profound thing that could be said of any church community is that the Holy Spirit can be found working among its members. This is precisely what the Catholic church said in *Lumen Gentium* about Protestant churches: "...we can say that in some real way they are joined with us in the Holy Spirit, for to them too he gives his gifts and graces whereby he is operative among them with his sanctifying power" (*LG*, 15).

Often movements in the church are attributed to the work of the Spirit. Many people today point to the explosion of lay ministries, the developing body of Catholic social teaching, the ecumenical movement, and the tendency toward more sharing of authority as evidence of the Spirit's work. Some liberal theologians are fond of claiming that in these days the Spirit prefers to work from the bottom up, moving the church through its people.

It is even said that the Holy Spirit is behind the current shortage of priests. People who reason this way foresee the resulting changes in church structure, such as the need to rely more and more on the laity, as ultimately good things in harmony with God's plan. Personally, I stay away from interpretations such as these. Maybe the Holy Spirit is behind the priest shortage and maybe the Holy Spirit is not. It is at least as likely that the shortage of priests is the result of people not listening to the Spirit as vice-versa.

This brings us to an important point: Not everything attributed to the Holy Spirit is from the Holy Spirit. The Catholic tradition has had to fight unbridled enthusiasm that sees the Spirit in everything, just as it has had to fight complacency that is inattentive to the Spirit's workings. An old Buddhist saying illustrates the need to be cautious about claims to religious authority: "If you meet the Buddha on the road, kill him." Why? Because the person claiming to be Buddha has got to be an imposter. I would not suggest killing everyone who claims that the Spirit is working through them or that they are the one most capable of interpreting the Spirit; I will simply encourage the dictum that all spirits are to be tested.

There is no single, clear formula for the testing of spirits. For starters, I would suggest asking the following: Does a particular claim align with the best of my religious tradition? Does it square with empirical facts? Does it find harmony with my own religious, moral, and intellectual conversion? Does it seem to continue to make sense as I live with it? Does it draw me outside of myself toward a new appreciation of others? A list of such questions could go on and on.

Current Task:
Be the Potential for God's Love in All Human Beings

Many Catholic theologians, among them Bernard Lonergan and Karl Rahner, speak of the basic orientation of all human beings toward the transcendent mystery whom Christians know as God.[2] All people are drawn in self-transcendent motion in the direction of goodness, truth, and love. No matter one's religion, even if one has no religion at all, everyone is capable of growing in the direction of God when one moves beyond selfishness to embrace higher values, openness, honesty, and loving human relationships. These theologians are further inclined to attribute this orientation to the presence of the Holy Spirit in all human beings, whether people call it that or not.

For this reason, many Christians who engage in inter-religious dialogue draw upon the concept of the Holy Spirit to talk about what is authentic in all of the religions of the world.[3] Only Christianity sees God in Christ. Some religions do not expressly believe in a God. It is the Holy Spirit, understood as the presence of the divine within us, that seems to provide the best starting point for a dialogue (though, of course, most religions do not call this divine presence the "Holy Spirit").

Summary

In this chapter we have reviewed the workings of the Holy Spirit in individuals, in groups, in the church, and in the world. It appears that the Holy Spirit has a lot of work to do. Yet the Catholic tradition expresses full confidence in the power of God. What we need to worry about more is our own willingness to listen to the promptings of the Spirit and make them a reality in our lives.

One part of the Spirit's job that I failed to mention is the element of surprise: The Spirit blows freely in astonishing ways. I believe that Vatican II is an example of this. I disagree with that minority of Catholics who thought the Spirit absent from the unanticipated wonder of Vatican II; that happens to be one of the main places that I look for the entry of the Spirit into the world of today.

In the next chapter we will examine the life of religious brothers and sisters who take vows and form communities.

FOR FURTHER REFLECTION

1. Do you find the concept of the Holy Spirit to be more helpful or more confusing?

2. Does the Holy Spirit have a function in your own prayer life?

3. Are you able to use the concept of "conversion" in talking about your own life-journey?

4. Have you ever experienced a "group conscience" that seemed to be greater than the sum of the individuals present?

5. How is the concept of the Holy Spirit important for the Catholic church?

SUGGESTED READINGS

Burns, J. Patout and Gerald M. Fagin. *The Holy Spirit.* Wilmington, Del.: Michael Glazier, 1984.

Chinnici, Joseph P. *Devotion to the Holy Spirit in American Catholicism.* Mahwah, N.J.: Paulist Press, 1985.

Congar, Yves. *I Believe in the Holy Spirit.* 3 Vols. New York: Seabury, 1983 [1979, 1980].

Conn, Walter. *Christian Conversion: A Developmental Interpretation of Autonomy and Surrender.* Mahwah, N.J.: Paulist Press, 1986.

SECTION SIX

RELIGIOUS

CHAPTER 19

RELIGIOUS COMMUNITIES

A student recently asked me why any man would choose to be a religious brother when he could be a priest instead. Immediately I remembered asking the same question of a religious brother who taught me science in high school. I also vaguely remembered his response as having something to do with different people having different callings.

In the same split second I blurted out my own personal response to the student's question: It could be great to live in community with a group of people who share similar interests and goals. During a couple of periods of my life, particularly in high school and in graduate school, I said, I had been part of a highly supportive circle of friends. It was wonderful to have a lifestyle that allowed close, family-like intimacy with a good number of people. One could feel drawn to such a community that bases itself on a religious lifestyle without experiencing a call to be a priest.

Once I had made this response, however, I could feel how personal, how relevant, and yet how insufficient and partial it was. I had struck upon something: Religious communities can be attractive environments within which to live for many reasons. This attraction can be part of an authentic call to live such a life. My response, however, focused too much on the attractiveness of community life to the neglect of the distinctively religious reasons why a person would choose such a life. Yes, community life can be attractive; why not, then, simply live in a commune? Why live in a community founded by a follower of Jesus Christ?

This Chapter

Chapter six of *Lumen Gentium* (taken together with section 42 of chapter 5) offers different reasons why men and women would experience a call to live in a religious community as "brothers" and "sisters." These reasons do not detract from the attractiveness of community life, but they provide a deeper foundation. Religious life includes mutual support, broad-based intimacy, and inspiring lifestyles. In this chapter, however, we will explore even deeper motivations against the background of some scriptural, historical, and contemporary reflections.

Extraordinary Love

In the Catholic tradition it has been held that, since there are different ways of following Jesus, it is appropriate to distinguish between different states of life in the church. Each path of discipleship, be it lay, clerical, or religious, is designed for people who are seriously focused on following Jesus. Although reality is rarely so clear-cut as the ideal vision, the laity represent the many people who are committed to Christ but who do not leave behind their everyday lives; the clergy represent the inner circle of the twelve apostles who carry on the authority of Jesus; religious brothers and sisters represent those who have abandoned the things of this world out of their desire to follow the Lord. (Of course, many male members of religious communities are also priests; diocesan priests, on the other hand, are sometimes called "secular" priests.)

Lumen Gentium 42, which is the conclusion of chapter five but which provides the lead-in to chapter six, speaks of the love that is expected from all Christians. All Christians are called to accept the will of God. The mark of the true disciple is the love of God and the love of neighbor.

The passage then goes on to speak of some extraordinary forms of love. Martyrdom is described as an "exceptional gift and as the fullest proof of love." It is a means of being transformed into the image of Jesus who really accepted death for the salvation of the world. All Christians are to be prepared for this possibility.

Following the paragraph on martyrdom are two paragraphs that discuss the evangelical counsels of chastity, poverty, and obedience. Their connection with martyrdom has long roots in the Catholic tradition: Death for one's faith has been called "red martyrdom," and life according to the evangelical counsels has been called "white martyrdom." Following the evangelical counsels represents a form of martyrdom in that it entails a renunciation of or a "dying to" certain worldly values.

The Evangelical Counsels		
Poverty	Chastity	Obedience

All Christians are called to reject materialism and consumerism and to have a special concern for the poor; all are called to be chaste insofar as sexual activity is reserved for the most appropriate of contexts; all are called to be obedient to the will of God. What distinguishes those who join religious communities and take vows is their extraordinary form of adherence to these principles. Although religious communities differ in their interpretations, basically the call to chastity is for them a call to celibacy; the call to poverty is a call to own nothing themselves but to give all to the community; the call to obedience is a call to renounce one's own will in deference to the will of one's religious superior. These principles are adhered to not for their own sake but because they can function as liberating helps to living a life based on love.

Leave Everything Behind

Lumen Gentium combined a new emphasis on the universal call to holiness given to all Christians in all states of life with a traditional reaffirmation of the extraordinary nature of the evangelical counsels. There exists something of a tension between, on the one hand, the notion that a person who lives a lay life is called to pursue and experience holiness as devotedly and intensely as any other Christian, and, on the other hand, the notion that life in religious community is somehow more extraordinary or special or heroic. Recent biblical scholarship sheds some interesting light on this tension.

Several stories in the New Testament present a contrast between an ordinarily good way of life and a more radical lifestyle based on an intense following of Jesus. Scripture scholar John Meier has argued that such stories were originally intended to distinguish between what is meant to be a good Jewish person who follows the law and what it meant to be a follower of Christ.[1] Read in this light, these stories can be seen to apply in some sense to every Christian.

Take, for example, the story of the rich young man in Matthew 19:16–22. The man asks Jesus what he must do to inherit eternal life. Jesus at first responds simply that he should keep the commandments. The man replies that he has kept the commandments from his youth; what more should he do? Jesus then tells him that he should sell all that he has, give the money to the poor, and follow him. At that the young man became sad and walked away. In Mark 10:29-30, following Mark's own version of the story of the rich young man, Jesus is portrayed as saying, "Amen, I say to you, there is no one who has given up house or brothers or sisters or mother or father or children or lands for my sake and for the sake of the gospel who will not receive a hundred times more now in this present age."

As Meier interprets this story, the rich young man represents for the gospel writer any Jewish person of the first century who is confronted by the challenge to follow Jesus. To follow the law is good; to become a disciple of Jesus represents the fulfillment of what the law is all about. Becoming a disciple, however, may involve being rejected by one's own family and the loss of one's inheritance. The passage thus interpreted is about Christian discipleship and can apply to any Christian in any state of life.

As different states of life developed within the early church, however, the story of the rich young man came to be interpreted as distinguishing between the ordinary lay way of living a good life and the extraordinary religious way of following Jesus by renouncing the things of this world. Thus interpreted, the passage is read as referring explicitly to those who take religious vows and implies that their path is a special or more heroic one.

I would not reject either interpretation of this story, but I would place the "religious" interpretation that arose within the tradition against the background of the earlier and deeper "discipleship" interpretation. That is, I think that the most important call to holiness is the one given to all Christians regardless of state of life. This call reflects a fundamental equality in spiritual dignity among all who are baptized; within that context I recognize the call to a vowed religious life as representing in some sense a more radical renunciation of certain worldly values.

A similar issue arises in the gospel of Matthew where Jesus seems to be advocating the renunciation of sex and marriage: "Not all can accept this word, but only those to whom that is granted. Some are incapable of marriage because they were born so; some, because they were made so by others; some, because they have renounced marriage for the kingdom of heaven. Whoever can accept thing ought to accept it" (Matthew 19:11–12). In the Catholic tradition this passage has at times been interpreted as seeing in celibacy a "higher" calling. Meier points out, however, that this passage is linked in the Gospel with Jesus' prohibition against divorce and with his affirmation of marriage as part of the Father's plan of creation (19:3–6). Meier says that "marriage without divorce or celibacy chosen for the Kingdom: these are the signs of a community which lives by the powers of the age to come" (p. 138). It is thus possible to read the passage as endorsing chaste marriage and celibacy as two extremely good paths to holiness. As with the issue of poverty I experience a tension here. I do not wish to suggest that celibacy is higher than marriage (although Thomas Aquinas as well as the majority of church Fathers were convinced that it was); at the same time I want to recognize that celibacy can represent a heroic sacrifice for a particular individual who decides to give up marriage for the sake of the kingdom.

Obedience is the third of the evangelical counsels. Jesus is portrayed throughout the gospels as one who renounces even his own will in deference to the will of his Father, although ultimately this path leads to his death. Mark depicts Jesus in the garden of Gethsemane, praying "Abba, Father, all things are possible to you. Take this cup away from me, but not what I will but what you will" (Mark 14:36). Jesus challenged his own disciples to do the same: "Can you drink the cup that I drink or be baptized with the baptism with which I am baptized?" (Mark 10:38). He counseled them: "No one has greater love than this, to lay down one's life for one's friends" (John 15:13).

Many other references could be made to passages in the New Testament that connect the call of some Christians with an explicit renunciation of the world. The areas cited above deal specifically with riches, sex, and personal choice. They form the backdrop of the vows of poverty, chastity, and obedience taken by members of religious communities. Yet they also form the backdrop of the call of all Christians to reject materialism, dehumanizing sex, and a life obsessed with personal gratification. They are ultimately connected with a total giving of oneself, even to the point of death.

Why Join?

Most of the time the majority of human beings act out of mixed motivations. All at the same time, we might be operating out of high principles, concern for others, a desire to serve God, a drive to contribute to society, love, honesty, self-concern, fear, boredom, greed, and the need for security. Some events in life offer us a clear choice between sets of motivations; most do not.

People who join religious communities usually do not leave all of their personal needs and reasons behind. A religious sister recently remarked to me that a problem facing her community is that many new inquirers seem to be seeking refuge from broken or dysfunctional families. Such people can be good candidates, but they will need to overcome any tendencies to find in religious life simply an escape from a world that they could not handle. Personal refuge is acceptable as one level of motivation for joining a religious community, but only if it is ultimately combined with a desire to serve God and others out of a sense of self-sacrificing love.

Section 44 of *Lumen Gentium* speaks of the ideal level of motivation of one who professes religious vows:

> Indeed through baptism a person dies to sin and is consecrated to God. However, in order that one may be capable of deriving more abundant fruit from this baptismal grace, one intends, by the profession of the evangelical counsels in the church, to free oneself from those obstacles, which might draw one away from the fervor of charity and the perfection of divine worship. By one's profession of the evangelical counsels, then, one is more intimately consecrated to divine service.

In other words, a person joins a religious community because that person perceives such life as a better way for himself or herself to be dedicated to the love and service of God. Other reasons can and will be present, but this is the highest reason. The document speaks approvingly also of religious communities as "religious families [that] give their members the support of a more firm stability in their way of life..." (*LG*, 43). That is, the many attractions of a life lived in intimate community can be an authentic reason for joining a religious order.

Origins of Religious Community

Religious communities find the beginnings of their way of life in Jesus' ministry and death. They also find much support in the example and advice of St. Paul. The martyrs of the first few Christian centuries, as well as those throughout history until the present day, provide further example of lives of extraordinary sacrifice.

During the fourth century, however, Christianity shifted from being an underground, often persecuted religion, to being the official religion of the Roman empire. Martyrdom was left to the missionaries who preached in foreign cultures. Christians no longer needed to live in small, secret communities. Professing Christianity even came to be an advantage in public life.

The impulse to purer, more countercultural forms of Christianity found an outlet in ascetics who fled the life of the city to dwell in the desert.[2] Some Christians, such as St. Anthony (c. 251-355), began to live in the desert long before the persecutions were over. However, the rise of the first desert monasteries in the fourth century roughly parallels the emergence of Christianity as a publicly acceptable religion. Those who discerned in Christianity a personal call to flee from the world could no longer do so just by living their faith in the city.

Monastic life flourished throughout the Middle Ages. Monasteries functioned not only as desert or rural refuges, but also as centers of learning. The Benedictines were founded by St. Benedict at Monte Cassino near Naples about 525. The famous "Rule of St. Benedict," noted for its sensible balance of work, leisure, and prayer, stood in contrast to the more severe rules of other monasteries at the time. To this day, Benedictines are noted for their balanced approach to spirituality and for their excellent liturgies.

Literally thousands of religious orders have existed in the history of the church. Each order has a founder whose special gifts and ideas form the vision and goals of the society. The Dominicans, founded by St. Dominic, are known for their preaching and teaching. The Jesuits, founded by St. Ignatius Loyola to further the cause of the Catholic counter-reformation, are today famous for their scholarship and high standards in education. The Franciscans, founded by St. Francis to bring the ideals of the monastery into life in the city, are today recognized for their social concerns and their activity among the poor. The Maryknolls, founded by Father Thomas Frederick Rice and Bishop James Edward Walsh as the official missionary society of the United States, are known for their support of social and spiritual activity throughout the world.

The Marianists, founded by Father William Joseph Chaminade to respond to the needs of post-Revolutionary Europe, are known today for their educational efforts, their spirit of collaboration, their artistic achievements, their family-like community, their commitment to service, and the special character of their devotion to each member of the Holy Family.

Not all Franciscans work with the poor; not all Jesuits labor as scholars; not all Marianists teach or produce works of art. These characteristic tendencies are associated with each order, but do not dictate the exact contribution of every member. It might be claimed that today each order has its own *esprit*, but that its individual members might engage in a wide variety of activities. What most characterizes the work of members of religious communities is that the great majority of them are engaged in lives of direct service to others. Whether it be ministry in a parish, hospital, or nursing home; teaching in a grade school, university, or prison; working among the poor in hostels, soup kitchens, or employment training; working in a rural area, an urban area, or a foreign culture, those who take religious vows are most often found engaged in activities that render help to others. They do this with the aid of a community lifestyle of renunciation that finds its multifaceted roots in the history of the Catholic tradition.

Current Issues

Religious communities today are beset with many challenges and difficulties. On a practical level, there has been the problem of decreasing membership with a corresponding rise in the median age of those who belong. Health care costs, retirement, and management of properties often crowd the agenda of community meetings.

Members of religious communities also struggle to define their identities in a rapidly changing world. Some communities, for example, accept the order of the pope that traditional dress is to be worn as normal garb. Other communities leave this question up to the individual brother or sister.

In our age, which places special stress upon the importance of the autonomy of the individual, the meaning of the traditional vow of "obedience" has been placed in question.[3] Is self-direction in response to one's conscience and calling as important as obedience to one's religious superior? Can responsible obedience be distinguished from blind obedience?

These issues are especially important today in communities of religious women. Catholic men have the possibility of requesting to be a priest, but Catholic women who feel called to roles of leadership do not have such a choice. Many persons today are challenging a church system that calls on communities of women to answer to structures of authority made up by men alone.

Any challenge has its positive and negative sides. Many who belong to religious communities today find that they live in interesting and exciting times. Many also believe that they could hardly find a better path for their struggle to follow the Lord.

Summary

In this chapter we have explored the evangelical counsels, the motivations for joining a religious community, the history of religious life, and some issues of current concern. The next time that a student asks me why a man would choose to be a brother rather than a priest, I will try not to leap to any conclusions. I will mention the attraction of a communal lifestyle, as well as the notion that different people have different callings. My main emphasis, though, will be on the need for each person to find the best way in which he or she can respond to the gospel's call.

In the next two chapters we will study liberation theology as an approach to faith that places a special emphasis on community.

FOR FURTHER REFLECTION

1. What would most attract someone to life in a religious community?

2. What have been your own experiences with people who are members of religious orders?

3. What does it mean to have a "call"? Does everyone have some type of calling in life?

4. Do you find it surprising that some people may be drawn to religious life for other than religious motivations?

5. Are the evangelical counsels "weird" in today's world?

SUGGESTED READINGS

Arbuckle, Gerald A. *Out of Chaos: Refounding Religious Congregations.* Mahwah, N.J.: Paulist Press, 1988.

Armstrong, Philip. *Who Are My Brothers?* Staten Island, N.Y.: Alba House, 1988.

Balthasar, Hans Urs von. *The Moment of Christian Witness.* Glen Rock, N.J.: Newman Press, 1969 [1966].

Chittister, Joan. *Winds of Change: Women Challenge the Church.* Kansas City: Sheed & Ward, 1986.

Merton, Thomas. *The Silent Life.* New York: Farrar, Straus & Cudahy, 1957.

Wynne, Edward. *Traditional Catholic Religious Orders: Living in Community.* New Brunswick, N.J.: Transaction Books, 1988.

CHAPTER 20

LIBERATION THEOLOGY
AND CHURCH COMMUNITY

Many books and films can help us grow by allowing us to see what reality looks like from a different perspective. *Driving Miss Daisy* shocks many white people into a recognition of their own sometimes subtle prejudices by letting them see the world through the eyes of a black chauffeur. Few straight people who see what the world looks like from the point of view of the gay men in *Boys in the Band* can come away without having some of their prejudices about homosexuals shaken. Many women secretaries suggest to their bosses that they see *9 to 5* in order to get a comic but nonetheless real view of what abusive power relationships look and feel like to them.

The Scottish poet Robert Burns wrote:

"Oh wad some Power the giftie gie us
To see oursels as ithers see us!"[1]

To see ourselves and the world through the perspective of another may indeed be a great gift, but it can also be a terrible one. If we see reality differently we might have to change. We might have to adopt new values, make new decisions, and alter the way we live and behave.

A relatively new way of doing theology that is popular today in Latin America and growing throughout the world is called "liberation theology." Liberation theologians call upon all people to see things through a very particular perspective: the eyes of the poor. The more a person becomes aware of this perspective, the more that person will change and grow.

This Chapter

This chapter will introduce some of the basic concepts of liberation theologians, with a primary focus on their ideas about the church. I will rely most on a controversial work by Brazilian theologian Leonardo Boff, *Church: Charism and Power*.[2] Liberation theology places a strong emphasis on new forms of Christian community, and hence can be related to chapter 6 of *Lumen Gentium*. Liberation theology can also be related to the emphasis on social justice that pervaded Vatican II.

Intolerable Conditions

Liberation theology advocates political action ultimately in the name of Christian love; it has its beginnings, however, in outrage over the condition of the poor in the countries of Latin America. Boff speaks of his own country of Brazil:

> For example, in Brazil, 75 percent of the people live in relative economic marginalization; 43 percent are condemned to a minimum salary in order to survive. A worker from São Paulo, Manuel Paulo, says it best: "What I earn is so little it only proves that I am alive. . . ." 40 percent of all Brazilians live, work, and sleep with chronic hunger; there are 10 million who are mentally retarded due to malnutrition; 6 million suffer from malaria; 650,000 have tuberculosis and 25,000 suffer from leprosy.[3]

Liberation theologians believe that the gospel must have something to say about such miserable conditions. Could it be the will of a loving God that so many millions live in abject poverty? Or is there a call in the Christian faith to work to alleviate this misery?

Base Ecclesial Communities

Boff claims that liberation theology has its roots not in the speculations of theologians, but in the experience of Christians who come together in prayer to read and reflect on the meaning of the Scriptures. These groups usually consist of about fifteen to twenty families. Boff offers the following description of what are called *communidades ecclesiales de base*, or base ecclesial communities:

> Initially, such a community serves to deepen the faith of its mem-

bers, to prepare the liturgy, the sacraments, and the life of prayer. At a more advanced stage these members begin to help each other. As they become better organized and reflect more deeply, they come to the realization that the problems they encounter have a structural character. Their marginalization is seen as a consequence of elitist organization, private ownership, that is, of the very socioeconomic structure of the capitalist system. Thus, the question of politics arises and the desire for liberation is set in a concrete and historical context. The community sees this not only as liberation from sin (from which we must always liberate ourselves) but also a liberation that has economic, political, and cultural dimensions.

Although it is still by far the minority of Latin Americans who are organized in base ecclesial communities, these groups have spread rapidly in countries such as Brazil, Colombia, and El Salvador. They combine a reading of the Scriptures with an analysis of the economic and social causes of their difficulties to inspire them into organized political action. Although some liberation theologians have advocated violence, most of them strongly favor non-violent revolutionary activities.

According to Boff, the base ecclesial communities have worldwide implications for the nature of the Catholic church. He criticizes current church operations for being top-heavy and bureaucratic, drawing their inspiration more from Roman and feudal structures than from the gospel. He sees the church in his own country as one that has historically sided with the rich against the interests of the poor. The base ecclesial communities, on the other hand, represent an ideal, classless society in which all members can participate fully. These communities care for the dispossessed and celebrate the true meaning of Christian liberation.

Boff highlights this contrast by describing two kinds of power. _Dominating_ power is the power of the oppressive ruler who wants to take power away from those who are ruled. The more power the ruler has, the less the subjects have. The ruler gets to control others in order to accomplish tasks in the ruler's best interest. In contrast to dominating power is _empowering_ power, the power of Jesus, the power of love. Those who possess this type of power want to share it with others. This type of power empowers others to be able to work for themselves and for the common good. The more power one person has, the more power all have.

In Boff's vision, the base ecclesial communities provide the starting point for the rebirth of the Catholic church from the bottom up. That is,

Boff envisions a worldwide networking of base ecclesial communities that will infuse a new spirit of egalitarian love throughout the entire church. He draws upon the image of Sara, Abraham's wife, who at one hundred years old thought that she was incapable of conceiving. The old church of dominating power is like Sara; the base ecclesial communities are the new life within its womb:

> Smile, Sara, because once sterile you have become fertile, you have become a new creation! Sara has already conceived. There, in Sara's womb, the signs of new life are already beginning to appear: a new church is being born, in the dark recesses of humanity.[4]

Liberating Scriptures

Liberation theologians look to the Christian Scriptures as the source of their faith. They have given special attention to the story in Exodus of how God took the side of the oppressed Hebrew slaves over their oppressor, the Egyptian Pharaoh. God heard their groaning, raised up a leader, and visited plagues upon the oppressor until God's people were finally released from bondage.

Liberation theologians cry out along with Moses, "Set my people free." They compare the situation of the poor in Latin America with the situation of the Hebrew slaves. They interpret the salvation that comes from God not simply as a spiritual matter concerning a final judgment for an individual, but also as a political, economic, and social matter that has implications right here and right now.

The story of Jesus has also been of special interest to liberation theologians, who have focused on Jesus' function as one who sets people free. They highlight Jesus' warnings to the rich, his special concern for the poor and the socially disenfranchised, his clashes with established religious and political authorities, and the power of his resurrection as the ultimate liberation from death. Jesus sets us free not only from personal sin but from the institutionalized structures of sin that mar human relationships by keeping people in horrible conditions of poverty and hopelessness.

Preferential Option for the Poor

Liberation theologians draw upon the Scriptures to speak of what they call the "preferential option for the poor," a phrase that has made its way into some official church documents, including speeches by Pope John Paul II. The phrase takes its inspiration from the manner in which God is portrayed—in the Jewish law and in the teachings of the prophets, as well as in the person and teachings of Jesus—as having a special concern for the poor. The phrase has been interpreted in many ways. Some say that "poor" can refer to many types of poverty, including not only material poverty, but loneliness, alienation, and depression. In this way one can say that God has a special concern for all people in response to their deepest needs.

I once offered this interpretation to a liberation theologian who was visiting the university at which I teach. He practically spit out his answer in contempt: "Phooey! You want to know what poverty is? Come to my country and I will show you what poverty is." He believed I was watering down the meaning of "poverty" to stop it from challenging my way of thinking. Real poverty is the horror of material deprivation that his people experience. If I redefine poverty to include the loneliness of people who are materially well off, I take away from the urgency to do something about the problems of his people.

A common question that my students raise at this point is whether God does not have a special concern for all human beings. The answer that I have heard a liberation theologian give to this is that the option for the poor includes a special concern for all human beings. This is because no one is ultimately served well by oppressive situations. The oppressor is as bound and limited by the situation as the oppressed person is. The slave-owner is made a small human being by the very fact of owning slaves. When the slaves are set free, the former slave-owner is set free from the bondage of being an oppressor. The former slave-owner is now open to new possibilities of entering into more authentic human relationships with those who used to be slaves.

In this interpretation, the "option for the poor" requires that one view reality through the eyes of the poor. To be unaware of what reality looks like through the eyes of the poor is to be out of touch with reality. Decisions must, therefore, be made taking the perspective of the poor into consideration. The lawyer Robert Rodes interprets the option for the poor in this way: It is to "discern the special interests of the dominant class *and then decide against those interests.*"[5] Whether or not one is personally poor, one must stand in solidarity with the poor and work to transform society with the well-being of the poor in mind. In this way, liberation theologians advocate the transformation not only of the church, but of society itself, from the bottom up.

Another question commonly raised about the option for the poor is whether it represents a glorification of poverty. Anyone who reads more than a page written by any liberation theologian would stop asking this question. Liberation theologians despise material deprivation. What they advocate is not poverty but justice. They love the poor not because of their poverty but because they represent the face of Christ who appears in all who are needy. Liberation theologians call for working to reverse injustices that contribute to human degradation. They do not glorify poverty in any way.

Model of the Church I:
Community of the People of God

In their emphasis on base ecclesial communities and the local church, liberation theologians have stressed a version of what Avery Dulles has called the "mystical communion" model of the church. Proponents of a "mystical communion" model can be divided into those who favor the "Body of Christ" image and those who favor the "People of God" image. Leonardo Boff is representative of liberation theologians in general in the way that he focuses on the church as "People of God." He interprets the emergence of this image as one of the most important events at Vatican II for two reasons.

First, the "People of God" signals a shift from a church too centered on the hierarchy and organizational structures to a church centered on the people with their everyday problems and struggles. Boff does not advocate doing away with the hierarchy, but he does want to see the leadership function of the hierarchy contextualized within the various functions performed by the people of God. For Boff, the hierarchical function of leadership is but one charism among many charisms. It is to be appreciated but not abused. Leaders should function as servants of the people, and not act as though they are higher or better than other Christians. The "People of God" image evokes a picture of a church with a radically egalitarian spirit, a church that is being reborn from the bottom up.

Second, the "People of God" names a church that must be open to change. In Boff's view, the church was founded by the apostles under the inspiration of the Holy Spirit on Pentecost. The Spirit guided the apostles in building a church that could respond to the needs of their time. That same Holy Spirit is still with the church today, helping the people of God respond to our changing needs. Boff uses this vision to criticize views that he believes are overly bound to past decisions of church leaders.

The practical implication of Boff's view of the Holy Spirit guiding the people of God is that he thereby favors many changes in the church today, such as the ordination of women, married priests, and the celebration of the Eucharist by local church leaders who may lack seminary training and an ordination with church-wide validity. Boff's argument is that we can be faithful to our heritage only if we imitate the leaders of the past by making decisions in accordance with our needs; to bind ourselves to past decisions that do not meet our needs is to create a static church unfaithful to our dynamic tradition.

Model of the Church II:
Servant and Instrument of Liberation

Even more important to liberation theologians than the "mystical communion" model is the "servant" model of the church. Here again liberation theologians offer their own very particular version. Dulles's original model stressed service in a world viewed optimistically as evolving toward ever greater achievements. It was represented by *avant-garde* thinkers such as Pierre Teilhard de Chardin and Harvey Cox. The liberation version of the servant model sees a world of systematic corruption built upon the oppression of a multitude of impoverished peoples.

Boff offers two complementary ways to think about the church as servant. First, the church is a "community and sign of liberation." Within its own internal framework, it strives to be an intimate and familial community. It offers help to its members, and also offers services to the larger society, such as education and health care. Boff believes these services are especially important when they are not duplicating services already provided by society.

Second, the church should be a "prophet and instrument of liberation." Boff warns of the danger of overemphasizing the communitarian aspects of the church. It is not enough to be satisfied with internal improvements that give people a homey feeling. Boff uses the example of inmates in a prison whose living conditions are improved. Such improvements are good as far as they go, but they do not compare with being released from the prison. In order for people to be set free, the church must work toward structural change in society:

> This process of liberation demands a much more detailed analysis of society: how the production of wealth functions, how wealth is distributed, the place of individuals in relation to capital, employment, and participation. The community that is awakened to this reality is already conscious of the violation of human rights, of structural poverty, of the social injustices that are the fruits of the organization of an entire system that is often presented as good,

Christian, democratic, and so forth. Christian faith awakens one to social justice, to the true meaning of the global liberation of Jesus Christ that demands the transformation, the conversion, not only of the individual but also of the structures.[6]

Members of base ecclesial communities are therefore called upon to organize politically to work against the forces of oppression. They balance social analysis and action with a spirituality of "faith, hope, love, trust, and patience." Boff points out that this path often leads to persecution and martyrdom.

Summary

In this chapter we have investigated some of basic dimensions of liberation theology: overcoming oppression, base ecclesial communities, liberation in Scripture, the option for the poor, and the church as People of God and Instrument of Liberation.

Liberation theologians make many claims and demands upon the people of the first world. I take all of these claims seriously. I agree with some, but not all, of them. What I take most seriously of all, though, is the demand that I try to see things through the eyes of the poor. The more I do that, the closer I will be to reality and to God. And the more I will change and grow.

In the next chapter we will explore some of the critical discussion concerning the value and role of liberation theology.

FOR FURTHER REFLECTION

1. Does liberation theology tie religion too closely with politics?

2. How do you personally interpret the concept that God has a special concern for the poor?

3. Is liberation theology useful for the U.S.? If so, how might it be apply?

4. Have you ever experienced what Boff calls dominating power? Have you ever experienced what Boff calls liberating power?

5. Should church leaders today feel more free to make changes to respond to new situation?

SUGGESTED READINGS

Berryman, Phillip. _Liberation Theology_. Oak Park, Il.: Meyer-Stone Books, 1987.

Boff, Leonardo. _Church: Charism and Power_. New York: Crossroad, 1985 [1981].

Ferm, Deane W. _Profiles in Liberation: 36 Portraits of Third World Theologians_. Mystic, Conn.: Twenty-Third Publications, 1988.

Gutierrez, Gustavo. _Liberation Theology_. Maryknoll, N.Y.: Orbis Books, 1973 [1971].

CHAPTER 21

LIBERATION THEOLOGY:
CRITIQUES AND APPRAISALS

Once I was talking with a student on a crowded elevator in our university library. The student remarked that when he was in high school he had expressed in class a political opinion about needing to be concerned about the poor; his teacher responded by calling him a Marxist.

When we got off the elevator, a man who had ridden with us walked up to my student. He was a short, dark man, about half my student's height. He pointed his finger way up toward my student's face, and said emphatically, in a heavily Latin American accent: "You did not say those things because you are a Marxist; you said them because you are a Christian."

The man started to walk away, but I could not let it end there. I walked along with him and asked who he was. He was a professor of languages from Colombia. He went into a short speech about how there are no real Christians around: "Do I love you? Do you love me? This is not a Christian society. This is a society where people look out for themselves. Tell me, who really lives the Christian life?"

My student's remark had triggered quite a reaction. The professor was not just being philosophical; he was angry and indignant at the very thought that a student who would express concern for the poor would be labeled a Marxist. That sounded too close to what often happens in his own country in response to the liberation theologians.

This Chapter
Liberation theology has many critics and many admirers. This chap-

ter will review some of the major critiques and assessments of liberation theology, such as its connection with Marxism, its utopian thinking, and the response of the Vatican. This material continues the introduction to liberation theology begun in the previous chapter, and is related to *Lumen Gentium* chapter 6 because of its stress on Christian community.

The Marxist Label

The term "Marxism" can refer to many different things. Pope Paul VI, in *Octogesima Adveniens* (1971), speaks of four meanings:

1. The active practice of class struggle.
2. The collective exercise of political and economic power under the direction of a single party.
3. A socialist ideology based on historical materialism and the denial of everything transcendent.
4. A rigorous method of examining social and political reality that links theoretical knowledge with the practice of revolutionary transformation. (section 33)

Most liberation theologians are not Marxist by definition 1. Very few if any liberation theologians are Marxist by definitions 2 and 3. If by "Marxism," however, one means definition 4, then most liberation theologians have taken some inspiration from a method of social analysis and transformative praxis that is historically linked with Marxism. Liberation theologians have often been given to sweeping generalizations about capitalism that have a Marxist ring to them. Capitalism and the exploitation of the third world by the first world are sometimes named as the causes of Latin America's economic woes. Social structures are often analyzed in terms of class struggle. These links to Marxism have been a central focus of critics of liberation theology.

Even on these points, however, the connection of liberation theology with Marxism is a highly qualified one. The connection is modified especially by the strong affirmation that liberation theologians give to belief in God, human transcendence, and the Scriptures. Simply labeling liberation theologians "Marxist" is therefore misleading and unhelpful in coming to a clear picture of what they are saying.

Jesuit theologian Arthur McGovern, an expert on the relationship between Christianity and Marxism, draws the following contrasts:

Liberation theology makes use of Marxist concepts, but these concepts do not retain the same meanings they have in classic Marxism. "Praxis" connotes the living out of the Christian faith, not Marxist tactics of change. "Class struggle" expresses the reality of social conflict in Latin America, not a program to stir up hatred or to eliminate some ruling class. Liberation theologians speak of the "poor" of Latin America, with a special emphasis on landless peasants, and those left marginalized and excluded from real participation in the economic-political life of Latin America. They do not focus on the industrial "proletariat" that Marxists have viewed as the bearer of emancipation.[1]

McGovern also points out that, since the 1980s, liberation theologians have been growing beyond the uncritical social analysis that blanketly condemns capitalism as the root of all problems, and some have talked about the need to build participatory democracies.

A test case for sophistication in the application of social analysis by liberation theologians is their use of what is called "dependency theory." In one form, dependency theory is an ideological and unscientific charge that the ongoing colonialism of the first world, especially the United States, is the major cause of all of the economic and social problems of Latin America. McGovern, however, is able to distinguish between this naive form of dependency theory and a more nuanced form that places a stress upon internal as well as external factors.[2] This more refined version of dependency theory analyzes complex forms of dependency and cites a variety of causes of deprivation without simplistically laying all of the blame at the first world's doorstep. McGovern argues that some liberation theologians, such as Leonardo Boff, seem to draw upon a mixture of the two versions; others, such as Gustavo Gutierrez, more clearly use the more nuanced, sophisticated version.

Any gross generalizations or labels concerning the use of social analysis by liberation theologians will not usually stand up to close inspection. Political philosopher John R. Pottenger has assessed liberation theology to be a developing movement with the potential to overcome traditional dichotomies between value-stances and objective analysis and between religion and politics.[3]

Yes, the liberation theologians draw upon Marxism for vocabulary, concepts, tools of analysis, and sometimes even political prejudices. A few of them even call themselves "Marxist." Upon examination, however, liberation theologians are far from Marxists in their belief in God, Scripture, transcendence, and even in the way they use the concepts and tools that they borrow.

Utopian?

A well-established critique of Marxism is that it is "utopian" because it offers an unrealistic view of a perfect future while sacrificing what good exists in the present.[4] The classic formulation of the anti-utopian position is the saying paraphrased from Voltaire's *Dictionnaire Philoso-phique*: "Don't make the best the enemy of the good." In other words, do not trade an imperfect but tolerable situation for an intolerable situation by insisting upon unattainable perfection.[5]

Some scholars, most notably Michael Novak,[5] have drawn upon the tradition of anti-utopianism in formulating their criticisms of liberation theology. Using data concerning prosperity in capitalist and socialist countries, Novak contends that any development program that favors socialism is not favoring economic progress. As Novak points out, his question, ironically, is not one of ideology but of praxis: Will liberation theology work? Novak believes that progress in Latin America will be attained only through the adoption of liberal, democratic institutions that foster political and economic freedoms. It is not capitalism but the absence of true capitalism that has so far hindered development in these countries.

Liberation theologians have tried to distinguish their use of "utopia" from the kind of idealistic usage criticized by Novak. They draw upon the work of sociologist Karl Mannheim, who distinguishes "ideological" thinking that simply supports the existing order from "utopian" thinking that criticizes the existing order.[6] In line with this tradition, Gustavo Gutierrez contrasts his own usage of "utopia" with idealistic interpretations. For him, "utopia" is not an impractical, unrealistic dream. It is a dynamic way of thinking that draws upon the social sciences to create more human living conditions; it receives its verification in praxis.[7]

Within this framework of concepts, therefore, "utopian" does not mean being wildly idealistic; rather, it means being open to needed changes. It does not try to impose a pre-set picture of a perfect reality onto the present system, but instead works to change the system one step at a time. Liberation theologians do not think that they are trading an imperfect but tolerable situation for a worse one; they believe that the situation in which they live is absolutely intolerable and that whatever emerges has got to be better.

For his part, Novak can point to some socialist rhetoric on the part of some liberation theologians that does not meet the criteria of open-minded praxis. For their part, liberation theologians can point to the way that their thinking has been changing through the praxis of recent years, including their assessment of capitalism and the causes of third world deprivation. Both Novak and liberation theologians agree that drastic changes are called for; where they disagree is in their judgment concerning whether "utopian" thinking can help the situation.

Response of the Vatican

In 1984, the Congregation for the Doctrine of the Faith published an "Instruction on Certain Aspects of the 'Theology of Liberation.'"[8] This document issued a stern warning about the connection of liberation theology with Marxism, especially the danger of distorting traditional Christian doctrines in a way that limits their meaning to political matters in this world. A related document, "Instruction on Christian Freedom and Liberation," was published in 1986.[9] This second document was much more moderate. Although it made but scant mention of liberation theology, it affirmed in general many of the basic themes concerning human freedom and social development that underlie liberation theology, while alluding to the dangers of such thinking in a less stern manner.

It was reported by Vatican sources that it was John Paul II's own idea to issue first a stern warning followed by a more moderate appraisal.[10] The second document states clearly that "Between the two documents there exists an organic relationship. They are to be read in the light of each other" (2). For this reason, it is possible to talk about an overall response of the Vatican to liberation theology.

The Vatican acknowledges the contemporary need to stress the importance of human freedom, beginning with freedom from sin through Christ, and including freedom from political and economic oppression. The struggle for justice, including change in social structures, is not an added extra to the gospel, but an essential part of it. The option for the poor, in which "poor" is understood as including all human afflictions and miseries, expresses an authentic dimension of the Christian message, especially as found in the spirit of the Beatitudes. The base ecclesial communities represent a source of hope for the future of the church. Human solidarity, the interconnectedness of all people in a way that is prior to divisions into nations and classes, is an important Christian virtue that should motivate people to take seriously their obligations to share the goods of the earth with each other. By affirming these points, the Vatican has made room within official church teaching for some of the basic thrusts of liberation theology. Many of the concerns of the liberation theologians have deep intersections with the concerns expressed in the long tradition of Catholic social teaching.

At the same time, the Vatican's cautions about some aspects of liberation theology remain. Although the church must preach a message that ultimately has serious political implications, getting involved on the level of partisan politics remains the job of the laity, not the clergy or religious. Theologians are warned not to become too closely allied with systems of thought that are atheistic or that advocate systematic recourse to violent revolution. Recognizing the need to change unjust social structures should not lead to deemphasizing the basic truth that sin has its roots in the hearts and choices of individuals. In the end, though, these cautions do not erase the acknowledgment of the authenticity of several of liberation theology's main themes.

Responses from liberation theologians have followed a pattern similar to that of the Vatican documents themselves: stern followed by moderate. That is, liberation theologians reacted sternly to the first document, and accepted the second document with cautious optimism as representing approval of many of their central ideas. In response to the first document, Juan Luis Segundo wrote a book that charged that the Vatican was not only reacting to a caricature of what liberation theology really is, but was in general trying to take back many of the progressive developments put forth by Vatican II.[11] The second document, though, is being read as one that at least leaves room for liberation theology.[12]

Will It Play in Peoria?

A question raised frequently about liberation theology is its usefulness outside of a Latin American context. Does liberation theology have a contribution to make to the church in North America? Early reports about liberation theology often stressed that it was intended to address only the conditions of the poor in Latin America. More recently, however, Leonardo Boff has written that liberation ecclesiology has important implications for the entire church.[13]

There have been some attempts at forming base ecclesial communities in the United States. More common, however, have been attempts to draw inspiration from the base ecclesial communities to experiment with structures more suitable to the United States' context.[14] This is especially true of many of the programs of parish reform, such as Renew, that encourage people to form small faith-sharing groups that read the Scriptures and that are motivated to action. Although some commentators would be more inclined to point out the contrasts between liberation theology with its radical social analysis and the activities that Renew groups actually tend to engage in, it is worth noticing the similarities of people networking, praying, and trying to address social problems.

Summary

In this chapter we have examined some of the common criticisms of liberation theology as well as some defenses of it. We focused on the charges of Marxism and utopianism, the attitude toward capitalism, the Vatican reaction, and the question of liberation theology's adaptability outside of Latin America.

I take seriously the criticisms of liberation theologians that question their willingness to depend on Marxist analysis and socialist theory. I take even more seriously, however, the defenders of liberation theologians who sympathetically interpret their attempts to articulate the Christian dimensions of the plight of the poor in Latin America. There *is* a class struggle in Latin America. Latin America *has* in many ways been dependent on first world countries, and has not often benefitted from the relationship. If we believe in a God who cares about justice, then perhaps the liberation theologians are right that God is howling in anguish over the conditions under which many human beings are living. I hope that liberation theologians will continue to listen and change in response to their critics. But I hope even more deeply that people and structures throughout the world will be changed in response to the calls of the liberation theologians.

FOR FURTHER REFLECTION

1. How do you think that recent world developments such as the collapse of Marxist economies might influence assessments of liberation theology?

2. Do you think that there are legitimate grounds for third world peoples to complain about their relationship with the first world?

3. Do you get the impression that liberation theology is utopian in the sense of being dangerously idealistic?

4. Which of the Vatican's warnings about liberation theology do you think is the most important?

5. Which of the basic themes of liberation theology do you think is most important in a positive sense?

SUGGESTED READINGS

Congregation for the Doctrine of the Faith. "Instruction on Certain Aspects of the "'Theology of Liberation.'" *Origins* vol. 14, 13 September 1984, pp. 193-204.

Congregation for the Doctrine of the Faith. "Instruction on Christian Freedom and Liberation." *Origins* vol. 15, 17 April 1986, pp. 713-28.

Novak, Michael, ed. *Liberation Theology and the Liberal Society.* Washington, D.C.: American Enterprise Institute, 1987.

Novak, Michael. *Will It Liberate? Questions about Liberation Theology.* Mahwah, N.J.: Paulist Press, 1986.

Pottenger, John R. *The Political Theory of Liberation Theology.* Albany: SUNY Press, 1989.

Segundo, Juan Luis. *Theology and the Church: A Response to Cardinal Ratzinger and a Warning to the Whole Church.* Minneapolis: Winston Press, 1985.

Section Seven

The Eschatological Nature of the Church

CHAPTER 22

THE PILGRIM CHURCH

"**B**ecause we've always done it that way" is a phrase that reminds me of explanations I got in my childhood when I asked why we did certain things. Why do we abstain from meat on Fridays? Why do we pray the Stations of the Cross during Lent? Why are we obliged to go to Mass on Sundays? The answer, and the great assumption, was that we had always done these things. We thought of the church in the same way that we prayed to the three persons in one God: "Glory be to the Father, to the Son, and to the Holy Spirit. As it was in the beginning, is now, and ever shall be, world without end. Amen."

Many people today tend to be critical of any notion of "tradition." Tradition is often presented as a storehouse of hang-ups that holds one back from growing as a person. I think my religious tradition is a wonderful and mysterious gift. It is something within which I dwell and upon which I draw as I live my life. My religious tradition opens up to me the meaning of my life. I generally do not find that it holds me back in my human relationships; rather, it encourages me to forgive and love people.

I now know the origin of and the reason for many things in my faith, such as the obligation to attend Mass on Sunday. There remain things that are part of my faith that I accept but have not yet investigated historically, such as the origin of the Stations of the Cross.[1] The origin of many practices, such as priestly celibacy and the exclusion of women from the priesthood, are hotly debated topics today. But one thing I have definitely learned since I was a child is that my religious tradition has changed over time. Catholic belief and practice differ in striking ways from century to century.

This Chapter

Chapter 7 of *Lumen Gentium* talks about a church that changes. It introduces the concept of the pilgrim church, one of the most important images of the church that emerged from Vatican II. A pilgrim is a person who undertakes a journey. A pilgrim is someone who is on the way. Far from being a perfectly complete church, the church that is emerging from Vatican II is not finished yet.

This chapter will investigate the meaning and the significance of the image of the pilgrim church. We will examine the relationship between continuity and change in the church with a final consideration of the dark side of church history.

Perfection Only in Heaven

The comedian George Carlin once pointed out that the very language of football tends to be rough: block, tackle, sack. Baseball, in contrast, sounds almost pastoral: walk, shag a fly, go home. The language expresses intangible differences in attitude and mood surrounding the games.

The first draft of *Lumen Gentium* spoke of the church militant and the church triumphant. The church triumphant was the church considered in its perfect, ideal state in heaven. The church militant was the church still fighting its battles in the course of this world. Although the terms have their own justifiable history, in the twentieth century such language betrayed a mood of triumphalism, an attitude that placed an overemphasis on the achievement of the church to the neglect of the church's imperfections. A triumphal attitude is one lacking in self-criticism while being disdainful of anyone different from oneself. It is the attitude of one who has all the answers.

By the final draft of *Lumen Gentium*, the language of the document had changed dramatically. The church triumphant became the church in the glory that it will not know fully until the end of time. The church militant became the pilgrim church. The two ideas of church were bonded together by the traditional concept of the Communion of Saints, which includes those who have died and are in glory, those who are being purified (purgatory, though the word was not used), and those church members who are alive now. All of us are bonded in that we share the same grace and love of God.

The shift to speaking of the pilgrim church brings with it revolutionary connotations, attitudes, and moods. There is the exhilaration of a shared journey and a shared quest. There is the bond of a common past and an as-yet-to-happen future. There is the anticipation of the arrival at one's destiny. If the pre-Vatican II church could harmonize with battle marches, the post-Vatican II church is off to see the world. Life is more than a test and a battle; it is an exciting adventure.

Chapter seven puts an end to any pretensions the church might have to a current perfection:

> The church...will attain its full perfection only in the glory of heaven....the church already on this earth is signed with a sanctity which is real although imperfect...the pilgrim church, in her sacraments and institutions, which pertain to the present time, has the appearance of this world which is passing....*(LG,* 48)

Continuity Deeper than Change

Does my emphasis on change mean that I think that the basic message of the gospel has changed? Wilfred Cantwell Smith, a scholar of world religions, has argued that Christian tradition has differed so much through the centuries that we cannot claim that Christians have "believed" the same things. This a striking, thought-provoking claim that is true in some respects, but false in some other, very important, ones. It is most likely true regarding the religious sensibility people develop in relating their faith to the modern world. But it is false when one considers how strong are the links that bind Christians of today with Christians of the past. The faith in Jesus Christ and the transforming power of the gospel should not be underemphasized as points of continuity. Smith holds that the way in which Christians today believe in these concepts is so different as to be further evidence of discontinuity:

> What all Christians have in common is that they have shared a common history. They have participated in a common process: namely, the Christian church in its ever-changing multiformity. They have in common also, no doubt...something transcendent. Yet to say what that transcendent reality is—the Real Presence, Christ, God; or to say that the church, in whose on-going life they variously participate, is itself the body of Christ; or however one conceptualise it—is to employ formulations that in turn are themselves not transcendent, and that historically are not stable.[2]

I argue, admittedly on risky philosophical grounds, that it is ultimately the same Christ whom we encounter through our tradition. Part of my belief in the church is that it does not just help put me in touch with the transcendent in a general sense, but that it puts me in touch with a particular relationship with God the Father through Jesus Christ who sends the Holy Spirit. This relationship with the triune God has deep commonalities with the relationship available to Christians throughout the history of the church.

Smith may want to emphasize that throughout the ages we have understood Father, Son, and Spirit so differently that in any particular sense we are no longer talking about the same concepts or realities. Again, he would be making a challenging point that needs to be taken seriously. I do not think it enough to state simply that I believe otherwise. I need to study the Christian tradition in a critical manner that acknowledges changes and even aberrations. But again, my difference with Smith concerns what I believe the church to be. Is the church simply a fellowship of men and women who share the same resources but who understand them so differently as to have virtually unrelated beliefs from generation to generation? Or, is the church in a mystical sense the continuation of the presence of Christ through the Holy Spirit in its journey through this world? Is the pilgrim church a chameleon, or is it founded on a cross and a rock?

In this brief discussion, I have done more to raise this issue than to settle it. Like the church itself, the discussion is unfinished. I simply wanted, in this chapter on change, to mention a scholar who puts a premium on change, and to put in a personal word for continuity.

Change and Freedom

Many issues could be used to illustrate clear and profound change in the church. I choose to focus on the way that religious freedom is treated in official Catholic teaching in Pius IX's *Syllabus of Errors* (1864) and in Vatican II's Declaration on Religious Liberty (1965). These teachings illustrate a dramatic reversal on an important issue: whether people should be free to worship in whatever religion they choose.

In the nineteenth century, the official Catholic stand was consistent with a theology that stressed "no salvation outside the church," but inconsistent with a theology that stressed human freedom and dignity. The church insisted that Catholics in non-Catholic countries should be free to worship as they chose, but also held that in Catholic countries it was permissible to exclude other forms of worship. This position is expressed clearly in Pius IX's *Syllabus of Errors*, in which he condemns eighty propositions representing modern errors, among them:

> Every person is free to embrace and profess that religion which, led by the light of reason, that person may have thought true.

> In this our age it is no longer expedient that the catholic religion should be treated as the only religion of the State, all other worships whatsoever being excluded.

> Hence it has been laudably provided by law in some catholic countries, that people thither immigrating should be permitted the public exercise of their own several worships.[3]

It is important to recognize that the above statements are not being taught by Pius IX as truth; they are being condemned as falsehoods. In fairness to Pius IX it should be noted that he saw the church threatened by a rationalism associated with the French revolution that was hostile to religion, and he thought that he needed to do whatever he could to protect the church's mission. Few minds of the time were able to envisage a synthesis of church teaching with the concerns of the modern world. Yet the stands that he took against freedom of religion are in clear contradiction to the teaching that emerged at Vatican II.

Vatican II's Declaration on Religious Liberty begins by affirming the basic dignity of human beings and the importance of human freedom. It argues that people must not be coerced to practice a particular religion; truth has its own power of gentle persuasion. Although the document does not rule out the possibility of an official religion of the State, people have the right to worship as they choose:

> One of the key truths in Catholic teaching, a truth that is contained in the word of God and constantly preached by the Fathers, is that a person's response to God by faith ought to be free, and that therefore no one is to be forced to embrace the faith against one's will. The act of faith is by its very nature a free act. (section 10)

The document itself points out that in taking this position it is "developing" the doctrine, although it stresses continuity with Scripture and tradition and papal teaching concerning freedom and dignity without mentioning the reversal of the *Syllabus of Errors*.

This shift was thus not only significant for the issue of religious freedom, but also for affirming that church teaching can indeed grow and change. John Courtney Murray, an American Jesuit whose theological works enabled him to champion the cause of religious freedom at Vatican II, wrote:

> The course of the development between The Syllabus of Errors (1864) and Dignitatis Humanae Personae (1965) still remains to be explained by theologians. But the Council formally sanctioned the validity of development itself; and this was a doctrinal event of high importance for theological thought in many other areas.[4]

Theologians today no longer argue about whether or not church teaching can change; rather, they argue about how to distinguish the essential from the non-essential and the truth from the particular formulation. A recent document from the Vatican's International Theological Commission states that the basic truth of the gospel contained in church teaching remains always the same; the particular ways in which this teaching is expressed will reflect the limitations and biases of various cultures and philosophical systems. Although interpretation is an intricate and often subtle affair, "What was once recognized as truth must . . . be acknowledged as true in an enduringly valid way."[5] That is, there is a fundamental insight in any church teaching that remains true even though it may have to be seriously reinterpreted within a new cultural context.

Does this mean that there is something in Pius IX's condemnation of religious freedom that is to be sifted out of its cultural context and preserved as truth? Is it possible to argue that what Pius IX mistook religious freedom to be, a rebellious notion based on reason alone, deserved to be condemned until more nuanced concepts of religious freedom grounded in the dignity of the person could be developed? Perhaps there is something in that argument. I prefer to go a different route. I seek out what might have been legitimate in the document taken as a whole, but I feel no need to justify each statement on a line by line basis in the way some fundamentalists read the Bible. The Syllabus of Errors is ordinary papal teaching that reflects a mid-nineteenth century overreaction to modern developments. It is not an infallible proclamation, nor does it have the same status as a declaration of Vatican II. Pius IX was wrong. This does nothing to change the enduring truth of the gospel. This shift in doctrine bolsters my confidence in church teaching; I trust our leaders more if they sometimes admit that they have been wrong. The traditional belief in the indefectibility of the church does not mean that the church will never make a mistake; it means that the church will basically remain on the true path.

The Dark Side of Church History

When I was in my early twenties I took on a renewed interest in the Catholic church. I wanted to find out as much as I could about my new-found love. I picked up a popular work on church history written by Philip Hughes.[6] I read it with a deep hunger; unfortunately much of it tasted bitter. I do not remember whether I really cried or not, but I remember that I wanted to. The church that I had thought was perfect had feet of clay. The spotless bride of Christ had been dragged through the mud. Rather than the story of glorious and civilizing love that I had expected, I read of heresies and condemnations, disagreements and wars, corruption and reformation. Hughes' style lent itself to apologetic understatement, in this case, for example, of the Catholic reformation:

> The popes continued to be, in many respects, the children of the age in which they fought to restore Catholic ideals, and they continued to make use of all the means open to them, the secular weapons of diplomacy and even war, and not merely the war of defence. (p. 162)

In other words, Hughes is politely saying that popes started wars of aggression over matters of church doctrine and government. Hughes barely alludes to things that I was to learn about later: the persecution of the Jews, the horrors of the crusades, the corruption of the Renaissance popes, the tortures and executions of the Spanish Inquisition.

It seems as though the church has not always been a good pilgrim. How is a Catholic to come to terms with this dark side of the church's history?

I have no final answers for this problem. I think of Hans Küng's suggestion that in the face of the centuries of Christian persecution of the Jews, "Shame and guilt must be our silent reply. . . ."[7] I can also think of some other suggestions, though.

First, it should be remembered that the dark episodes in church history are balanced by a long and glorious history of an institution that has accomplished immeasurable good over the centuries in areas such as education, health care, social work, art, and culture. Perhaps the truly balanced history of the church has yet to be written. Second, the history of the church is not to be assessed simply in terms of its institutional achievements, but also in terms of the lives of countless individuals for whom the church has opened tremendous potential for holiness. Of course, the lives of individual Christians also have their own dark side. Third, it is important to distinguish between what can be attributed to the Catholic church and what can be attributed to individuals or groups who may be unfortunately acting in the name of the church. There have been times when even popes have not seemed to take the will of God into their deliberations. Fourth, we should not expect the human elements of the church to be perfect. This does not mean, however, that at certain points in history we should not have expected a lot better than what was delivered.

There remains room for the shame and guilt of which Küng speaks. Yet what is the purpose of shame and guilt other than to help us to grow so that we can leave them behind? The Christian tradition calls us beyond our sins to a life of faith, hope, and love. The church is an important dimension of that tradition; like Christ, the church is a commingling of human and divine elements. The human side of the church, however, often messes things up, at times in major proportions. We are a pilgrim people, not yet finished, journeying along with the treasure of our faith, which in the most important respects has remained the same throughout the ages.

Summary

In this chapter we have discussed the pilgrim journey of the church. We focused on Vatican II's acknowledgment of imperfection, on change and continuity, on the specific case of religious liberty, and on the dark side of church history. Tradition remains crucially important to the Catholic church, yet Catholics are more aware today that tradition does not cancel out all change. We no longer simply buy the argument, "because we have always done it that way." In the words of theologian Monika Hellwig, "Tradition implies change in continuity with the past."[8]

In the next chapter we will discuss the meaning of life.

FOR FURTHER REFLECTION

1. Have you ever been taught that the Catholic church is supposed to be perfect?

2. Is the image of the "pilgrim church" too mundane to get across the

majesty of the church? Is it going to the opposite extreme of the more triumphal images?

3. Amid all the changes, what in Christianity stays the same? What do Christians of the twentieth century share with Christians of the first century?

4. How do you feel about the Catholic church reversing itself on a position such as in the case of religious liberty? Does it weaken the credibility of the church to reverse itself like that?

5. How aware are you of the dark side of church history? How do you react to it?

SUGGESTED READINGS

Bausch, William J. *Pilgrim Church: A Popular History of Catholic Christianity.* Mystic, Conn.: Twenty-Third Publications, 1989 [1981].

Dulles, Avery. *The Survival of Dogma.* Garden City, N.Y.: Doubleday, 1971.

Küng, Hans. *The Church Maintained in Truth.* New York: Crossroad, 1980 [1979].

Murray, John Courtney. *We Hold These Truths: Catholic Reflections on the American Proposition.* New York: Sheed & Ward, 1960.

CHAPTER 23

THE MEANING OF LIFE

B y the time I was in college I had rejected my religion. I wanted
to know the true meaning of life. I majored in English literature
because I thought that perhaps those recognized as great authors would teach me something about the meaning of life. I also became interested in philosophy for the same reason. I learned a great
deal in my studies, for which I will always be grateful, but when it
came to the meaning of life I did not have much luck. Perhaps it was
because I was searching for an "answer" to a question that doesn't have
a clear, set one. Why do human beings exist? Why does any reality exist at all? Is there a purpose to my life?

I became especially concerned about an area known as general se-
mantics, where philosophy and linguistics intersect. To find out the
meaning of life, I would first need to know the meaning of "meaning."
If I could know what meaning "meaning" itself had, I would be in a
better position to know the meaning of life. What does it mean to
"mean?" Why is there such a thing as "meaning?"

For various reasons my college years were intense and depressing. I
reache a breaking point in my early twenties. Through group support,
I was led to reach out to God in prayer. Through continuing support, I
learned how to grow in faith. After a time, I again sought out the religion of my youth. Eventually, I made the academic study of religion, especially Catholicism, my main occupation.

It is through faith and prayer that I have come to trust that life does
indeed have meaning. The academic study of religion is important to
me, but it would mean much less to me if it were not related to my personal faith.

So what, after all of that, is the meaning of life? I still do not have an "answer." What I have found is that by striving to live a Christian life, by seeking the will of God, by struggling to live my life on a spiritual basis, I have come in contact with the meaning of life. I experience meaning within the context of my life journey. I do not "know" the meaning of life. It is not something that I could write out definitively in a paragraph or two. It is more something that I have an inkling of as meaning spills over into my daily activities. The less I anguish intellectually about the meaning of life, and the more I reach outside of myself to God and to others, the more I experience the rich and deep meaning there is to be had in this great gift of life.

I have trouble relating with Albert Camus's claim that life is absurd because the human heart cries out for meaning in a universe that gives no reply. Whether it be in the midst of the most wonderful things in my life or in the midst of the deepest sufferings I have had to face, I have become more and more convinced that life has an ultimate meaning and purpose. It is as though I cannot quite see or hear it, but I can taste, smell, and touch it. I know it is there, but I cannot describe it in any final or definitive way.

This Chapter

Chapter 7 of *Lumen Gentium* talks about the meaning of life in a way that I can relate to. After proclaiming the ongoing activity of Christ in the world through the church and through the Eucharist, it goes on to say:

> Therefore the promised restoration which we are awaiting has already begun in Christ, is carried forward in the mission of the Holy Spirit and through Him continues in the church in which we learn the meaning of our terrestrial life through our faith, while we perform with hope in the future the work committed to us in this world by the Father, and thus work out our salvation. (LG, 48)

That is, by living a life in which one follows Christ, seeks the will of the Father, and listens to the promptings of the Spirit, one will learn the meaning of life, which allows one to carry on one's earthly work with hope for the future.

In this chapter we will explore two themes from chapter 7 of *Lumen Gentium* that help to illuminate the meaning of life: eternal life and the Communion of Saints.

Eternal Life

If this life is all there is, then it has little if any ultimate meaning. Does life end in death? Are we simply snuffed out of existence? Will the universe trudge on for all eternity, never to hear from us again?

Catholic teaching about the afterlife prior to Vatican II tended to be exceedingly clear. Heaven and hell were presented as the two ultimate choices, with purgatory as a temporary but harsh middle ground and limbo as a neutral place for unbaptized infants and other innocent non-believers. Although it was always acknowledged that the actual nature of these places or states of being were far beyond our imaginations, the ways in which they were talked about was often quite detailed and concrete.

In *A Portrait of the Artist as a Young Man*,[1] James Joyce offers an exaggerated yet telling depiction of the kinds of things a Catholic retreat preacher might say about hell in 1916. The preacher reports that "Hell is a straight and dark and foulsmelling prison, an abode of demons and lost souls, filled with fire and smoke." He tells how the walls of hell are said to be four thousand miles thick; how horrible is the stench; how despicable the company of demons; how boundless and intense the fire; how painful to be deprived of divine light; how insufferably long is eternity. On each of these points the preacher goes into an extended, vivid description designed to drive home the fear of hell to his school-aged listeners. Although what is being presented is much more extreme than ordinary Catholic preaching of the time, it is fair to say that Catholics tended to operate with a fairly clear idea of what heaven and hell were like and even who was likely to go where.

Contemporary Catholic teaching about the afterlife has tended to focus on the *mystery* of it. There is much less of an immediate stress on what heaven and hell are like and much more emphasis on the coming of the kingdom that Jesus preached. There is an attempt to balance any focusing on individual souls with a focus on human relationships and social issues. There is an attempt to balance talk of afterlife with talk of the kingdom having its roots in this world, wherever the will of God breaks in to transform people and social structures for the better. The kingdom is both individual and social; it is both here and yet to come; it is a reality we experience and a mystery we hope for.

Kingdom of God
both individual and social
both here and yet to come
both a reality and a mystery

Some theologians, writers, and artists have been drawn to an emphasis on the experience of the eternal dimension of reality as we encounter it *now*. They can be said to emphasize the "already present" aspect of the kingdom. William Blake wrote of experiencing the whole universe in a grain of sand.[2] In *Our Town*, Thorton Wilder depicts a world whose present moments go by largely unappreciated unless it be by a poet or by someone who has returned from the dead.[3] T.S. Eliot writes in *Four Quartets* of "a lifetime burning in every moment."[4] In *Total Presence*, T.J.J. Altizer speaks of the contemporary experience of an immediacy that signifies the death of interior consciousness and the end of history. He claims that "the only regained paradise is the final loss of paradise itself."[5] These authors challenge us not to simply put heaven off to the day when we die but to appreciate the depth dimension of our lives as we live them.

Other theologians and artists remind us more of the *not yet* aspect of the kingdom. Picasso's *Guernica* stands as a symbol of the terrible reality of modern warfare. Elie Wiesel's *Night* helps us to keep in mind the horrors of the Holocaust and of human hatred.[6] Gustavo Gutierrez's classic *A Theology of Liberation* tells of a world that has too much human suffering to simply lend itself to acceptance and appreciation.[7] These thinkers remind us that the fullness of the kingdom is still a long way off.

As was the case with the mystery of the church itself, *Lumen Gentium* speaks about the afterlife in images and symbols drawn from the Scriptures. There is no attempt at an overly clear definition or description. The reader is told:

> Since however we know not the day nor the hour, on Our Lord's advice we must be constantly vigilant so that, having finished the course of our earthly life, we may merit to enter into the marriage feast with Him and to be numbered among the blessed, and that we may not be ordered to go into eternal fire like the wicked and slothful servant, into the exterior darkness where "there will be the weeping and the gnashing of teeth." (*LG*, 48)

In the original text this single sentence contains five footnotes to scriptural passages, drawing heavily from Matthew 25, but referring also to Matthew 22 and Hebrews 9. It is surrounded by other heavily footnoted sentences that borrow liberally from the letters of Paul and John. In other words, when it comes time to discuss the afterlife, the document relies exclusively on highly symbolic images from the New Testament.

Such a reliance does two things. It helps to reestablish the afterlife as a mystery of the faith rather than as some piece of information that we know all about. Gone are the days that a retreat master might be tempted to speak of heaven and hell as literally as if describing the house down the street. Catholics still believe firmly in the reality of heaven, but we are inclined more to remember the symbolic and analogous nature of the language that we use to talk about it.

At the same time, though, the reliance on scriptural texts reinforces the importance of this mystery in the total scheme of our beliefs. As Catholics, we are called to remain vigilant as we live in the confident hope for eternal life. In our hope, at least, we have not changed.

Communion of Saints

My father died some years ago. Where has he gone? Will I ever meet him again?

When I was a child I did not tend to think of the Communion of Saints as having to do with ordinary people that I had known. I thought mainly of the saints as amazingly holy people to whom one would pray because they had the power to grant special favors. For example, if I lost something, I prayed to St. Anthony. If I found it, I would pay St. Anthony by putting a dollar in the poor box at church. (Today, if I am really desperate, I may still resort to doing this.)

Lumen Gentium, drawing upon the depths of the Catholic tradition, includes in the Communion of Saints not only those addressed as "Saint," but all those people who have died and are now with God. It also includes those who are struggling to live lives of holiness now. That is, the Communion of Saints includes not only those extraordinarily holy people who have been canonized, but also people like my father and myself. The point of the belief in the Communion of Saints is that we are all joined with one another in that we share the same grace of our loving God. We remain related to each other in a community. My father and I are still both part of the Mystical Body of Christ; the fact that he has died and that I remain alive has not erased our continuing relationship. Only death separates us; we are united through our love of God. I know nothing concrete of what eternal life is like, but I know that I believe in it and that I hope to meet my father again.

Lumen Gentium still talks about the saints as those who through their merits can intercede for us with God; this belief, however, is complemented by an even greater emphasis on the role of the saints as inspiring examples and as companions in a fellowship of love. Vatican II did not come right out and tell me to stop praying to St. Anthony when I lose something; what I hear the document saying, however, is that my prayers for intercession should be complemented by a knowledge of the life of the particular saint and an openness on my part to become a more open and loving person through that saint's example. In other words, for me to receive the grace of God through the intercession of a saint is connected with my knowledge of that saint and my openness to being inspired. In this light the document calls for growth in the way we relate with saints:

> . . . we urge all concerned, if any abuses, excesses or defects have crept in here or there, to do what is in their power to remove or correct them, and to restore all things to a fuller praise of Christ and of God. Let them therefore teach the faithful that the authentic cult of the saints consists not so much in the multiplying of external acts, but rather in the greater intensity of our love, whereby, for our own greater good and that of the whole church, we seek from the saints "example in their way of life, fellowship in their communion, and aid by their intercession." *(LG, 51)*

This passage suggests that we avoid superstitious petitioning of saints through repetitious prayers. Saints are a help in relating with God, not a substitute. We should study the life of any saint to whom we pray, sense our connectedness with him or her, and be open to be inspired.

Functions of the Saints
intercede for us with God
inspire us by example
strengthen fellowship in love

The church also still holds a special place for those saints who have been canonized. It is hoped that many, many people, both those alive and those who have gone before us in death, can qualify for the generic title, "Saint," but there have been some people who have led such recognizably holy lives that they stand out as shining lights for the rest of us. These people are canonized by the church much in the way that baseball players are inducted into the Hall of Fame. They are proposed to a committee, investigated and reviewed, and finally voted and decided upon. The pope has the final say. To be canonized a saint is to receive an official endorsement by the Catholic church that you are a fit model for veneration and inspiration. Unlike the Hall of Fame, people are not eligible for canonization until after they have died.

Pope John Paul II has beatified and canonized holy Christians at a pace more rapid than his recent predecessors.[8] Part of his motivation for doing so has been to expand the types of saints that the faithful have available to them, for one of the functions of saints is to show how the Christian life can be lived faithfully in a variety of life situations and circumstances. Some commentators have called for even more expansion of the canon of saints, with a yet deeper emphasis on bringing in more women, more non-Europeans, more middle-class, and more married people. Some liberation theologians have argued that the church should give more emphasis to reformers and political activists who work for systemic change than to "saints of the system" who do not challenge the status quo.[9] It is important to remember, however, that the number of saints in the Catholic church (and, I would add, beyond) is far greater than the number of those who have been canonized.

Summary

In this chapter, we have discussed the meaning of life in relation to Catholic belief concerning eternal life and the Communion of Saints.

I am fairly certain that my father will never be officially canonized; I live in hope, though, that he is now with God as sure as is St. Peter, and that someday we will meet again.

In the next chapter we will examine different styles of theology that have emerged in the Catholic church since Vatican II.

FOR FURTHER REFLECTION

1. What do you think of when you hear the phrase, "the meaning of life?"

2. The journey theme is very popular in contemporary spirituality. What are its limitations? Does it need to be balanced by other images?

3. Some art and literature stresses the need to appreciate life now. Other works stress the horrors of the realities we face. How might these contrasting emphases fit together?

4. Do you know anyone whom you think of as a "saint?" What is that person like?

5. Do you believe in eternal life?

SUGGESTED READINGS

Cunningham, Lawrence. *The Meaning of Saints*. San Francisco: Harper & Row, 1980.

Hellwig, Monika. *What Are They Saying about Death and Christian Hope? Mahwah*, N.J.: Paulist Press, 1978.

Küng, Hans. *Eternal Life? Life After Death as a Medical, Philosophical, and Theological Problem*. Garden City, N.Y.: Doubleday, 1984 [1982].

Sherry, Patrick. *Spirit, Saints, and Immortality*. Albany: SUNY Press, 1984.

Thompson, William M. *Fire and Light: The Saints and Theology*. Mahwah, N.J.: Paulist Press, 1987.

CHAPTER 24

PILGRIMS AND SAINTS

C onflicts sometimes arise between people in the Catholic church who represent different points of view. It was reported that church representatives at an international conference on AIDS held at the Vatican in 1989 objected to a slogan carried on many posters: "The Body of Christ has AIDS." Their objection was that when the church is referred to as the Mystical Body of Christ, it is understood as being without sin or stain or blemish.

The Body of Christ image has functioned in a way similar to the image of the church as the "spotless bride of the spotless lamb"—it is the church understood in an ideal, mystical sense. The church in this sense is a great gift to us from God, something more than simply a human invention. It is Christ's continuing presence, the way of salvation, the fountain of grace, the light of the peoples that remains ever untarnished. Church officials, understanding the Body of Christ in this manner, were offended at the suggestion that the Body of Christ has AIDS.

The people who carried the signs at the AIDS conference were most likely operating out of a contrasting set of images of the church. These people would tend to think more of the unfinished and changing Pilgrim church than of the spotless bride of the spotless lamb. They would resonate more with the church as the People of God ever in need of reform and renewal than with the church as an untarnished ideal. They would be more inclined to focus on the Body of Christ as broken and bloody than as risen and glorified. They might recall the words of Paul about the Body of Christ:

God has so constructed the body as to give greater honor to the lowly members, that there may be no dissension in the body, but that all members may be concerned for one another. If one member suffers, all the members suffer with it; if one member is honored, all the members share its joy. (1 Corinthians 12:24–26)[1]

Seen in this perspective, to say that the Body of Christ has AIDS is simply another way of saying that we all share in each other's suffering.

Both perspectives, it seems, can find much support in Scripture and in church tradition.

This Chapter

In the first chapter of this book we raised questions about current issues and divisions within the Catholic church. In subsequent chapters, theological conflicts, both past and present, have often surfaced.

In this chapter we will explore more deeply some of the differences between contrasting schools of thought in the Catholic church today. For the sake of simplicity, I identify only two such schools of thought, although in reality there exists a wide spectrum of approaches. The main point of difference on which we will focus is the manner in which Vatican II is interpreted by each group. We will close with a consideration of the "Extraordinary Synod" of 1985, a Vatican meeting that tried to create harmony among the often cacophonous voices.

This material is related to chapter 7 of *Lumen Gentium* insofar as that chapter introduced and harmonized two images of the church that tend to be favored respectively by the two schools of thought: the Pilgrim Church and the Communion of Saints. For this reason, I will call one group the "Pilgrims" and the other group the "Saints." Most Pilgrims would be among those who would support the slogan, "The Body of Christ has AIDS"; most Saints would be among those who strongly object.

Pilgrims

Theologians who tend to favor images such as the "Pilgrim Church" and the "People of God" identify the major gains of Vatican II as a whole set of progressive changes: the ecumenical openness, the more positive attitude toward other world religions, the focus on the laity, the emphasis on religious freedom, and the special concern for matters of peace and economic justice. For these theologians, such as Edward Schillebeeckx and Leonardo Boff, the major shift at Vatican II was from a church too concerned about itself as an institution to a church trying to reform itself and to engage in constructive interaction with the world. The church was no longer a fortress over against the world but a force within the world working toward social change.

For Pilgrims, the basic theological shift that underlies the changes at Vatican II is *from* the Catholic faith considered as a systematic and complete "package" that was delivered intact from Jesus and passed down through the apostles *to* an understanding of the Christ-event in more historical and social terms. The focus is on human experience. Thus, Schillebeeckx begins his theology not with a Jesus who "comes down" from heaven but with the man Jesus who has a unique experience of transformation through his encounter with his "Abba" or Father. Jesus' "Abba experience" becomes the experiential basis for his ministry and mission. After Jesus' death, the experience that the disciples have of Jesus as Lord transforms them and becomes the basis of the Christian community. Today the continued experience of Jesus as Lord brings people together in communities based on a love that leads them to engage in transforming society.[2]

Pilgrims stress the ability of the church to change and adapt as it faces new situations. For this reason, both Schillebeeckx and Boff focus on the role of the Holy Spirit in the founding of the church. Rather than emphasizing the church as established by Jesus and therefore not subject to change, they emphasize that the disciples founded the church by addressing new situations with the aid of the Holy Spirit. Therefore, as new situations arise today, church leaders should feel capable of making necessary changes. Both Schillebeeckx and Boff, for example, favor allowing married priests and the ordination of women.

Pilgrims are people who strike out for new territories. Both Schillebeeckx and Boff sense an urgent need for change in church and society. It is not surprising that they should focus on those elements of Vatican II that represent social progress.

Saints

Theologians who tend to favor less historical, more mystical images of the church, such as the "Communion of Saints," the "Bride of Christ," and the "Mystical Body of Christ," identify two distinct sets of progressive changes at Vatican II, and then subordinate one set to the other. For these scholars, such as Hans Urs von Balthasar and Joseph Ratzinger, the shift from an overemphasis on the hierarchy to a concept of church as including the whole people of God was a useful but relatively minor change. The major shift at Vatican II was from a church too concerned with the juridical and the official to a church aware of itself as a mystery that expresses the love of God for humankind. These theologians neither ignore nor reject the progressive teachings of Vatican II about ecumenism, the laity, religious freedom, or peace and justice, but they interpret these teachings within a framework that emphasizes the church as the Mystical Body of Christ with a hierarchical structure.

For Saints, the basic theological shift that underlies the changes of Vatican II involves the church becoming newly aware of its mission to evangelize the world with its message of the love of the three persons in God made known through Jesus, the Incarnate Word of God. It is a matter of the same church that has been in existence since Christ being awakened to its pastoral charge. The shift in understanding the church is not a shift away from an institutional model toward some other type of model, but rather a shift from an overly juridical institutional model to a model still significantly institutional but set afire by the love of Christ. A church that does not emphasize the importance of Jesus becomes simply another social service organization.

Saints stress the ability of the church to face new situations in ways that remain faithful to the tradition that has been handed down intact throughout the ages. For this reason, von Balthasar and Ratzinger emphasize that it is Christ who founded the church and that the human beings running it should be extremely hesitant to change it. Ratzinger's emphasis leads him to a position in contrast with that of Boff:

My impression is that the authentically Catholic meaning of the reality "church" is tacitly disappearing, without being expressly rejected. Many no longer believe that what is at issue is a reality willed by the Lord himself. Even with some theologians, the church appears to be a human construction, an instrument created by us and one which we ourselves can freely reorganize according to the requirements of the moment.[3]

Ratzinger sees this view as undermining the Catholic faith itself:

... the church is indeed composed of men who organize her external visage. But behind this, the fundamental structures are willed by God himself, and therefore they are inviolable. Behind the human exterior stands the mystery of a more than human reality, in which reformers, sociologists, organizers have no authority whatsoever. If the church, instead, is viewed as a human construction, the product of our own efforts, even the contents of the faith end up assuming an arbitrary character: the faith, in fact, no longer has an authentic, guaranteed instrument through which to express itself. Thus, without a view of the mystery of the church that is also supernatural and not only sociological, Christology loses its reference to the divine in favor of a purely human structure, and ultimately it amounts to a purely human project: the Gospel becomes the Jesus-project, the social-liberation project or other merely historical, immanent projects that can still seem religious in appearance, but which are atheistic in substance.[4]

For Ratzinger, then, the church, including its most fundamental structures, is in an important sense a mystery beyond this world that remains untouchable by merely worldly criticisms.

Communion Ecclesiology

The theological differences between Pilgrims and Saints result in many practical differences. Pilgrims are often perceived as liberals who want the church to keep changing in dialogue with the world. Saints are often perceived as conservatives who wish to maintain a distinctively Catholic identity in the face of a world that is overly chaotic. Pilgrims tend to see Saints as backward and repressive theologians who are trying to reestablish the Catholic faith as an ideology that is unresponsive to changing human experience. Saints tend to see Pilgrims as loose, dangerous villains who would water the faith down to nothing in hope that the world find them acceptable. These tensions among theologians are often reflected in similar liberal-conservative tensions throughout the church.

In the beginning of this chapter I referred to the problem of putting everyone in two groups and thus painting an overly polarized picture that does not capture the complexity of the situation. The world of Catholic theologians cannot really be divided into the Pilgrims and the Saints; these are simply explanatory categories that may distort as much as they reveal. In reality, Catholic theologians are spread out along a wide spectrum of positions. Most of them are somewhere in the middle. This is true also of the church as a whole. The liberal-conservative polarizations fade when they are placed against the background of the reality of a wide spectrum of positions, again with most people falling somewhere in the middle.[5]

In 1985 a meeting of bishops was held in Rome that is known as the Extraordinary Synod. What technically made it "extraordinary" was that it was held as a special event in addition to the now "ordinary" synods that convene once every three years. The main purpose of this meeting was to review and assess the progress that the church has made since Vatican II. Some Pilgrim theologians at the time were afraid that the Saints were going to march in and try to take back the progress that Vatican II had achieved. Most commentators after the fact believed that this did not happen at all. The Extraordinary Synod resoundingly reaffirmed Vatican II, while issuing some cautions and suggestions concerning its implementation.

A major theme put forth by the synod was called "communion ecclesiology." This concept is presented as the key to interpreting Vatican II: "The ecclesiology of communion is the central and fundamental idea of the council's documents."[6]

Communion ecclesiology is an understanding of the church that has roots in the early Christian centuries. It sees community first of all in the love of the three persons of the Trinity for each other; the church is a community that reflects this love. Through the Eucharist, "holy communion," people are brought together in Christ's love.

Communion ecclesiology also emphasizes that the church is a communion of local churches. It has some elements that Saints find very satisfactory, such as a stress on unity through Christ and the hierarchy. It has other elements that Pilgrims find very satisfactory, such as a stress on the legitimate diversity and pluraformity of local churches.

The Extraordinary Synod promoted communion ecclesiology as a bridge between differing theological approaches. It called for an end to approaches that ideologically give preference to some Vatican II statements over others; in their place, it called for approaches that respect each document as a whole, the interrelationship among the documents, and the intentions of those who wrote and affirmed them:

> The theological interpretation of the conciliar doctrine must show attention to all the documents, in themselves and in their close interrelationship, in such a way that the integral meaning of the council's affirmations—often very complex—might be understood and expressed.[7]

The synod thus called for a higher vision that moves beyond partisan theological concerns to an attentive listening to the multidimensional teaching of Vatican II.

Some Saints might want to smugly and triumphantly declare victory through the synod insofar as it warned against overly optimistic views of the world and overly loose interpretations of the council. Some

Pilgrims might want to announce, against the background of their own sometimes irrational fears, their great relief that the synod affirmed rather than withdrew Vatican II. Some commentators might want to point out that "communion ecclesiology" at this point remains a somewhat vague category that allows itself to be interpreted by Saints in one way and by Pilgrims in quite another.

My own optimistic view is that the synod did indeed call for a higher vision and provided at least a start in the direction of achieving one. I am glad that we have some people in the church who carry signs that read: "The Body of Christ has AIDS." At the same time, I am glad that we have other people who object to that. Both of the groups have much of value to share; neither has a corner on the market in truth or theological appropriateness. This is not to say that I am a relativist. I believe that the Christian message is true. I also believe that some theological approaches are better than others. On so many issues, though, there is plenty of room for a legitimate spectrum of positions. I embrace both Pilgrims and Saints in our church, a few who are even more extreme, and the many who stand somewhere in the middle.

Summary

In this chapter we have examined two contrasting schools of thought that have emerged since Vatican II. The Pilgrims tend to think that the church has not changed enough; so much needs to be done regarding issues of justice, gender, and internal church reform. The Saints tend to think that the church has changed enough already; it is now time to put a lid on the madness and concentrate on the simple basics. Somewhere in the tension between these two visions, the future of the church is being worked out.

In the next chapter we will discuss the place accorded to Mary in the Catholic vision.

FOR FURTHER REFLECTION

1. In what ways have you been aware of theological tensions within the Catholic church?

2. How do you react to the slogan: The Body of Christ has AIDS?

3. Are you more of a Pilgrim or a Saint?

4. If two statements in a Vatican II document seem to be in conflict, what might be a good way to arrive at an interpretation?

5. What dangers are there in seeing people as categorized into two polarized groupings?

SUGGESTED READINGS

Albegio, Giuseppe, Jean Pierre Jossua, and Joseph A. Komonchak. *The Reception of Vatican II*. Washington, D.C.: The Catholic University of America Press, 1987.

Hastings, Adrian. *Modern Catholicism: Vatican II and After*. New York: Oxford University Press, 1991.

Hebblethwaite, Peter. *Synod Extraordinary: The Inside Story of the Rome Synod*. Garden City, N.Y.: Doubleday, 1986.

Küng, Hans, and Leonard Swidler, eds. *The Church in Anguish: Has the Vatican Betrayed Vatican II?* San Francisco: Harper & Row, 1987.

Neuhaus, Richard John. *The Catholic Moment: The Paradox of the Church in the Postmodern World*. San Francisco: Harper & Row, 1987.

Rynne, Xavier. *John Paul's Extraordinary Synod: A Collegial Achievement*. Wilmington, Del.: Michael Glazier, 1986.

Schillebeeckx, Edward. *Church: The Human Story of God*. New York: Crossroad, 1990 [1989].

CHAPTER 25

MARY AS SYMBOL OF THE CHURCH

I often go jogging with a friend of mine. When I jog alone, however, I pray the rosary.

The rosary is a series of prayers, most of which are addressed to Mary. Traditionally these prayers have been said while counting on prayer beads.

I do not carry rosary beads. I use my fingers, of which there are, conveniently, ten. I begin with the Apostles Creed, followed by an Our Father and three Hail Marys. Then for each of the five decades (units of ten prayers) I say an Our Father, ten Hail Marys, and a Glory Be to the Father. While I say (silently) the prayers, I meditate on the mysteries of the rosary. There are three different sets: the Joyful, the Sorrowful, and the Glorious. I meditate on only one set each time I jog. I close with a prayer that begins, "Hail, Holy Queen."

I learned to pray the rosary as a child. I rejected the rosary with the rest of my faith somewhere in my teenage years. I tried the rosary again when I re-embraced my faith in my early twenties. I had some ambivalent feelings about it. I started out saying the prayers by concentrating on asking Mary for help and favors. I treated the rosary as if it were a magic formula prayed over magic beads. At times it embarrassed me (although I always said it silently as I jogged). I remember on one occasion angrily throwing my beads in the back of a drawer and slamming it. To this day, I prefer to go without the beads.

The prayer itself is something else. It has become less and less a magical incantation and more and more a deep meditation on my life in relation to Mary and the church. The rosary comforts me as it connects me with my own past. It challenges me as it connects me with a long tradition of prayer that I share with others. When I say the opening prayers, I concentrate on consciously intending the words. Once I move into the five decades, though, I am meditating. The words of the prayers resound quietly in my consciousness like a mantra. I think about the scriptural and traditional events of each mystery, but at the same time I think about the things of my everyday life in relation to these events. I review my human relationships, work life, personal goals, feelings, and upcoming decisions as I explore what I have come to think of as the "dynamics" of each story.

Take, for example, the story of Finding Jesus in the Temple. This "joyful mystery" refers to the story from Luke 3:41–52 in which Jesus' parents search for him for three days and finally find him teaching in the temple. I tend to agree with those biblical critics who doubt the historical nature of this particular event. What is relevant for me is the dynamics of the story. Drawing upon what issues are currently important in my life, I can put myself in the place of Jesus, who says that he must be about his Father's business. I know that I am called to do what I have to do, even if at times it causes pain to others. (If one of my own boys did what Jesus did in that story, he would have a lot to answer for.)

I can also put myself in the place of Mary and Joseph. What must it be like to lose a child for three days? I once lost one of my boys in a mall for about twenty minutes. I was utterly heartsick and panic-stricken. I think of how many things in life are beyond my control. I think of how there are many things, often painful, that I have to accept in this life. I think of the joy of finding my lost child. I think of the objects, situations, and relationships in my life that I have lost and found, the many things over which I need to grieve and rejoice.

What I have written here barely begins to scratch the surface of what the rosary means to me. Yet I can say many of the same things about Mary herself that I have said about the rosary. Mary was an important part of my faith as a child. When I reembraced my faith I turned to Mary. At first I related to Mary in an immature way. For example, I once said a set of prayers that a pamphlet told me would guarantee my salvation through a special visit from Jesus and Mary fifteen days before I would die. The pamphlet is now way in the back of my drawer, far beneath my rosary beads (which really do not deserve such treatment). Through the years I have grown more to appreciate Mary both as an inspiring historical person to whom the Scriptures testify and as a symbol of the church.

The Catholic church as a whole has traveled a journey in relation to Mary that is similar to my own experience. It would be difficult to underestimate the importance of Mary in the church prior to Vatican II. Sometimes we Catholics paid more attention to Mary than we did to God. There was not only the rosary, but also processions, medals, hymns, and various prayers and devotions honoring Mary.

Yet after the council Catholics seemed to put Mary in the back of a drawer for a while. Devotion to Mary seemed to be superstitious and non-ecumenical to many. In recent years, however, the church has brought out devotion to Mary as a newly polished treasure. The approach to Mary has been more scriptural and more Christ-centered, with more attention to her symbolic and potentially ecumenical aspects.

This Chapter

This chapter will examine the treatment of Mary in *Lumen Gentium*, with some comments on how Mary has functioned in relation to God and church. This material is related to chapter 8 of *Lumen Gentium*.

An Integral Chapter

It was debated at Vatican II whether the chapter on Mary should be part of *Lumen Gentium* or whether it should be made into its own document. Some favored making the chapter into its own document because they felt it would highlight Mary's importance. Others wanted the chapter out of *Lumen Gentium* because they felt that focusing on Mary distracted from the document's ecumenical flavor. The majority thinking, which obviously won out, was that the chapter on Mary should be included in *Lumen Gentium* because it is appropriate to highlight Mary's role as an essential part of the church. John Paul II, who was a bishop at the council, argued that the chapter on Mary should come much earlier in the document in order to emphasize the significance of her role in the church.

The brief chapter on Mary is divided into five sections. *Section I* emphasizes that Mary is truly the Mother of God, and as such, although she is at one with all other creatures, holds a privileged place both in heaven and on earth. She is honored "with filial affection and piety as a most beloved mother" (*LG*, 53). She plays an integral part in the mystery of salvation that is continued in the church.

Section II outlines the specific nature of Mary's role in the history of salvation. Like other sections of *Lumen Gentium*, it relies on many references to Scripture and the use of carefully phrased symbolic language. The section tells of how Mary is foreshadowed in the Old Testament, of her own immaculate conception, of her faithful acceptance of God's will, of her virginal conception of Jesus, of her pilgrimage of faith, of her role in the public life of her son, of her sorrow at the cross, of her presence at the birth of the church at Pentecost, of her assumption into heaven, and of her final exaltation. Throughout this section, Mary's relationship with Jesus is highlighted.

Significant emphasis in section II is given to Mary's *fiat* (let it be), her response to the angel of the Annunciation. Mary's freely chosen acceptance of the will of God is contrasted with the disobedience of Eve.[1] As a woman was connected with the Fall, so a woman is at the heart of the process of redemption. Like Jesus in the Garden of Gethsemane when he accepts God's will rather than his own, Mary allows God's will to be done. Her faithful, courageous decision stands at the core of the Christian faith.

Section III directly examines the connection between Mary and the church. Before it does so, however, it spends time addressing the relative ranking of Christ and Mary. For ecumenical purposes, the section greatly stresses that Christ is the one Mediator and that Mary is subordinate to Christ. Within this context, it is appropriate to honor Mary as the creature above all other creatures, with traditional titles such as "Advocate, Auxiliatrix, Adjutrix, and Mediatrix" (*LG*, 62).

Although the motivations for dealing with the issue of ranking are understandable, one wonders what Jesus might think about the stress on his mother's subordination to himself, even when limited to the realm of salvation and divinity. This is less an issue of technically acknowledging the problem of the worship of Mary in place of God than it is an issue of good taste.

How the Church is Like Mary
Mother: brings forth children to eternal life
Virgin: remains faithful to spouse in charity

The main images that the section uses to connect Mary with the church are those of mother and virgin. The church is a mother in that it brings forth sons and daughters to a new immortal life through baptism and the Holy Spirit. In other words, as Mary gave life to Jesus, so each of us are born anew through the church, our mother. As Jesus lived a totally graced life, so the church opens up to us the life of grace and the way of salvation. The church is a virgin in that it remains faithful to Christ, its spouse. The church "keeps with virginal purity an entire faith, a firm hope and a sincere charity" (*LG*, 64).

These two images of Virgin and Mother are explored further in this section. Calling Mary the type (symbol) of the church, the document connects Mary's *fiat*, her virginal faithfulness, with the calling of all Christians:

> Seeking after the glory of Christ, the Church becomes more like her exalted Type, and continually progresses in faith, hope, and charity, seeking and doing the will of God in all things. (*LG*, 65)

In other words, when Christians seek and do the will of God in their lives, they are imitating Mary. The document then explicitly calls all Christians to be, symbolically speaking, mothers:

> The Virgin in her own life lived an example of that maternal love, by which it behooves that all should be animated who cooperate in the apostolic mission of the Church for the regeneration of men and women. (*LG*, 65)

I find it very meaningful that the church calls me, a man, to be animated by maternal love. There is a strong feminine dimension to the love that guides one in Christian activities.

Section IV of *Lumen Gentium's* treatment of Mary deals with the tradition of prayers and devotions to her. As in the previous section, there is a stress placed on Mary's subordinate ranking to Christ. Given this qualification, the document encourages devotion to Mary, especially through liturgy. At the same time, the document warns against abuses:

> . . . the magisterium of the Church . . . exhorts theologians and preachers of the divine word to abstain zealously both from all gross exaggerations as well as from petty narrow-mindedness in considering the singular dignity of the Mother of God. (*LG*, 67)

In other words, Christians are encouraged neither to overdo nor to unreasonably object to Marian devotions. As with other saints, we are exhorted to ground our prayers in a true relationship that leads us to imitate Mary's virtues. We need to grow in our knowledge of Mary if we are to imitate her.

It would be hard to dispute the statement that devotion to Mary has at times been exaggerated. An example of this is the art work on the back wall of the sanctuary of the Shrine of the Immaculate Conception in Washington, D.C. Mary is in the foreground, with the Jesus of the

Last Judgment in the background. The underlying message, as I interpret it, is that mild Mary is going to save us from her angry son. The painting points up distortions in the Catholic consciousness concerning both Jesus and Mary. Jesus is unapproachable as he strikes us with fear. Mary is little like the courageous woman of faith portrayed in the New Testament.

Yet, while abuses should be acknowledged, the Catholic emphasis on Mary rests on the strong grounds that she truly is the Mother of God who is remembered in our community above all for who she really is and the life she lived. The Catholic imagination throughout our history has discerned a richness associated with Mary that is beautifully expressed in prayers, in teachings, and in art. As David Macaulay put it in his video program, *Cathedral:*

> Most of the prominent cathedrals of [the medieval] period were dedicated to Notre Dame, Our Lady. In an age of chivalry and exalted womanhood, it is as if an entire society had fallen in love. Mary is perceived as the Mother of God and as the human vessel through which God became flesh. She is therefore both of heaven and of earth, just like the cathedrals that bear her name.[2]

The Middle Ages had a love affair with Mary. This love affair continues in the Catholic tradition, although it takes different forms as it develops.

Section V closes the chapter with a final comparison between Mary and the church as figures of hope, and with a prayer for Mary's intercession that all families of people may be gathered in the one people of God.

The chapter leaves the overall impression that the church cannot be given a justified treatment without a consideration of Mary, and that the role of Mary cannot be appreciated apart from the context of the church.

What Is Said about Mary Is Said about the Church

Mary has been so closely associated with the church throughout the history of Christianity that many scriptural sayings and traditional teachings about Mary can also be understood as sayings and teachings about the church. Many regard Mary as "the first Christian." She gave birth to Jesus and raised him. She was with him during his public ministry, and she was there at the foot of the cross. Mary was with the apostles on Pentecost when the Holy Spirit descended. Mary played an important role in each moment of the church's birth.

The Catholic Marian scholar and feminist theologian Elizabeth Johnson has investigated the symbolic nature of speech about Mary. She begins with the premise that Marian statements refer to both Mary and the church. Throughout the Christian tradition, Mary has served as a vehicle for the church to express its ideal self-realization. This is appropriate because of who Mary truly is as the mother of Jesus and because of how Mary is really remembered for her actual role in the earliest of Christian communities. Thus, in the Christian tradition, memories of Mary and beliefs about the ideal Christian community are mixed together; this is not a bad thing, however, because what can be said about one can also be said about the other.

Many Scripture passages about Mary are often interpreted as being about the church as well. For example, I have heard Luke 2:51, "his mother kept all these things in her heart," interpreted as foreshadowing the way the church has developed and enlarged its body of teachings throughout the centuries. The church is pondering what it already knows in its heart. Mary's order to the servants at Cana in John 2:5, "Do whatever he tells you," has been interpreted also as the advice of the church to each individual Christian. Jesus' words from the cross to Mary and John in John 19:26–27: "Woman, behold, your son; [to John] Behold, your mother," have been interpreted as referring to the relationship between the church and each Christian disciple. Mary's Immaculate Conception, that she herself was conceived without sin, has been interpreted as referring not only to Mary but also in an ideal sense to the graced life that is offered to every person. Mary's Assumption, her being taken bodily into heaven at the completion of her life, has likewise been interpreted as signaling in some way the fate that awaits all redeemed persons.

In the Catholic tradition, one must be careful to remember that the belief in Mary's Immaculate Conception and her Assumption refer to her "privileges" that recognize her unique role in the plan of salvation as the Mother of God. At the same time, however, Mary's privileges are not intended to isolate her by cutting her off from the body of Christians; rather, these privileges signify things for which all Christians and people of good will have reason to hope.

Summary
In this chapter we have examined the treatment of Mary in chapter 8 of *Lumen Gentium*. We have also discussed the way that things said about Mary and things said about the church often have interchangeable applications.

I am glad that Mary seems to be making a comeback in Catholic devotion. Getting back in touch with who Mary is parallels our journey in articulating what we believe the church—and we ourselves—should be.

In the next chapter we will discuss some feminist views of contemporary issues in the Catholic church.

FOR FURTHER REFLECTION

1. Why do you think that Mary has traditionally played such an important role for Catholics? Do you personally feel comfortable with this importance?

2. Are you more inclined to think of the rosary as a meditative prayer or as a superstitious prayer?

3. Why is Mary's *fiat* (let it be) so important for understanding her role in Christian history? How does this apply to other Christians?

4. In what way are questions about Mary *ecumenical* issues?

5. Why is it important to understand some of the things said about Mary as being "symbolic?"

SUGGESTED READINGS

Brown, Raymond, et. al., eds. *Mary in the New Testament: A Collaborative Assessment by Protestant and Roman Catholic Scholars.* Philadelphia: Fortress Press, 1978.

Buby, Bertrand. *Mary: The Faithful Disciple.* Mahwah, N.J.: Paulist Press, 1985.

Greeley, Andrew M. *The Mary Myth: On the Femininity of God.* New York: Seabury Press, 1977.

Jelly, Frederick M. *Madonna: Mary in the Catholic Tradition.* Huntington, Ind.: Our Sunday Visitor, 1986.

Lappin, Peter. *First Lady of the World: A Popular History of Marian Devotion.* New York: Don Bosco, 1988.

Moloney, Francis J. *Mary: Woman and Mother.* Collegeville, Minn.: Liturgical Press, 1988.

Ruether, Rosemary Radford. *Mary—The Feminine Face of the Church.* Philadelphia: Westminster Press, 1977.

CHAPTER 26

FEMINISM AND CHRISTIAN TRADITION

I n a recent discussion with a male theologian friend of mine, we remarked how a great shift seemed to take place in Catholic theology in the mid-1960s, coinciding with the completion of Vatican II. Surely many classic and useful theological texts were written before that time, but the great majority of theological writings before 1965 struck us as recognizably outdated. Most of the books and articles written in the late 1960s, however, are as useful as the ones written today.

Something big had happened. Vatican II represents a major turning point in Catholic theology, a dividing line, a watershed. Theology was one way before; now everything is different. Some theologians warn quite rightly against taking this view too far. For all of the changes that Vatican II brought about, the elements of continuity with the tradition are much deeper and much more important. Also, many of the so-called changes of Vatican II have their own long history that led up to their official acceptance. Nonetheless, the differences between pre- and post-Vatican II theology are real. To someone working in the field the differences are unmistakable.

My friend and I both began to remark at the same time how once that major shift had taken place, things stayed pretty much the same; theologians are now just playing out the diverse options and deepening the various directions that Vatican II had laid out. But we caught ourselves as we started to do this. One of us said, "But what about liberation theology?" Then all of a sudden we both blurted out, "What about *feminism?*"

It could be argued that insofar as Catholic theology is concerned,

Vatican II laid out much of the groundwork that allows for feminist perspectives and contributions to be taken seriously today. Such an argument, however, does not appreciate how little feminism is reflected in the documents, how recently feminism has entered the center stage in Catholic theology, and how dramatic and far-reaching is its impact.

This Chapter

This chapter looks at patriarchy in the Christian tradition, the woman-church movement, and some feminist concerns about images of Mary. Since much feminist writing about the Catholic church has addressed the issue of Mary, we link this material with chapter 8 of *Lumen Gentium*. Throughout this chapter I often rely on substantial quotes from authors in order to allow feminist theologians to speak for themselves.

Patriarchy

As I understand it, the central theme of the feminist movement as it has affected Catholic theology is the recognition that Western civilization and indeed much of global history have been patriarchal, and that patriarchy is a highly limiting and repressive system of human organization. This realization should lead not only to a massive reinterpretation of history, but to a contemporary challenging of institutions and social roles. Feminist social change looks toward a future that is non-patriarchal and thereby liberating for both women and men.

Feminist scholar Gerda Lerner defines "patriarchy" as:

> the manifestation and institutionalization of male dominance over women and children in the family and the extension of male dominance in society in general. It implies that men hold power in all the important institutions of society and that women are deprived of access to such power. It does not imply that women are either totally powerless or totally deprived of rights, influences, and resources.[1]

A non-patriarchal society would thus be one in which women and men are equal partners in the family and in which they share equal access to power in society at large.

More than power or justice is at stake, however. Many feminists claim that patriarchal beliefs and patriarchal thinking determine the very reality in which we dwell. A society transformed by feminism would not, therefore, simply be the world as we now know it with a dash more justice sprinkled on top. Feminist social change will involve a complete overhaul of our culture.

The following chart provides a highly abbreviated list of what Char McKee presents as "the partriarchal imagination" in contrast with "the feminist imagination"[2]:

Patriarchal	-	Feminist
logic only valid way of knowing	-	many valid ways of knowing
reality is mechanistic	-	reality is alive
hierarchical/polarized	-	systems within systems
our natural state is dangerous	-	our natural state is ecstasy
humans dominate the earth	-	humans care for the earth
not enough resources	-	there are enough resources
solve problems through science	-	solve by global cooperation
violence and war acceptable	-	only peaceful solutions

I want to emphasize that this highly abbreviated chart does not fully reflect how McKee spells out these contrasts. Nor is it intended to reflect a careful, scholarly approach to the subject. It does not even necessarily reflect what the majority of feminist thinkers would agree with. Personally, I find such generalizations to be highly questionable, and so do many feminists. I present the chart because it demonstrates something of the wide range of issues that feminists raise and the depth of change that is being called for. Feminists claim that whether we are female or male, because of our culture we tend to be patriarchal in our ways of feeling, thinking, imagining, and behaving. Overcoming patriarchy will involve radical changes in the ways that we feel, think, imagine, and behave.

Patriarchy in Christian Tradition

Feminist scholars have little difficulty finding evidence of a patriarchal culture being reflected in the Scriptures. But is the gospel message itself patriarchal? Does the basic Christian message need to be critiqued and revised according to feminist standards?

Radical feminist theologian Mary Daly, whose early work *The Church and the Second Sex*[3] called for equality within the church, came to reject her own early approach as not radical enough. In a later work, *Beyond God the Father*,[4] Daly finds sexism at the heart of the Judeo-Christian Tradition, starting with Eve and ending with a male God and a male redeemer. She calls for women to begin anew with a fresh naming of the forces of the cosmos. In her most recent works, *Gyn/Ecology*[5] and *Pure Lust*,[6] Daly undertakes this task by practically inventing a new language for articulating a feminist ethic.

Somewhat in contrast with Mary Daly's approach is that of the feminist biblical scholar Elisabeth Schüssler Fiorenza. Fiorenza presents one dimension of the original gospel message as radically egalitarian. She draws upon what has come to be known as the "women's passage" from Galatians 3:28: "There is neither Jew nor Greek, there is neither slave nor free person, there is not male and female; for you are all one in Christ Jesus." With this passage and other information from the New Testament, Fiorenza constructs a picture of some of the earliest Christian communities as preaching and living out a gospel that calls for inclusion of women on all levels of discipleship and leadership. In particular, in Mark and in John woman are portrayed as inspiring role models. Fiorenza speculates that it is likely that women also presided at the Eucharist, although this speculation is hotly debated today.

What happened to this gospel that included the equality of the sexes? Fiorenza argues that it struggled with a patriarchal culture and the culture won. She traces through the New Testament and through other early Christian documents how submission and patriarchy won out over altruistic love and service. In other words, Fiorenza is arguing that the last two thousand years of Christian tradition have been skewed by the submergence of the authentic egalitarianism of the basic gospel message.

Is this less radical than the position of Daly? Yes it is, insofar as it finds the grounds for an ultimate hope in the gospel itself. Yet in some ways it is not so very different in that it still calls for a rethinking and a reinvestigation of the ways that Christian symbols and power structures have been used and abused throughout the entire history of Christianity.

Women-Church

Fiorenza is one of the major voices articulating the experience of the movement that she calls "the *ekklesia* of women," more commonly known as "women-church." "Women-church" involves women gathering together to pray and to celebrate, to analyze the issues that they face together, and to support each other in their struggles. Fiorenza expresses the purpose of women-church in a forceful manner:

A feminist Christian spirituality, therefore, calls us to gather together the ekklesia of women who, in the angry power of the Spirit, are sent forth to feed, heal, and liberate our own people who are women. It unmasks and sets us free from the structural sin and alienation of sexism and propels us to become children and spokeswomen of God. It rejects the idolatrous worship of maleness and articulates the divine image in female human existence and language. It sets us free from the internalization of false altruism and self-sacrifice that is concerned with the welfare and work of men first to the detriment of our own and other women's welfare and calling. It enables us to live "for one another" and to experience the presence of God in the ekklesia as the gathering of women. Those of us who have heard this calling respond by committing ourselves to the liberation struggle of women and all peoples, by being accountable to women and their future, and by nurturing solidarity within the ekklesia of women. Commitment, accountability, and solidarity in community are the hallmarks of our calling and struggle.[7]

Fiorenza is here calling for women to gather together in worship communities in a way similar to the base ecclesial communities of Latin America. In this regard, feminist theology can be read as a form of liberation theology.

Theologian Anne Carr describes "women-church" in a way that captures this similarity to the base ecclesial communities:

> . . . the movement of various women's groups to join together in the search for ways of being church that are especially open to the experience of women. Their gatherings sometimes include men who share the hunger for more inclusive, relational, and communitarian expressions of Christian life. Activities take the form of new kinds of structure, decisionmaking, social action, and liturgy that can eventually be incorporated in ordinary parish communities. But at present, the existence of women-church simply allows for the time and space in which experimentation can occur and discoveries be refined. The very existence of women-church signals the determination of women, as the symbol of all the other groups who have been excluded from the life of the church, to find a Christian life that is concretely expressive in today's world of the message of the gospel.[8]

In other words, such groups of women (and some men) have been experimenting with what church and what spirituality might be like if fully informed by a feminist perspective. These groups tend to be ecumenical. They draw upon the Christian tradition and other sources to devise their own forms of prayer, support, and liturgy. Women and all others are included as co-equal partners.

Some feminist theologians do not explicitly include men at this time. Rosemary Radford Ruether gives this description of communities of women in her book, *Women-Church*:

> . . . the first step in forming the feminist exodus from patriarchy is to gather women together to articulate their own experience and communicate it with each other. Women assure each other that they really are not crazy, that they really have been defined and confined by systematic marginalization of their human capacities. They develop words and analysis for the different aspects of this system of marginalization, and they learn how to recognize and resist the constant messages from patriarchal culture that try to enforce their acquiescence and collaboration with it.[9]

Although Ruether's description may differ somewhat from Carr's because she does not explicitly include men, her description is very similar regarding the development of communities of liberation that will help women to bring about systemic changes.

Separation or Unity?

Fiorenza anticipates and addresses two common objections to women-church. First, the charge is made that women-church does not share in the fullness of the church. True, Fiorenza replies, but neither do hierarchical assemblies that are exclusively male. The Christian tradition has a long history of communities of women; the women-church movement seeks to reclaim these communities by freeing them from clerical control and making them accountable for their own decisions.

A second objection is that women-church represents reverse sexism. Fiorenza argues that the gathering of the exploited does not oppress the oppressors. The women-church movement is not over and against men, but rather is for the purpose of the spiritual survival of women. The goal is mutuality, not the subordination of one group by another. Fiorenza's final vision is one of unity:

> Only when the ekklesia of women is joined by all those in biblical religion who share the vision of the people of God as the discipleship of equals, only then is the gospel proclaimed in the whole world.[10]

It is worth noting that Fiorenza's final appeal is thus to the gospel, which she reads as proclaiming a discipleship of equals.

Rosemary Radford Ruether also takes a stand that combines a call for separation with the hope for a longer-range unity. Ruether recognizes separation as a necessary stage in the development of any individual or movement, but she rejects what she calls "separatism as total ideology." Women-Church is but one stage in a process that has yet to be fulfilled:

> One can see this begin to happen as women shape a sufficiently clarified critical culture so that some men feel compelled to try to understand it on its own terms and not simply to try to ridicule or repress it. What is required for the development of a new cohumanity of men and women liberated from patriarchy is that men begin to critique their own dehumanization by patriarchy and form their critical culture of liberation from it in a way that truly complements the feminist exodus and allows the formation of real dialogue. I assume the name for this liberated humanity would then no longer be "Women-Church," but simply "Church"....[11]

Ruether calls for feminists also to secure "footholds in existing Christian churches" so that they can share their vision with large numbers of people.[12] Both Ruether and Fiorenza, though they do hope for a future unity, envision a true unity of coequals, not just a few concessions from a church that will remain basically unchanged.

Feminism, Mary, and the Church

Many feminist theologians have been especially critical of the ways in which images of Mary have been used in Christian tradition for the suppression of women. The very characteristics of Mary held most in esteem in *Lumen Gentium,* her submission to the will of God and her being simultaneously virgin and mother, are seen by some as devaluing women by reinforcing their submissiveness and denying their sexuality. Theologian Mary Jo Weaver, for example, thinks that patriarchal religion has used the Virgin Mary as "an image of passive humility," a "reification of male power over women."[13]

In an article in the journal, *Thought,* professors Una Cadegan and James Heft review a wide range of feminist writings on this issue.[14] They find much of value in the feminist critiques, and agree that some images of Mary have been distorted and non-liberating. They argue further, however, that the submission to the will of God represented by

Mary is a central element of the Christian tradition that cannot be dismissed lightly. The paradoxical dimensions of this submission and the liberating empowerment that it brings are not in any way self-destructive: "When we submit to God, in the sense in which the New Testament intends, we discover our true selves"(p. 184). Cadegan and Heft agree with Ruether that images that have forced women into submissive roles need to be corrected, but they feel that this should be done without denying the value of submissiveness in one's relationship with God.

Concerning the interrelationship between virgin and mother, Cadegan and Heft argue that an understanding of this paradox that draws sympathetically upon a deep vision of the Christian tradition will value rather than devalue sexuality and the body. Elements of the tradition that have not done this are inauthentic, but one should not throw the baby out with the bath water. Taking a stance that remains within the traditional church, Cadegan and Heft represent the possibility of a newly emerging interchange between theologians of women-church and more traditional theologians who will dialogue with them seriously and respectfully.

Summary

In this chapter we have discussed patriarchy, the women-church movement, and current debate concerning images of Mary.

Much has changed in the thinking of women and men about feminist issues since Vatican II. To me, these matters are still new and confusing and exciting and sometimes difficult and often hopeful. I certainly do not feel, at this time, that I am in a position to make any comprehensive evaluative comments. Although I do not embrace all feminist perspectives uncritically, I have come to realize that neither do most feminists. Feminist perspectives present us with many opportunities for challenge and growth.

In the next chapter we will focus on the debate concerning the ordination of women.

FOR FURTHER REFLECTION

1. Is devotion to Mary more of an obstacle or more of an aid to the progress of women in church and in society?

2. Do you buy the argument that certain styles of thought are "male" and others "female"?

3. Do you agree that western civilization as well as most of global history have been tarnished by patriarchy?

4. Does the women-church movement sound attractive to you?

5. Is exposure to feminist ideas ultimately liberating for men?

SUGGESTED READINGS

Daly, Mary. *Beyond God the Father: Toward a Philosophy of Women's Liberation.* Boston: Beacon Press, 1973.

Fiorenza, Elisabeth Schüssler. *In Memory of Her: A Feminist Reconstruction of Christian Origins.* New York: Crossroad, 1984.

Lerner, Gerda. *The Creation of Patriarchy.* Oxford: Oxford University Press, 1986.

Ruether, Rosemary Radford. *Women-Church: Theology and Practice of Feminist Liturgical Communities.* San Francisco: Harper & Row, 1985.

Weaver, Mary Jo. *New Catholic Women.* San Francisco: Harper & Row, 1985.

CHAPTER 27

THE ORDINATION OF WOMEN

I n April 1988, the U.S. Catholic bishops released the first draft of a document that has come to be known, some think ironically, as the "women's pastoral." Called "Partners in the Mystery of Redemption," the letter sought to address the concerns of women in relation to church and society.[1] In April 1990, the bishops released a second draft,[2] "One in Christ Jesus," which incorporated some revisions in response to criticisms of the first draft. Each of the drafts attempts to address the concerns of women in four areas: as persons, in relationships, in society, and in the church. Sexism is clearly denounced as sinful, and its pervasive effects are explored. Perhaps the major difference between the first draft and the second draft is that the first tended to divide women against each other by pitting "voices of affirmation" against "voices of alienation." The second draft is less divisive because it includes the voices of a diverse range of women while emphasizing the major concerns that unite them: being treated as persons and having equal status in all areas of personal, familial, social, and ecclesial life.

The main reason why some people feel that it is ironic to call this document the "women's pastoral" is that its final approval depends on an authoritative body made up exclusively of men. In fact, there are those who oppose the very idea of this letter for that reason: No matter how far the letter goes, it cannot go far enough as long as women have no decisive voice in the final say. Until that changes, the letter can only try to make deeper concessions and accommodations within the present system without truly addressing the deepest, structural issue. The system of exclusively male dominance has to change; until that happens, whatever the bishops pay lip service to will not be enough. Many other people, however, believe that it is a fine letter that represents a much needed step in the right direction.

As of this writing, the bishops have yet to release a third and final draft. One of the reasons the letter is being delayed is that it is being circulated internationally to elicit the response of Catholics throughout the world. The Vatican is concerned that the bishops may be advocating directions that, while acceptable locally, may be at odds with the needs of the universal church. Perhaps not all cultures, for example, will welcome the U.S. bishops' suggestion for a study of the possibility of admitting women to the ordained diaconate. This is perceived to be an issue that to some degree will affect the entire church. At a conference in Rome in May 1991, Vatican officials expressed fears that the U.S. bishops were allowing church teaching to be influenced by whoever spoke with the loudest voice.

This Chapter

In this chapter, after a brief consideration of some of the main points of "One in Christ Jesus," we will focus on the issue of the ordination of women. This material is intended to continue the discussion of women's issues linked with chapter 8 of *Lumen Gentium*.

Major Themes in "One in Christ Jesus"

The United States bishops teach that sexism is a sin that is expressed subtly and pervasively in our society. Although the bishops acknowledge some differences between men and women, they stress that "women and men have the same nature, a common humanity, and a fundamental equality" (section 25). They reject any dual anthropology that implies superiority/inferiority or dominance/subjection. They affirm the roles of both married and single women, and urge men to become full partners in parenting.

The bishops call for more inclusion of women in the decision-making processes of the church. Although they repeat the arguments of papal and other Vatican documents limiting the ordained priesthood to men, they call for a thorough investigation by the Congregation for the Doctrine of the Faith, "without preconceived ideas," concerning the possibility of admitting women to the diaconate (section 120). This position is controversial, because, for centuries prior to Vatican II, the diaconate had functioned only as a step in ordination to the priesthood. Unlike other ministries now being opened to women, the diaconate requires a formal ordination and is one of the three fundamental ministries in the New Testament and in the early church. Although the bishops ask only for an "investigation" of the possibility of women in the diaconate and state their support of an all-male priesthood, many read their move as a step in the direction of women priests.

The bishops call also for sexually inclusive language in the church, such as not using "man" as a generic term when what is meant is "humankind." In November 1990, the bishops approved a new inclusive language lectionary for use in worship.

The final section of "One in Christ Jesus" deals with the role of women in society. The bishops decry discrimination against women in regard to jobs, poverty, and responsibilities in the home. They condemn violence against women. They denounce the often degrading depiction of women in media and advertising. They acknowledge problems in the way that women have been treated and continue to be treated in the church. They call for a deep conversion of heart and a change in social structures to address these problems.

This brief summary does not do justice to the letter itself. Whether one is for or against the release of the letter as an official church document, one can sense throughout the letter a tremendous effort to wrestle deeply with the issues and to address them as fully as possible within existing constraints.

Women's Ordination

A person can make two mistakes when assessing the importance of the question of the ordination of women within the Catholic church. The first is to see this as the only real issue regarding women. Some Catholic women have sensed that this issue seems to be a dead end for now, and so they are pursuing other paths for reform.

The other mistake is to underestimate how important this issue is and how deeply people feel about it. It is a given in many feminist contexts that *power* is the issue here and that the men who are in control do not want to share the power. From this perspective, official arguments against the ordination of women appear to be clever ideological cover-ups of what is really going on.

I am amazed by how many people I encounter, both women and men, both within the church and without, who dismiss the feminist movement as an outlandish gathering of oddballs who can hardly be taken seriously. This type of presupposition on either side does not provide the makings for a good dialogue.

For many issues, it can be misleading to lay out the arguments for both sides, because such an approach ignores the subtleties of middle positions. When it comes to the ordination of women, however, there is not much middle ground. One is either for it, against it, or not sure. In what follows, I will try to lay out as sympathetically as possible the arguments being made on each side.

Arguments Against the Ordination of Women

The most basic document that lays out the Vatican position on the ordination of women is *Inter Insigniores,* the "Declaration on the Admission of Women to the Ministerial Priesthood," issued by the Congregation for the Doctrine of the Faith in 1976.[3] The document begins with a strong statement against any forms of discrimination on the basis of sex followed by an affirmation of the important role played by women in the life of the church. It then recognizes the ecumenical nature of this issue insofar as many Protestant denominations have already ordained women.

The document explains the Vatican position by stating that "the church, in fidelity to the example of the Lord, does not consider herself authorized to admit women to priestly ordination" (section 332). In other words, it is not up to the church to decide this matter; it is the job of the church to safeguard the tradition that has been handed on and thus to pass it on faithfully. Many things come under the jurisdiction of the church and can be changed. The ordination of women, however, is not one of them.

The document argues that exclusively male ordination is an unchangeable matter because it is part of an unbroken tradition that represents the will of Christ. The church has never ordained women. Although women were ordained in some of the heretical gnostic sects in early Christian centuries, the church Fathers promptly condemned such a practice. The churches in the East have likewise maintained the unbroken tradition of ordaining only men. The medieval theologians also opposed it, although it is clear that many of their arguments for this are not acceptable today. Throughout the long history of the church, the magisterium has not seen fit to intervene on this matter.

In the New Testament, Jesus did not choose any women to be members of the twelve apostles. It is to the twelve apostles that Jesus gave the explicit charge to celebrate the Eucharist and to offer the forgiveness of sins. Whatever Jesus' reasons, they were probably not due simply to cultural restrictions. Jesus readily broke through many cultural barriers of his time and included women in many aspects of his ministry; it was probable, therefore, that Jesus had other reasons for not including women among the twelve apostles. The present-day church does not feel authorized to change organizational structures that may represent the intentions of Jesus. The disciples followed Jesus' lead and selected only men when it came to replacing members of the Twelve.

The document argues that not ordaining women is not a slight to women's dignity. They point out that Mary was not a priest and yet no one surpasses her "in dignity and in excellence" (section 335).

The document then goes on to address some of the most common objections to its arguments. Foremost among these is the charge that Jesus' actions reflect the culture of his time; he did what he did because of historical circumstances. The document argues that this cannot be proved; it is possible that Jesus had more in mind than simple expediency. The next objection is that not ordaining women reflects a time-bound cultural prejudice that is evident throughout the Scriptures. The document replies that Paul, who gave us the most important passages about the fundamental equality between men and women, cannot be said to be simply reflecting prejudice rather than the will of Christ. The final objection addressed by the document is that the church really does have the power to change on this issue because it primarily involves the administration of the sacraments over which the church is in charge. The document replies that although the church does have charge over the administration of the sacraments, it does not have charge over their substance; the issue of who is ordained involves the very substance, not just the administration.

The document then gives an illustration of the fittingness of its teaching, being careful to point out that it is offering not a demonstrative argument but only an analogy of faith. Basically, the document says that the priest at the altar represents Christ, and that it is important that as much as possible the priest bear a natural resemblance to Christ so that people can imagine Christ present through him as he pronounces the words of consecration. If a woman were to play such a role, "it would be difficult to see in the minister the image of Christ. For Christ himself was and remains a man" (section 339). This argument is similar to saying that the Mass is something like a play; would it be appropriate for a woman to play Hamlet or King Lear?

Yet the argument goes deeper than this. The document goes on to talk about the meaning of the Mass as containing a nuptial theme. We are told in the Scriptures that Christ is the bridegroom and the church is the bride. This nuptial theme, traced through various references to the Old and the New Testaments, symbolically expresses something about the nature of men and women in their relationship with each other. In other words, the Mass has not only a meal theme as a reenactment of the Last Supper in anticipation of the kingdom banquet, and not only a sacrifice theme as a reenactment of the death and resurrection of Jesus; the Mass has also a sexual theme that expresses the union of Christ, the bridegroom with the church, his spouse. From this intimate union issues the new life of grace. In a papal letter written in 1989, John Paul II is even more explicit than *Inter Insignores:*

> As the redeemer of the world, Christ is the bridegroom of the church. The eucharist is the sacrament of our redemption. It is the sacrament of the bridegroom and of the bride. The eucharist makes present and realizes anew in a sacramental manner the redemptive act of Christ, who "creates" the church, his body. Christ is united with this "body" as the bridegroom with the bride. . . .
>
> Since Christ in instituting the eucharist linked it in such an explicit way to the priestly service of the apostles, it is legitimate to conclude that he thereby wishes to express the relationship between man and woman, between what is "feminine" and what is "masculine." It is a relationship willed by God both in the mystery of creation and in the mystery of redemption. It is the eucharist above all that expresses the redemptive act of Christ, the bridegroom, toward the church, the bride. This is clear and unambiguous when the sacramental ministry of the eucharist, in which the priest acts in persona Christi, is performed by a man.[4]

One might ask: Should the one who presides at Eucharist then be Jewish and have a beard? *Inter Insigniores* replies that the sexual difference expressed even in the story of creation is deeper than any ethnic or grooming differences. Does not the priest act also as representative of the church, so that the symbolism could vary but still express the mystery? The document responds that it is precisely as representing the person of Christ that the priest represents the church; it is specifically in the person of Christ that the priest presides over the whole Christian assembly.

Is it not, however, an injustice to discriminate against women concerning this matter so important to our faith? The document argues that the church is not like other governments or states; its offices are not a matter of rights and privileges, but a matter of a call from God to a service. What then, about women who claim to experience a personal call to the priesthood? The document acknowledges that such an experience might stem from a true desire to serve Christ and the church, but that vocations "cannot be reduced to a mere personal attraction, which can remain purely subjective" (section 342–43).

The document closes with a call for women to become more greatly aware of the importance of their mission. The document's main arguments remain that Jesus intended the priesthood to be all male; that Christ probably had a reason for this that was more than practical expediency; that the reason probably had to do with the sexual dimension symbolically represented in the Eucharist; that this tradition has not been changed throughout the whole of Catholic or Orthodox tradition; that the church does not have the authority to change what Jesus may have explicitly intended; and that not ordaining women does not mean that women do not share equally in the dignity of all persons made in the image of God and redeemed by Christ.

Arguments in Favor of the Ordination of Women

Many of the more common arguments in favor of the ordination of women have already been mentioned in the form of objections to which *Inter Insigniores* has responded. What has not been done is to advance these arguments in a sympathetic context.

As mentioned above, some people who favor women's ordination forthrightly dismiss the Vatican's arguments as an ideological smoke screen for the simple fact that the men in charge want to hang on to their power. Others, however, are willing to engage the Vatican in a point by point debate. They argue that the church is engaging in unnecessary and demeaning discrimination against women, but at the same time are willing to address each argument individually.

From the pro-ordination perspective, the deepest argument is that not ordaining women reflects the patriarchal culture of the time of Jesus. Jesus, who operated within the confines of this culture, did all that he reasonably could to break through barriers and include women in his ministry. If Jesus were alive in earthly form today, there is much in the New Testament to suggest that he would favor and perhaps even demand that women be ordained.

There is a radically egalitarian dimension in the earliest gospel message. What has come to be known as "the women's passage," Galatians 3:28, variations of which appear in two other places in Paul's letters, is thought to have been part of an early baptismal rite:

> There is neither Jew nor Greek,
> There is neither slave nor free person,
> There is not male and female;
> For you are all one in Christ Jesus.

In other words, when one becomes a member of the church, one enters into a world in which there are no distinctions concerning equality of persons. What happened, argue some, is that the egalitarian gospel went up against a patriarchal culture and the culture won; at least for a couple of thousand years so far.

Some scholars, basing themselves on the ground-breaking work of Elisabeth Schüssler Fiorenza,[5] argue that women not only had leadership roles in the early church but perhaps even presided at the Eucharist. It is argued that some of the early house churches, where the one to preside would be the head of the household, were headed by women, usually widows. Fiorenza traces what she calls the patriarchalization of church ministries from a time when leadership rotated among all members to when it was gradually taken over by men. This movement was related to the establishment of bishops as heads of local churches in the first two centuries.

Inter Insigniores cited Paul's forbidding women to speak in church (1 Corinthians 14:34–35) as evidence that women, who were allowed to prophesy, were to be excluded from the official function of teaching in the eucharistic assembly. The document attributes this position to "exegetes" or Scripture scholars. Other scholars, however, interpret this passage differently. Vincent Branick, for example, points out that this passage seems to contradict clear evidence in the same letter that women do in fact prophesy in church. Branick suggests two possibilities. First, the passage calling for women to be silent may be a later interpolation that is foreign to the thinking of Paul. Second, it is quite possible that Paul was operating here with a distinction between the small house church and the large public gathering. His admonition for women not to speak in church applied to the public gathering only. In effect, Paul was presupposing the fact that women do regularly speak in the local house churches; they are not to speak at the large public gatherings because they might give scandal to others in their patriarchal culture and drive away prospective converts.[6]

Another Vatican position that receives serious challenge is the belief that the church is not free to change anything that might have been intended by Christ. Liberation theologian Leonardo Boff finds the beginning of the church at Pentecost, which represents the guidance of the Holy Spirit, to allow the church to address whatever new situations arise. Boff argues that Jesus founded the church insofar as he willed "grace, liberation, the irruption of the Spirit, the new creation, the heavenly Jerusalem, and the kingdom of God...."[7] However, Boff thinks that it is a mistake to believe that Christ founded the church in terms of its institutional structures and its sociological components. In other words, Boff takes the position that Jesus in a sense founded the church, but that he did not will for the church to have just one particular form. Christ's will is for the church to take on whatever forms are necessary to address current situations through the guidance of the Holy Spirit. Boff clearly believes that the current situation calls for the ordination of women:

> Woman's position in the church should keep pace with the evolution of her position in civil society. That society tends more and more to accord women an equality with men. Any discrimination on the grounds of biological or cultural differentiation becomes more and more unseemly and intolerable.[8]

Boff concludes his discussion by explaining why he agrees with theologian Karl Rahner that the arguments of *Inter Insigniores* "are not theologically convincing."[9]

The main arguments, therefore, of those who favor ordination and are willing to argue with the Vatican's position on a point by point basis, are that Jesus' selection of the Twelve probably reflects more the socio-historical situation of a patriarchal culture than some explicit intention of Jesus; that ordaining women would be in continuity with the main thrust of Jesus' ministry to include women in contrast with the cultural expectations; that women had leadership roles in the early church that were suppressed as church structures gradually conformed to the patriarchal culture; that the church has the power to make structural changes to address new cultural situations as they arise; and that the new recognition of the equality and dignity of women calls upon the church to practice what it preaches and to be an institutional role model rather than a regressive force in society. Added to these reasons are some practical concerns, such as that ordaining women would be of some help in addressing the shortage of priests; that some women do feel strongly that they are called to be priests; that women would bring dimensions to the priesthood that it is now lacking; and that ordaining women would be a good move in the direction of ecumenical unity.

A Difficult Issue

The Vatican has its own practical concerns to add to the pile of arguments: Ordaining women would not currently be in the interest of ecumenical unity with the churches of the East; ordaining women would be a practical difficulty in many cultures that strongly differentiate between the roles of women and men; and finally, the Vatican might have difficulty explaining why it had reversed itself on a stand taken so many centuries ago and buttressed by so many recent arguments.

Recently a colleague of mine said that it was the Vatican's deeply entrenched fear of women that held them back from doing the right thing. Another colleague said that he thinks that the Vatican sincerely believes that it has a two-thousand-year-old tradition to safeguard and thereby does not feel that it can change according to the cultural winds without knowing clearly that such is the will of God. In any case, it is difficult to make judgments concerning the inner disposition of Vatican officials.

Inter Insigniores admits that its own arguments are not compelling, but it finds the arguments of those who favor women's ordination themselves to be highly speculative and impossible to prove. Since it is a matter of doubt, it is better to rely on the tradition itself as most clearly representing the will of God. Leonardo Boff, on the other hand, believes that the burden of proof should be shifted to the Vatican to explain why they withhold ordination from women at the same time that they call for recognition of the equality and dignity of women in all other areas of life.

Concerning such a divisive issue, true dialogue that involves a sympathetic exploration of contrary positions is hard to find. A notable exception to this rule is an article that appeared in *Worship* in 1989 by Sara Butler, a theological consultant for the U.S. bishops' committee for the pastoral letter on women's concerns as well as head of a task force of the Catholic Theological Society of America that is studying women's ordination.[10] Butler, a long-time advocate of ordaining women, shares her journey from one of devastated rejection of the Vatican's position to one of serious engagement with arguments that she now recognizes to have a great deal of internal consistency and theological respectability. She explains that early on she had developed her own position from a context that was totally independent of the Vatican's position. From that perspective, the Vatican's arguments appeared to be little more than repressive nonsense. Although Butler has by no means changed her position on women's ordination, her current explorations more directly intersect with the types of issues that the Vatican raises. For example, she takes very seriously the importance of the maleness of Jesus and the richness of nuptial imagery in the Christian tradition; she simply does not arrive at the same conclusion as the Vatican that therefore only men should preside at the Eucharist. Butler's article has provoked some thoughtful discussion.[11] It is only when more and more voices on either side of the issue take the other side seriously that any true progress will be made.

Summary
After a brief overview of the U.S. Catholic bishops' draft letter on the concerns of women, we investigated both sides of the debate concerning the ordination of women in the Catholic church.

I do not foresee an easy resolution to this issue.

In the next chapter we will examine how at Vatican II the Catholic church emphasized its own role as a servant within the world.

FOR FURTHER REFLECTION

1. Does it bother you that an official teaching of the church about women depends for its approval upon the decision of a body made up entirely of men?

2. Is it important for the Catholic church to proclaim that sexism is a sin?

3. No matter which position you personally may take: Which arguments against the ordination of women are good ones? Which arguments are not good?

4. No matter which position you personally may take: Which arguments in favor of the ordination of women are good ones? Which arguments are not good?

5. Are you personally more for or against the ordination of women in the Catholic church?

SUGGESTED READINGS

Boff, Leonardo. *Ecclesiogenesis*. Maryknoll, N.Y.: Orbis Books, 1986 [1977].

Butler, Sara. "Second Thoughts on Ordaining Women." *Worship* 63 (May 1989):157–65.

Carmody, Denise Lardner. *The Double Cross: Ordination, Abortion, and Catholic Feminism*. New York: Crossroad, 1986.

Carr, Anne. *Transforming Grace: Christian Tradition and Women's Experience*. San Francisco: Harper & Row, 1988.

Congregation for the Doctrine of the Faith. *"Inter Insigniores."* In *Vatican II: More Post-Conciliar Documents.* Edited by Austin Flannery. Collegeville, Minn.: The Liturgical Press, 1982.

Hopko, Thomas. *Women and the Priesthood.* Crestwood, N.Y.: St. Vladimir's Seminary Press, 1983.

U.S. Bishops. "Partners in the Mystery of Redemption: A Pastoral Response to Women's Concerns for Church and Society." Washington: United States Catholic Conference, 1988.

PART THREE

GAUDIUM ET SPES:
THE CHURCH ENGAGING THE WORLD

———

SECTION ONE

CHURCH AND WORLD

28. The Servant Church

29. Atheism and the New Theism

30. Religious Pluralism

CHAPTER 28

THE SERVANT CHURCH

T he legend of St. Christopher, as I have heard it told,[1] goes something like this:

St. Christopher was a very large and strong man. When he was very young, he decided that he should serve only the greatest of kings. The king in his local area claimed that he was the greatest of kings, and so for some time Christopher served him.

One day Christopher found out that his king was frightened of the emperor. He therefore set off in search of this emperor. The emperor did indeed claim to be the greatest of rulers. Christopher served him for many years.

One day Christopher learned that the emperor was frightened of Satan. So Christopher set out in search of Satan. He found Satan riding at the head of a large army. Satan did claim to be the most powerful of rulers, and so Christopher entered his service.

One day when the army was marching through the desert, Satan altered the entire course of the march in order to avoid going near one small cross that was planted in the sand. When Christopher inquired about the reason, he learned that Satan was terribly afraid of Christ. So Christopher went out in search of Christ.

Christopher inquired after the whereabouts of Christ from a ferryman who took people across a river. Although the ferryman did not know where to find Christ, he suggested that if Christopher took over from him he might find out, since in time nearly everyone in the world would cross at that river.

Christopher served many years as a ferryman who took people across the river. He met none who could tell him of the whereabouts of Christ. Then one night, as a storm arose, a small boy asked for passage across the river. Christopher took the boy upon his back and began to cross. He found the boy to be surprisingly heavy. By the time he was halfway to the shore, the storm was raging mercilessly and the boy felt exceedingly heavy. Nevertheless, Christopher continued to struggle until he had reached the other side. By the time he put the boy down, he felt as though the weight of the world had been lifted off his shoulders.

The boy thanked him and then proclaimed that he himself was the Christ whom Christopher had been seeking. Christopher asked to accompany Christ on his journey and serve him. Christ replied that Christopher has been serving him all along, whenever he helped people to cross the river. Christopher asked again if now he might serve Christ more directly by going with him. Christ responded that the best help that Christopher could give to him would be to continue to help people to cross the river.

Christopher continued his work. To this day he is popularly known as the patron saint of travelers.

This Chapter

The legend of St. Christopher expresses a deep Christian belief that Christ can be served through one's work in the world. At Vatican II, this belief burst to the surface to become one of the major themes of *Gaudium et Spes*. The issue was addressed in terms of the relationship between the church and the world. In this chapter we will make some brief comments about the church-world relationship in the history of Christianity, examine the shift at Vatican II, and then discuss the assessment of the Extraordinary Synod of 1985.

The first twenty-seven chapters of this book took their basic organization and inspiration from *Lumen Gentium*. The remaining nine chapters follow roughly the organization of *Gaudium et Spes*. This chapter addresses an underlying theme that runs throughout the document.

Historical Background

The relationship between the Catholic church and the "world" has undergone many complex developments throughout Christian history. Strong strains that are world-affirming and strong strains that are world-denying can both be traced within the large Catholic-Christian tradition. New Testament communities often saw themselves as bastions of salvation from an evil world. Particularly in the Gospel of John, the world is a horrible place of lies and temptations. Yet it is in that very Gospel that we are told that "God so loved the world that he gave his only Son, so that everyone who believes in him might not perish but might have eternal life" (3:16). And in Acts of the Apostles we find frequent evidence of a God who calls the apostles to be more and more world-embracing as the Christian mission spreads. We also find evidence of a "natural theology" that identifies the God of Christians as the one anticipated in the pagan nature religions (Acts 17:22–29). The scriptural testimony concerning the goodness of the world therefore has its own tensions and ambiguities.

Christianity entered the fourth century as an underground, sometimes persecuted religion. Such a position profoundly affected the church's attitude toward the world. In 313, with the issuing of the Edict of Milan, Christianity was officially tolerated. In 380, Christianity became the official religion of the Roman Empire. Within the space of one century, Christianity was well on the way to becoming in many ways a "worldly" religion, insofar as it was related to the state and had concern for the temporal well-being of people. Over the years the offices in the church came more and more to resemble offices in the state.

By that same fourth century, however, there were monasteries in the desert that provided a home base for solitary monks who sought God by escaping city life. These monks developed many ascetical practices in the belief that worldly concerns would stand between them and God.

The tension between the worldly and the other-worldly in Christianity can also be seen in the attitude toward art. In the early Greek church there were clashes between those who favored the use of icons in worship and those known as the "iconoclasts" (literally, smashers of symbols). Iconoclasts believed that the injunction in the first commandment to "make no graven images" was as true for Christians as it was for the Jews who made the golden calf. They attempted to throw the art out of the churches, seeing attempts to represent the divine as offensive to God.

The church of the Middle Ages tended to choose the worldly option in regard to art and architecture but the other-worldly option in regard to lifestyle. The church of the Renaissance tended to choose the all-around worldly option more often. The great Protestant reformers, Luther and Calvin, perceived the Roman Catholic church to be worldly in a way that opposed the gospel.

Luther and Calvin each in his own way advocated an other-worldly approach to religion. Luther emphasized the salvation of the individual through faith alone rather than through works performed in this world. Calvin taught the predestination of the saved and the damned, which ironically led to a concern for one's status in this world as a sign of one's eternal destiny.

The Council of Trent, in reaction to Luther and Calvin, asserted a somewhat more positive understanding of the human person. The council agreed that original sin was very serious and that human beings had lost their holiness and righteousness thereby; but the Fall was not total, for human beings still retained a free will and still were made in the image and likeness of God. In other words, the Fall was seriously distorting, but not absolute. From the Catholic point of view, the issue was whether people could be said to be responsible for their eternal destiny, while at the same time acknowledging the necessity of grace. Trent's position is one classic articulation of the Catholic emphasis that human beings and the world are basically good.

For the Reformers, what they perceived as the Catholic overemphasis on sacraments and art was tied in with its worldliness. Protestants themselves have traditionally preferred crosses to crucifixes, sermons to sacraments, music to sculpture, and the Bible to great cathedrals. The Catholic emphasis has been on a sacramental sensibility: that God can be encountered in and through the things of this world.[2] The Protestant emphasis has been on the saving power of the Word proclaimed to sinners who otherwise would have no recourse but to be caught up in this treacherous world.

The parallel and often overlapping histories of Catholicism and Protestantism show wide varieties and complex shifts taking place within all denominations and local churches in regard to the status of the "world." If Catholic anthropology and art appreciation of recent centuries have been world-affirming, Catholic attitudes and policies have not. Perhaps somewhat ironically, Protestantism was seen from the Catholic perspective to be "worldly" in that it took both political and spiritual power away from the church and put it in the hands of the nation-states. The separation of church and state, which often took the form of the subordination of the church to the state, was strongly resisted by the Catholic church. From the Catholic standpoint, a balance of power could only be preserved by a relationship between nation-states and a universal church, not between nation-states and national churches.

As discussed in chapter two, for several centuries prior to Vatican II the Catholic church saw movement after movement arise that challenged its authority and its place in the world. From the Enlightenment with its emphasis on science and its hostility to religion, to the French revolution with its persecution of the church, to the rise of industrialization with its new forms of poverty and its philosophies of atheistic materialism, the Catholic church felt threatened. Thus, while retaining, in relation to Protestantism, a relatively positive theological view of humankind and the world, the Catholic church of the last few centuries saw the world in practical terms as an evil and ugly place. During the first half of the twentieth century, the Catholic church had developed what many commentators call a "fortress mentality" or a "ghetto mentality." It was the church over and against the world, presenting itself as the way to salvation for those who would escape the world's clutches.

Dialogue with the World

Vatican II attempted to bring the church beyond the fortress mentality. The openness of Vatican II represented a virtual about-face from a suspicious scrutiny of a world seen as hostile to a sensitive reaching out to a world seen as bursting with potential. Some commentators view this as the single most significant development of the council.[3]

Pope John XXIII helped to usher in this shift with his calls for *aggior namento* (updating) leading up to Vatican II. The most important achievement of Vatican II in regard to dialogue with the world was *Gaudium et Spes*, the Pastoral Constitution on the Church in the Modern World. *Lumen Gentium* stated its purpose as expressing the "nature and mission" of the church; *Gaudium et Spes* stated its own purpose as explaining "the presence and activity of the church in the world today" (*GS*, 2). The "world" in *Gaudium et Spes* is seen as a basically good though ambiguous place. It is full of potential, but also dangers: "The modern world shows itself at once powerful and weak, capable of the noblest deeds or the foulest; before it lies the path to freedom or to slavery, to progress or retreat, to brotherhood or hatred" (*GS*, 9). The document goes on to explain that the "religious" is not opposed to the "human": "...Christians are convinced that the triumphs of the human race are a sign of God's grace and the flowering of God's own mysterious design" (*GS*, 34).

Gaudium et Spes several times expresses the desire of the church to enter into conversation with the modern world:

> ...this Council can provide no more eloquent proof of its solidarity with, as well as its respect and love for the entire human family with which it is bound up, than by engaging it in conversation about these various problems. (*GS*, 3)

The gospel message needs to be reformulated in accordance with the "signs of the times" (*GS*, 4). Among the signs of the times is that the world has entered into a new stage of history characterized by rapid social change and tremendous potential for good and for ill. These times lead people to ask deep questions about why life is the way that it is. Is there hope? Is there ultimate meaning? What is any of this struggle for?

The role of the church is to address these questions by offering to the world its teaching about the saving mystery of Christ. This in itself is nothing new. What is most new in the document is the emphatic manner in which the church acknowledges that God can be served either through explicit witness or through service. People can do the will of God in many ways:

> Now, the gifts of the Spirit are diverse; while the Spirit calls some to give clear witness to the desire for a heavenly home and to keep that desire fresh among the human family, the Spirit summons others to dedicate themselves to the earthly service of human beings and to make ready the material of the celestial realm by this ministry of theirs. (*GS*, 38)

The world is good. Human beings possess a fundamental dignity as being made in the image and likeness of God. Yet individuals are not isolated; human beings are social by nature. Human efforts are not in vain; in spite of the dangers, God is on the side of those who work for human advancement. Human progress helps to lay a groundwork in preparation for the coming of God's kingdom. In Christ we find the assurance that life, which does not end in death, contains these meanings. Such is the message that *Gaudium et Spes* holds out to the world.

Church as Leaven in the World

Gaudium et Spes goes even deeper than seeing the world as a good place and engaging in conversation with it; it also recognizes the world as the main arena of human activity, and the church as a servant to the world. One way that the church expresses its message is to say:

> To those, therefore, who believe in divine love, God gives assurance that the way of love lies open to human beings and that the effort to establish a universal brotherhood is not a hopeless one. (*GS*, 38)

In the centuries prior to Vatican II, the church pictured itself mainly as a refuge from the world of vanity and temptation. In *Gaudium et Spes*, the church portrayed itself "as a leaven and as a kind of soul for human society as it is to be renewed in Christ and transformed into God's family" (*GS*, 40). In other words, the church approves of many elements of contemporary social movements and sees itself as wishing to collaborate and make a contribution to that which is already good.

To put it yet another way: prior to Vatican II, the leadership of the church tended to perceive its role as being servants to Christ and spiritual rulers of those who had converted to the church from the world. In *Gaudium et Spes*, the church is presented as the servant to what is good in the world, whether or not the world has explicitly converted to Christ. The sinful nature of human beings and the insufficiency of merely earthly progress are noted; however, working for peace and economic justice ceased being optional extras and were seen instead as integral to the gospel message. The opening lines of the document capture its overall stress on the importance of human solidarity:

> The joys and hopes, the griefs and the anxieties of the people of this age, especially those who are poor or in any way afflicted, these are the joys and hopes, the griefs and anxieties of the followers of Christ.

Message from the Sixties?

Gaudium et Spes was issued at the close of Vatican II in 1965. In the United States, the following years were to find hippies, Viet Nam War protests, Woodstock, and widespread social change often expressed through sex, drugs, and hard rock. It was the days of the early peace movement, of Martin Luther King, of landing on the moon. Electric bards told us to tear down the walls, to give peace a chance, to get together and try to love one another right now. The moon was in the seventh house, Jupiter was aligned with Mars, and many youth expected that it would not be so difficult to overthrow the corrupt world of our parents and build a new peaceful society based on justice and universal love.

Gaudium et Spes itself was not quite so optimistic. It discusses the sinful nature of human beings in three different passages (10, 13, 25). It never discusses the goodness of the world without mentioning also its ambiguities. It does not believe that any total human emancipation can be achieved through human effort alone. It stresses the importance of human progress, but in several passages it is clear that the world can also take quite a different turn if human beings do not take proper responsibility.

Yet, when measured against former church documents, *Gaudium et Spes* is extremely optimistic in its hope for human progress on a global scale. Some church leaders have felt that it was much too optimistic. The following passage from the final document of the Extraordinary Synod of 1985 tries to cautiously affirm *Gaudium et Spes* while reasserting the important role played by church authority:

> The church as communion is a sacrament for the salvation of the world. Therefore the authorities in the church have been placed there by Christ for the salvation of the world. In this context we affirm the great importance and timeliness of the pastoral constitution, Gaudium et Spes. At the same time, however, we perceive that the signs of our time are in part different from those of the time of the council, with greater problems and anguish. Today, in fact, everywhere in the world we witness an increase in hunger, oppression, injustice and war, sufferings, terrorism, and other forms of violence of every sort. This requires a new and more profound theological reflection in order to interpret these signs in the light of the Gospel.[4]

In the English version, this subsection of the document is ironically entitled "Importance of the Constitution, *Gaudium et Spes.*" As I read it, it says that *Gaudium et Spes* was too optimistic, that it needs to be read in a context that highlights the importance of church authority, that the world has not gotten better but indeed is much worse, and that we are in need of a more profound theology if we are to carry out our mission in the world.

The Synod document suggested that a theology stressing the goodness of creation needs to be balanced by a theology stressing the importance of the cross, and that regeneration of the world needs to take place through an encounter with the proclamation of the Good News. The document seems to present itself as more realistic than *Gaudium et Spes:* "When we Christians speak of the cross, we do not deserve to be labelled pessimists, but we rather found ourselves upon the realism of Christian hope" (section 449). The overall message of the Extraordinary Synod was a resounding affirmation of Vatican II; its reservations and qualifications, however, make for a strong undercurrent.

Summary

In this chapter we have examined some of the complex history of the various ways that Catholics and Protestants have viewed the relationship between the church and the world. Against that background, we discussed how Vatican II set a new optimistic tone for Catholic attitudes toward dialogue with the world. Finally, we looked at how a 1985 Catholic synod took a more pessimistic outlook toward the current state of world affairs. I suppose that the pendulum will keep swinging.

I can agree that the dream of a world united in peace and love seems farther off now than it did in the 1960s. I cannot help but think, however, that *Gaudium et Spes* is a deep reflection of the message of the gospel for our times. It has been extended but by no means surpassed by more recent documents. Many Christians can still hear the lesson of St. Christopher even as they listen seriously to the cautions of the Extraordinary Synod.

In the next chapter we will discuss Vatican II's response to atheism and the question of God.

FOR FURTHER REFLECTION

1. In what way does the story of St. Christopher speak to you?

2. Is it possible for religion to be too "worldly?" Is it possible for religion not to be "worldly" enough?

3. Have today's youth lost their idealism in contrast with the students of the 1960s?

4. Can one serve God just as well by working within the world as one can through explicitly religious ways?

5. If you had to choose, would you be more supportive of *Gaudium et Spes* or of the Extraordinary Synod of 1985 on points where they seem to be in contrast?

SUGGESTED READINGS

Cooke, Bernard. *Sacraments and Sacramentality.* Mystic, Conn.: Twenty-Third Publications, 1983.

Cunningham, Lawrence. *The Catholic Heritage.* New York: Crossroad, 1983.

Maritain, Jacques. *The Peasant of the Garrone.* New York: Holt, Rinehart, and Winston, 1968 [1966].

McBrien, Richard P. *Church: The Continuing Quest.* New York: Newman Press, 1970.

Metz, Johann Baptist. *The Emergent Church.* New York: Crossroad, 1981.

Mühlenberger, Richard. *The Bible in Art: The New Testament.* New York: Moore and Moore Publishing, 1990.

Mühlenberger, Richard. *The Bible in Art: The Old Testament.* New York: Moore and Moore Publishing, 1991.

CHAPTER 29

ATHEISM AND THE NEW THEISM

C hild psychiatrist Robert Coles reports the following statement from a thirteen-year-old Christian student in a private school near Boston:

You take the kids whose folks aren't into any religion; we have lots of them in our school, and they're no different from anyone, and some of them—I talk with them about what they believe—are really great, because they ask a lot of questions about life, and they want to stop and talk about things, about what's right and wrong, and what you should believe, and after I'll talk with them, I'll say to myself, hey, maybe if you have no religion, you end up being more religious. You know what I mean?[1]

I know what he means. Throughout my life I have wondered about the goodness of people who seem to hold beliefs not only different from my own but at times contradictory to them. For the brief period of my life when I was an atheist, I sometimes marveled at the wisdom and goodness of people who had not yet grown beyond their Catholicism. As a Catholic again, I am often impressed by the spiritual insight and moral integrity of people who label themselves atheists.

This Chapter
Something similar seems to have been on the minds of the bishops at Vatican II. In this chapter we will examine the challenge of Marxism and other philosophies that lurk in the background of *Gaudium et Spes*, investigate the approach to the question of God offered by the great

258

theologian Karl Rahner, and then see how Rahner's approach influenced Vatican II's interpretation of atheism.

This material is related to the discussion of atheism in chapter 1 of *Gaudium et Spes*.

The Systematic Expression of Atheism

Atheism can refer to any system of thought that includes the claim that there is no God. *Gaudium et Spes*, without mentioning any names of persons, singles out two types of atheism. The first type resembles most closely the existentialism associated with mid-twentieth century writers such as Jean-Paul Sartre and Albert Camus. Existentialism is a philosophy that places great emphasis on the freedom of human beings to shape reality without being hampered by pre-set categories. *Gaudium et Spes* says:

> Those who profess atheism of this sort maintain that it gives human beings freedom to be an end unto themselves, the sole artisans and creators of their own history. They claim that this freedom cannot be reconciled with the affirmation of a Lord Who is author and purpose of all things, or at least that this freedom makes such an affirmation altogether superfluous. (*GS*, 20)

The document's response to existentialism can be found in an earlier passage that links true freedom with God:

> ...human dignity demands that people act according to a knowing and free choice that is personally motivated and prompted from within, not under blind internal impulse nor by mere external pressure. People achieve such dignity when, emancipating themselves from all captivity to passion, they pursue their goal in a spontaneous choice of what is good and procure for themselves, through effective and skilful action, aids to that end. Since human freedom has been damaged by sin, only by the aid of God's grace can people bring such a relationship with God into full flower. (*GS*, 17)

Such a general discussion was not intended to be either a full presentation of existentialism or a full response to it. It was simply an allusion to existentialist philosophy and a statement that the key to disagreements lies in the meaning of "freedom" and in the relationship of freedom to God.

Gaudium et Spes gives a somewhat fuller (but by no means complete) treatment of a second type of atheism, Marxism:

> Not to be overlooked among the forms of modern atheism is that which anticipates the liberation of humankind especially through economic and social emancipation. This form argues that by its nature religion thwarts this liberation by arousing hope for a deceptive future life, thereby diverting people from the constructing of the earthly city. Consequently when the proponents of this doctrine gain governmental power they vigorously fight against religion, and promote atheism by using, especially in the education of youth, those means of pressure which public power has at its disposal. (*GS*, 20)

As is the case with existentialism, neither Marxism nor Marx is mentioned explicitly by name.

Gaudium et Spes takes very seriously the Marxist charge that the church's teaching about afterlife encourages people not to take this life seriously. It reaffirms that "...the church has been taught by divine revelation and firmly teaches that human beings have been created by God for a blissful purpose beyond the reach of earthly misery" (*GS*, 18). Yet in several passages it makes the point that a belief in eternal life should help rather than hurt one's motivation to work for the betterment of this world. The document states that "while we are warned that it profits a man nothing if he gain the whole world and lose himself, the expectation of a new earth must not weaken but rather stimulate our concern for cultivating this one" (*GS*, 39). An injunction often repeated in the document is that "a hope related to the end of time does not diminish the importance of intervening duties but rather undergirds the acquittal of them with fresh incentives" (*GS*, 21). The salvation of the human race remains clearly the mission of the church, but "salvation" is considered not simply as something that happens on the last day, but as a multidimensional process that has its roots in this life. We are to begin working toward the kingdom right here and right now.[2]

Although it is not a simple issue, it could at least be argued that Marxism has been one positive factor in motivating the Catholic church to emphasize the this-worldly dimension of the gospel message.

The Endpoint of Our Self-Transcendence

In order to understand the response of *Gaudium et Spes* to atheism, it will be helpful to examine the approach to the question of God taken by Karl Rahner, an influential figure at Vatican II as well as one of the most important Catholic theologians of the twentieth century.[3] Rahner is not so much interested in giving a classical "proof" for the existence of God as he is in demonstrating what believers appropriately mean when they speak of "God."

Rahner thinks that in order to talk about who God is, it is useful to begin with talking about who human beings are. The most important consideration here is that human beings are *self-transcendent*; that is, human beings are not purely self-contained within limited boundaries but have the capacity to move beyond themselves.

Our self-transcendence can be seen in our experience of knowing, willing, and loving. When we seek to know something, we are aware not only of our personal limitations but also of our awareness of an ultimate context within which some things are really true. When we know, we want to know not just things that seem true to us; we want to know what is really true in the highest possible context outside of ourselves. Within each of us, if we dig deep enough, we can get in touch with this inner drive toward self-transcendence, the desire to know what is really true, no matter what we might otherwise wish to be true for our own convenience.

Similarly, when we seek to do what is good, we seek a goodness that is beyond our own immediate desires and satisfactions. Within each of us is a desire to do what is truly good, even if this at times requires personal suffering. Likewise, when we truly love another person, we move beyond ourselves to a concern for that person as he or she is, not just for what that person can do for us.

None of us is at all times in complete touch with our inner drives toward self-transcendence. Some of us may rarely or even never consciously experience such drives. Yet Rahner believes that it is part of the nature of the human being to have this potential to transcend oneself. Human growth in general can be characterized as the experience of growing beyond one's narrow and limited concerns to a personal identification with higher perspectives that take the well-being of others into account.

Having established that human beings are self-transcendent, Rahner is ready to give an account of what we should mean by "God." I have constructed the following "definition" to try to represent what Rahner means:

God is the endpoint of our transcendence when we are moving beyond ourselves towards truth, goodness, and love.

I use the word "endpoint" to translate the German word, *"woraufhin."* *Woraufhin* has been translated as "whither," "term," and "orientation." What the definition is saying is that when we are transcending ourselves by moving in the direction of truth, goodness, and love, the One toward whom we are ultimately moving is God. God is the endpoint of our inner drive toward self-transcendence.

Rahner emphasizes that each one of us must come to grips with our relationship with God in our own way. The following passage, though long and difficult, illustrates this point:

> The individual person, of course, experiences this [awareness of relation to God] best in that basic situation of his own existence which occurs with special intensity for him as an individual. If, therefore, he is really to understand this reflection on "proofs" for God's existence, the individual person must reflect precisely upon whatever is the clearest experience for him: on the luminous and incomprehensible light of his spirit; on the capacity for absolute questioning which a person directs against himself and which seemingly reduces him to nothing, but in which he reaches radically beyond himself; on annihilating anxiety, which is something quite different from fear of a definite object and is prior to the latter as the condition of its possibility; on that joy which surpasses all understanding; on an absolute moral obligation in which a person really goes beyond himself; on the experience of death in which he faces himself in his absolute powerlessness. Man reflects upon these and many other modes of the basic and transcendental experience of human existence. Because he experiences himself as finite in his self-questioning, he is not able to identify himself with the ground which discloses itself in this experience as what is innermost and at the same time what is absolutely different. The explicit proofs for God's existence only make thematic this fundamental structure and its term.[4]

In other words, each of us needs to find a way to come to grips with our own self-transcendence. When we do this, we can come to a recognition of what it means to say that in our experience of self-transcendence we become aware of a mysterious ground beyond ourselves that makes self-transcendence possible. This infinite mystery that grounds our ultimate questioning, striving, suffering, and loving, is what we mean by "God."

Rahner believes that this God of infinite mystery has been unsurpassably revealed in the person of Jesus Christ, and that it is most appropriate to relate to God as "personal." However, on the basis of the structure of our own experience, we encounter God first as the infinite mystery that calls us forth toward truth, goodness, and love.

Anonymous Theists?

Have you ever known something to be so, but in a way that you could not yet put it into words? I remember the first time I heard a lecture on family systems analysis. I had never even heard of this topic before, and yet the lecture so spoke to my own experience of family that I realized that in a way I had known these things all along. The inklings that I had of this prior knowledge through my own experience is what Karl Rahner calls *pre-reflective* knowledge. The clear concepts and tools of analysis discussed in the lecture represent what Rahner calls *categorical* knowledge.

Rahner uses a similar distinction to talk about two different levels on which we "know" God. We do not simply deduce logically that God is the term of our transcendence; on a deep level of consciousness we actually experience God in this way as the one toward whom we are drawn. According to Rahner, *transcendental* knowledge of God refers to this basic experience of God prior to any reflection or conceptualization. It is a pre-reflective experience of God. *Categorical* knowledge of God refers to our ideas and concepts of God in a way that we can clearly think about and communicate with others.

Rahner's distinction can be helpful for understanding what he means by God. To accept God on a *transcendental* level is to embrace the call to respond to life's challenges in an open, willing, and loving manner. It is to be disposed to choose truth, goodness, and love over self-deceit, narrowness, and selfishness. To reject God on a transcendental level is to refuse to affirm life or to accept life's challenges for growth. It is to be closed inward upon one's own narrow world, being disposed to act most often simply in one's own selfish interests without regard for others.

To accept God on a *categorical* level is to have some notion or idea of God and to say, "I believe in God." To reject God on a categorical level is to say, "I do not believe in God. I am an atheist."

Here is where Rahner's analysis becomes especially interesting. It is possible, as many people do, to accept God on both a transcendental and a categorical level. Such is a good theist. It is also possible to reject God on both a transcendental and a categorical level. Such is the stereotypical atheist.

It is also possible, however, as Rahner argues, to accept God on a transcendental level through one's commitment to truth, goodness, and love, while at the same time rejecting one's concept of God on a categorical level. This person says, "I am an atheist." At the same time, though, this person lives life in an ongoing affirmation of the transcendent mystery that Christians call "God." In a sense, according to Rahner, such a person accepts God but without knowing it. Rahner labels such a person an "anonymous theist."

How does it happen that a person becomes an anonymous theist? Usually it is because that person rejects the more common concepts of God that are available in that person's milieu. In other words, the more that inadequate concepts of God are preached and lived out by Christians, the more likely it is that basically good people will become "atheists." Anonymous theists reject not the one who God really is, but their own inadequate concepts of God.

Yet Rahner's analysis does not end here. Rahner also takes the position that on a categorical level most Christians believe not in the true God of infinite mystery but in an inadequate concept of God, something of an idol. That is, most Christians have tended to settle for a nice old man or a fearsome judge rather than the infinite One who calls them forth in their deepest being. Yet Rahner also believes that the majority of such people do accept God on a transcendental level; that is, they are basically good people who could do with a few major adjustments in the ways in which they think about God.

	Transcendental	Categorical
Christian believer	Yes	Yes to mystery
stereotypical atheist	No	No
anonymous theist	Yes	No
many Christians	Yes	Yes to idol
another possibility?	No	Yes to idol

A Catholic Response to Atheism

Gaudium et Spes shows the influence of Karl Rahner in its approach to God and atheism. On the one hand is a clear rejection of atheism:

...the church has already repudiated and cannot cease repudiating, sorrowfully but as firmly as possible, those poisonous doctrines and actions which contradict reason and the common experience of humanity, and dethrone human beings from their native excellence. (*GS*, 21)

On the other hand, however, is a sincere reaching out to atheists, an explicit acknowledgment of the profound issues raised by atheism, and an attempt to explore sympathetically the causes of atheism.

The document mentions several causes of atheism:

1. The use of philosophical methods that are locked into their own skeptical presuppositions.
2. The belief that science can explain everything.
3. An extravagant affirmation of human beings without leaving room for God.
4. Some people do not seem to experience religious stirrings.
5. The rejection of fallacious ideas about God.
6. A violent protest against the existence of evil and suffering.
7. Putting certain human values (e.g., nationalism, social status) in the place of God.
8. Willfully shutting out God from one's heart.
9. A critical reaction to certain religious beliefs and practices, sometimes against the Christian religion in particular. (adapted from *GS*, 19)

The influence of Rahner can be seen throughout these reasons, particularly in what I have listed as reasons 4 and 5. In Rahnerian terms, reason 4 says that many people are out of touch with their own inner drives toward self-transcendence. Reason 5 says that some people reject on a categorical level the ideas and concepts of God to which they have been exposed.

An even more important influence of Rahner can be detected in the document's discussion of what I have listed as reasons 8 and 9. As I read the document, it is saying that although some people who are atheists may truly know what they are doing when they reject God, it is also likely that many atheists are basically good people who have been presented with an inadequate picture of religion, particularly Christianity. The document says that "believers themselves frequently bear some responsibility for this situation" (*GS*, 19).

In other words, following Rahner, the document is critical of believers whose own categorical concepts of God and whose own lifestyles may contribute to the existence of atheism. Thus it says: "The remedy which must be applied to atheism, however, is to be sought in a proper presentation of the church's teaching as well as in the integral life of the church and her members" (GS, 21).

Although it rejects atheism, "root and branch," *Gaudium et Spes* says that all human beings, "believers and unbelievers alike, ought to work for the rightful betterment of this world in which all alike live; such an ideal cannot be realized, however, apart from sincere and prudent dialogue" (GS, 21). The comments on atheists conclude with an expressed hope for their salvation: "since Christ died for all human beings, and since the ultimate vocation of human beings is in fact one, and divine, we ought to believe that the Holy Spirit in a manner known only to God offers to every person the possibility of being associated with this paschal mystery" (GS, 22).

Summary

In this chapter we have investigated Vatican II's response to atheism, with special emphasis on the theology of Karl Rahner and his influence on *Gaudium et Spes*.

Rahner's explanations concerning God and atheism are very intriguing. His ideas on these issues have influenced me more than those of any other theologian. But his positions also have their own significant limitations. His focus on the experience of God through our own self-transcendence can too easily be used to overlook the political realities of the concrete world in which we find ourselves. Also, his position that good atheists are really unwittingly good Christians does not seem to do justice to what atheists themselves have to say. I am certain, however, that Rahner would find in my dissatisfactions and in my hope for an even better explanation a sign of my self-transcendent questioning, which will ultimately bring me face to face with the experience of infinite mystery that we call "God."

In the next chapter we will discuss the relationship of Christianity with other world religions.

FOR FURTHER REFLECTION

1. Have you ever encountered the phenomenon of the "good atheist?"

2. Have you ever encountered someone who talked a lot about God or who quoted the Bible frequently but who did not seem to be a good person?

3. Do you agree with Karl Rahner that on a categorical level many people worship an "idol?"

4. Did Vatican II go too far in suggesting that some atheism may be caused by the failings of Christian believers?

5. In what ways have you grown in your own life concerning how you think about God?

SUGGESTED READINGS

Greeley, Andrew M. *God in Popular Culture.* Chicago: Thomas More Press, 1988.

Haught, John F. *What Is God? How to Think about the Divine.* Mahwah, N.J.: Paulist Press, 1986.

Küng, Hans. *Does God Exist? An Answer for Today.* Garden City, N.Y.: Doubleday, 1980 [1978].

McFague, Sallie. *Models of God: Theology for an Ecological, Nuclear Age.* Philadelphia: Fortress Press, 1987.

Phillips, J.B. *Your God Is Too Small.* New York: Macmillan, 1953.

Rahner, Karl. *Foundations of the Christian Faith.* New York: Crossroad, 1978 [1976].

CHAPTER 30

RELIGIOUS PLURALISM

When I had completed the majority of my doctoral work in religious studies, I took a trip to Egypt. While I was there I visited several mosques. Most of the mosques I entered were large ones accustomed to receiving tourists. There were designated places to leave one's shoes outside.

One afternoon I was walking down a narrow back street in Cairo when I came upon a small, neighborhood mosque. I was curious, so I took off my shoes and went in. Several people were sitting on the ground praying. I put my shoes down and did the same.

While I was in prayer, a young man of about twenty came up and asked me if I was a Muslim. I said no, I was a Christian. He shooed me out of the mosque by motioning with his hands, saying, "Muslims only. Muslims only." I apologized and was out the door before I knew it.

A few moments later, as I was tying my shoes, the young man and a companion came out to talk with me. The companion asked what I had been doing in the mosque. When I told him I was praying, he invited me back in.

The three of us sat down together and were quickly joined by three more young men. The man who had chased me out explained to me that I must place my shoes down with the soles facing each other; when he had seen my shoes sole-side down, he knew something was wrong, because such was an insult to God.

These young men were all of college age. One was studying to be a veterinarian. Another was studying to be an aeronautical engineer. All knew some English, and a few were fluent in it.

They asked me what I thought about their holy book, the Qur'an. Because I had recently been studying academic perspectives on world religions (from a somewhat sociological point of view), I felt comfortable saying that "The Qur'an is the word of God." In saying this, I was not intending to give personal testimony, but simply to acknowledge that I recognize how the Qur'an authentically functions as the word of God for many millions of people.

The young men were getting excited. They wanted to know what I thought of Muhammad. From the same perspective that I had affirmed the Qur'an, I repeated another of their formulas: "Muhammad is God's prophet."

After a brief consultation in Arabic, one of them ran out and came back a couple of minutes later with three books, each of which had Arabic on one side and English on the other. They made a present to me of these books, and asked me to read aloud some basic professions of faith from one of them.

It was at this point that I realized that they did not think, as I did, that we were simply engaging in interreligious dialogue. They thought that they had a convert on their hands, and they were formally welcoming me into their religion by having me make a public profession of faith. For a moment I was scared. Ancient images flashed through my mind of Muslims using large saber swords to lop off the heads of infidels. But I summoned the courage to say, "No, no, you misunderstand. I respect and revere your religion, but I wish to remain Christian."

It was as though a sigh of disappointed relief swept through the mosque. Without uttering a word, the looks on their faces read, "But why didn't you say so in the first place?" I had gotten them all excited, but their making of a new Muslim was not to be.

Our conversation soon recovered from this low point, however. We had an interesting discussion about religious beliefs. They brought up the ridiculousness of the Christian belief in the Trinity. I assured them that Christians profess ultimately to believe in one God. I explained to them that Jesus functions in our religion something like the way that the Qur'an functions in theirs; that is, just as they believe that God's word has come to them most fully in the Qur'an, Christians believe that God's word has come to them most fully in the person of Jesus. Most Christians do not place the Bible on as high a level as Muslims place the Qur'an. No Muslim places Muhammad on the same level that Christians place Jesus. From my point of view, I explained, the doctrine of the Trinity is not at all ridiculous; it is a formal way for Christians to express their experience of Jesus as Lord and their belief that the Spirit is at work within them.

My new friends were surprised to hear that Christians believed in hell. In retrospect, I think that their surprise stemmed from a combination of thinking that their own most basic beliefs are unique and that the Western world is too corrupt to be populated by any large number of people who are aware that hell is a possibility.

I corresponded with one of these young men for a couple of years afterward. I look back on the incident fondly as a wonderful religious interchange and as a reminder that what begins in misunderstanding can end in fruitful conversation.

This Chapter
In this chapter we will investigate how the official attitude of the Catholic church toward other religions shifted at Vatican II. We will begin with a brief look at some prior attitudes, examine the position taken at Vatican II, and finally discuss various stances that Christians take concerning this issue.

This chapter is related to *Gaudium et Spes* insofar as that document calls for dialogue with the world; it is more directly related, however, to the Council's Declaration on the Relation of the Church to Non-Christian Religions (*Nostra Aetate*).

The One True Faith
Throughout the history of Christianity, the majority of Christians have held that Christianity is the one true faith and that Jesus is the savior of the world in a cosmic sense. The quantity and seriousness of this testimony is something that no Christian can afford to take lightly. There are many lines in the New Testament that have been interpreted as buttressing this view:

No one can enter the kingdom of God without being born of water and Spirit. (John 3:5)

Whoever believes in him will not be condemned, but whoever does not believe has already been condemned, because he has not believed in the name of the only Son of God. (John 3:18)

Jesus said to [Thomas], "I am the way and the truth and the life. No one comes to the Father except through me." (John 14:6)

There is no salvation through anyone else, nor is there any other name under heaven given to the human race by which we are to be saved. (Acts 4:12)

Some Christians have believed that only Christians can be saved at the end of the world. Many other Christians have maintained that whereas Christ is the only real savior, many non-Christians can be saved because the grace of God that comes through Christ is somehow made available to all. That is, many people are saved by embracing the grace that is available to them, even though they may not know the name of Christ or have perhaps rejected an inadequate presentation of Christianity.

Both of these positions share the belief that all salvation ultimately comes through Christ. Although these positions may have their drawbacks, their clear strength is their fidelity to the long-standing Christian claim that Jesus came not just to save a few but to effect the salvation of the human race from the original sin that continues to distort it. Jesus did not just teach a good path, but is in himself the incarnation of God, who set right the relationship between God and the human race. Those who are quick to embrace other religions as equal have a lot of explaining to do about their own faithfulness to the Christian tradition.

I do not in any way mean to imply here that the explanations offered by theologians who argue for the salvific potential of other religions are not often good ones. Christian language that seems to imply that other religions are false can often be interpreted as encouragements to insiders not to abandon their faith in the face of pagan cults; they were not originally intended to be universal condemnations of other world religions. Also, such language can be interpreted as being like love language; to say to a lover, "you are the only one," or "you are the most wonderful person in the world," is to express something real without pretending it to be a fully objective statement. Another explanation of such statements is that they reflect the intensity of the experience of the early Christians; one can embrace the Christian experience today without embracing exaggerated implications of the ways in which it was expressed.

Those who say that Christianity is necessarily the only real path to salvation have had their own set of problems that need explanation. How can one account for the goodness and wisdom of the long and often venerable religious traditions of the world? Catholic textbooks written prior to Vatican II at times reflected more prejudice than accuracy when describing other world religions.

Although the following example is a bit extreme, it represents the kind of attitude that can develop. In a 1939 Irish textbook for a first-year college theology course, Bishop Michael Sheehan gives a very unflattering description of the origin and teaching of Buddhism, and then

offers the following as one of the main reasons for Buddhism's popularity:

> its toleration of sin, for it taught that those who indulged their
> passions did not lose, but merely delayed, their final happiness.[1]

After a likewise unflattering description of Islam, Sheehan accounts
for its popularity by:

> its pandering to base passions; but above all to the might of the
> sword.

Sheehan goes on to say that, unlike Christianity, neither Buddhism
nor Islam have ever "received the divine testimony of manifest and
well authenticated miracles." Sheehan's presuppositions about the in-
adequacies of other religions prevent him from giving a fair or accurate
assessment.

Vatican II on Other Religions

Vatican II's Declaration of the Relation of the Church to Non-
Christian Religions differs greatly in approach and tone from Michael
Sheehan's textbook. The document begins with an affirmation that human beings form but one community and that we share a common destiny in God. It then gives a very sympathetic description of various
world religions, especially highlighting Hinduism and Buddhism:

> Thus, in Hinduism people explore the divine mystery and express
> it both in the limitless riches of myth and the accurately defined
> insights of philosophy. They ask release from the trials of present
> life by ascetical practices, profound meditation, and recourse to
> God in confidence and love.

> Buddhism in its various forms testifies to the essential inadequacy
> of this changing world. It proposes a way of life by which people
> can, with confidence and trust, attain a state of perfect liberation
> and reach supreme illumination either through their own efforts
> or by the aid of divine help. (section 2)

The document then expresses the new openness in attitude of the
church:

> The Catholic church rejects nothing of what is true and holy in

these religions. The church has a high regard for the manner of life and conduct, the precepts and doctrines which, although differing in many ways from its own teaching, nevertheless often reflects a ray of that truth which enlightens all people. (section 2)

Now, read closely, the above passage is not an overwhelming endorsement of these religions. Taken out of its historical context, it might be read as "damning with faint praise." After all, it merely says that these religions reflect "a ray" of the truth to which all people have access. The paragraph goes on to remind Christians that it remains the duty of the church to proclaim Christ, who is the way, the truth and the life.

Read within its historical context, however, the passage represents a major shift in the Catholic position in the direction of openness and dialogue. Indeed, the document urges Christians to engage in discussion and collaboration with people of other faiths.

Muslims and Jews

The declaration has a separate section for Islam and another one for Judaism. This is because of the special ties between Christianity and these other Western, monotheistic religions. In regard to Islam, the document notes its many links with the faith of Christians, and expresses regrets for past quarrels and dissentions.

In regard to Judaism, the document discusses at some length the deep ties formed within a shared religious heritage. It mentions that the initiating figures of Christianity were all of Jewish descent; that although the Jews did not accept Jesus they remain dear to the God who has not taken back his promise of the covenant; that it is inappropriate to speak of the Jews as rejected or accursed; that although some Jewish authorities pressed for the death of Jesus, Jews cannot be indiscriminately charged with this crime today; that the church reproves all religious persecution, particularly any that has been leveled from any source against the Jews.

The declaration closes with a rejection of any discrimination against anyone on the basis of race, color, condition in life, or religion. Overall, its outlook toward other religions is very positive, looking forward to dialogue and collaboration.

Contemporary Positions

The position represented by Michael Sheehan and others who reject other religions as false and misleading is known as *exclusivism*. The

position that one's own religion is the highest religion but that other religions are basically good insofar as they reflect truth in a partial way is
known as *inclusivism*. That is, one's own religion is extended in a broad
way as including all people of good will.

Karl Rahner proposed a well-known form of inclusivism by claiming
that people of other faiths who live a good life are actually Christian although they do not know it. Rahner believed that the Christ event is
the highest and unsurpassable expression of the drama that underlies
every life story. Anyone who affirmatively answers the call to embrace
the mystery of life has thereby accepted Christ. At first Rahner referred
to such a person as an "anonymous Christian," one who is a Christian
without knowing it. He later dropped the term because some people
found it offensive, although he still defended the basic concept. (Those
who found the term offensive thought that it showed disrespect for
other religions in and of themselves.)

The documents of Vatican II represent a shift from an *exclusivist* position to an *inclusivist* position. Christianity is still presented as the final, cosmic truth about the meaning of life. Vatican II says little to emphasize that other religions must still be second best, but such a
position is clearly implied in a close reading of the documents.

Many theologians and scholars of religion do not believe that an inclusivist position goes far enough. Few scholars would hold a position
traditionally known as *indifferentism*, which is the belief that all religions are really just basically the same. Many scholars, however, operate
out of what I will call a *comparativist stance*. This position acknowledges
great differences among religions, but also presumes that one cannot
make prior judgments about one religion being superior to another.

This is the position that I associate most with Raimundo Panikkar,
whose mother was a Catholic and whose father was a Hindu. In his
work *The Intra-Religious Dialogue*,[2] Panikkar gives several images that
try to illustrate analogously how the various religions are related: They
are like bands of color in the rainbow; they are like different types of
maps for the same territory; they are like different languages. Panikkar
encourages dialogues in which people try in a sense to trade faiths for a
while and to speak to each other from within the other's faith.

Many academic scholars operate out of a comparativist stance. Wilfred Cantwell Smith, a well-known Christian scholar of Islam, spent a
good portion of his academic career wrestling with the question of how
faiths that are so different can express ultimate truth in such a personal
way to various peoples.[3]

Some theologians, however, do not find it satisfactory to simply put on the shelf the matter of the ultimacy of their own faith. Yet some of them, too, want to move beyond an inclusivism that presumes superiority. Such is the position of Dutch theologian Edward Schillebeeckx,[4] who takes what I label a *dialogic stance*. This is the position that one testifies to the belief or experience of ultimacy within one's own tradition, but remains willing to engage in dialogue with people of other faiths without assuming their inferiority. Schillebeeckx says, "I believe in Jesus of Nazareth." He is then ready to engage in interreligious discussion without presupposing that another religion could not also in some way be authentically experienced as ultimate.

A dialogic stance is a delicately balanced position that can easily collapse back into an inclusivism or a comparativism. Schillebeeckx, for example, after laying out a dialogic approach, seems often to arrive at the advantages of Christianity when he does in fact engage in comparative discussions.

exclusivist	=	other religions are false and misleading
inclusivist	=	my religion is the highest; others are good
indifferentist	=	all religions are basically the same
comparativist	=	religions are different; study open-mindedly
dialogic	=	my religion has ultimacy; I'm open to the possibility of ultimacy in other religions

Summary

In this chapter we have discussed the shift at Vatican II from an exclusivist position concerning other religions toward an inclusivist position. We also discussed the range of positions that are reflected in theology today.

Interreligious dialogue raises great questions about truth and the meaning of life. After my interreligious dialogue with the Muslim students in Cairo, I am convinced of one thing: I do not know the final answers to these questions; probably only God does.

In the next chapter we will examine the underlying principles of Catholic social teaching.

FOR FURTHER REFLECTION

1. Are you satisfied with the type and amount of exposure to world religions you were given in your own education?

2. If Christians believe that Jesus Christ is God incarnate, does it necessarily follow that other religions cannot be quite as good?

3. What do you think is the best way to interpret the exclusivist language often used within the history of the Christian tradition?

4. Do all religions boil down to basically the same principles?

5. What is your own position concerning the relationship among the major religions of the world?

SUGGESTED READINGS

Biallas, Leonard J. *World Religions: A Story Approach.* Mystic, Conn.: Twenty-Third Publications, 1991.

Johnston, William. *The Mirror Mind: Spirituality and Transformation.* San Francisco: Harper & Row, 1981.

Knitter, Paul F. *No Other Name? A Critical Survey of Christian Attitudes Toward the World Religions.* Maryknoll, N.Y.: Orbis Books, 1985.

Panikkar, Raimundo. *The Intra-Religious Dialogue.* Mahwah, N.J.: Paulist Press, 1978.

Smith, Huston. *The Religions of Man.* New York: Harper & Row, 1958.

Smith, Wilfred Cantwell. *Religious Diversity.* New York: Harper & Row, 1976.

SECTION TWO

PRINCIPLES, FAMILY, CULTURE

CHAPTER 31

UNDERLYING PRINCIPLES
OF CATHOLIC SOCIAL TEACHING

I n her short story, "Revelation,"[1] Flannery O'Connor tells of Ruby
Turpin, a Southern white woman of the 1950s who has the world
divided into neat rankings of people:

> Mrs. Turpin occupied herself at night naming the classes of peo-
> ple. On the bottom of the heap were most colored people, not the
> kind that she would have been if she had been one, but most of
> them; then next to them—not above, just away from—were the
> white trash; then above them were the home owners, and above
> them the home-and-land owners, to which she and Claud be-
> longed. Above she and Claud were people with a lot of money
> and much bigger houses and much more land. But here the com-
> plexity of it would begin to bear in on her, for some of the people
> with a lot off money were common and ought to be below she
> and Claud and some of the people who had good blood had lost
> their money and had to rent and then there were colored people
> who owned their own homes and land as well.

Mrs. Turpin uses this mental diagram to convince herself of what a
good person she is. O'Connor gives us this further peek at her mind:

> To help anybody out who needed it was her philosophy of life.
> She never spared herself when she found somebody in need,

whether they were white or black, trash or decent. And of all she had to be thankful for, she was most thankful that this was so. If Jesus had said, "You can be high society and have all the money you want and be thin and svelte-like, but you can't be a good woman with it," she would have had to say, "Well don't make me that then. Make me a good woman and it don't matter what else, how fat or how ugly or how poor!" Her heart rose. He had not made her a nigger or white trash or ugly! He had made her herself and given her a little of everything. Jesus, thank you! she said.

Mrs. Turpin's rationalizations make her blissfully unaware of her own deep prejudices.

In the course of the story, Mrs. Turpin has a soul-shaking encounter with a young woman who calls her a wart-hog from hell. The superstitious Mrs. Turpin takes this to be a revelation from God. In the end of the story she has a vision of many people marching through the sky toward heaven. At the front of the line are black people and white trash. Bringing up the rear are the people like Ruby Turpin.

The story brings to mind several passages from the New Testament, such as "the last will be first, and the first will be last" (Matthew 20:16). The ranking of those who have the most dignity in the eyes of God are not likely to match up well with the rankings that are most common to people in our society.

Most people operate with categories of social ranking that place some types of people above others. Perhaps a few people in history, like St. Francis of Assisi, escape such prejudices, but the great majority of people do not. Ruby Turpin may be less sophisticated than many of us, but for that very reason her rankings may be less insidious than our own rationalizations along these lines.

This Chapter

Who ranks as an important person? What is the source of human dignity? What is it about any person that might make him or her worthy of respect? Am I worthwhile? If so, why? How do I rank in relation to other people? Am I a valuable creature in the eyes of God?

Gaudium et Spes addresses these questions. The responses that it gives form the underlying basis of Catholic social teaching, whether in regard to family, race relations, peace, or social justice. In this chapter we will examine the teaching of Vatican II concerning the dignity of the human person, the social nature of the human person, and the existence of one human family.

These themes are drawn from throughout the first four chapters of *Gaudium et Spes*. These four chapters make up part 1 of the two major parts of the document. These principles lay the foundation upon which the more specific teachings in part 2 are based.

The Dignity of the Human Person

The other day my wife and I were talking about mutual acquaintances of ours who are having marital difficulties. My wife mentioned that the woman in question, whom we will call Sylvia, had remarked that she simply had no respect for her husband because he is still making the same amount of money that he did ten years ago. When I heard that, I had trouble maintaining my respect for Sylvia. I knew that her husband, who makes about three times as much as I do, is in a profession that is experiencing many shifts and transitions. He is an honest, intelligent, hardworking man. As I perceived it, his wife is too interested in surrounding herself with material trifles and in keeping up with her rich neighbors. I wondered aloud what kind of respect Sylvia must have for *me*.

At that point, however, I caught myself using my own categories to rank Sylvia in a way similar to the way that she ranks me and her husband. In my own personal "Ruby Turpin diagram," people like her are way at the bottom, while people like her husband and myself are near the top. Is my system of ranking morally higher than hers? Somehow I suspect that it is not.

Gaudium et Spes draws upon Genesis to teach that human beings are made in the image and likeness of God. It quotes Psalm 8 to the effect that human beings are made little less than the angels, crowned with glory and honor. This teaching applies across the board to all human beings. Our being made in the image and likeness of God is the source of the basic dignity of each one of us.

Thus the most basic source of our dignity is something that we share with all other human beings, not something that divides us or makes some of us better than others. Among our most precious qualities are our intellects, our emotions, our consciences, and our freedom, yet even those human beings who lack one or more of these are recognized as being of inestimable value. Although the presence of sin is pervasive, each human being is called to share in the divine life.

Does this mean that I need to respect Sylvia and all that she says and thinks? No. Traditionally, Christians have distinguished the sinner from the sin. I need to respect Sylvia, but not all that she says and thinks. It means, too, that I need to love myself, but I have to examine critically the things that I say, think, and do.

This is particularly true when I catch myself losing all respect for Sylvia in a way that I mentally rank myself above her. What makes me worthwhile in the first place is the same thing that makes Sylvia worthwhile. If I deny her basic dignity, I end up implicitly denying my own. When I do that, I begin to falsely value myself solely for my personal achievements and accomplishments, and I lose touch with the true source of my dignity through my relationship with God. When that happens, I am in the grips of a subtle self-rejection that will continually try to cover itself with more and more personal achievements and glory. The great paradox here is that my ability to love and accept myself as worthwhile is directly related to my willingness to love and accept others.

Does this mean that I think that I can draw none of my own dignity from my personal achievements or status? I do not think so. Rather, it means that the personal worth that I draw from such things must remain grounded in my grateful awareness of being a creature made in the image and likeness of my Creator. What is good in me ultimately comes from God. What socially recognizable "success" I may have in life does not make me fundamentally better than other people.

The more that I am able to recognize that Sylvia is to be treasured beyond measure as one of God's creatures and that she herself is trapped by her materialistic values, the more I am able to treasure myself and to realize the prejudices and traps set within my own value system.

The Social Nature of the Human Person

If the dignity of the human person is the first principle of Catholic social teaching, then the social nature of the human person follows a close second. Catholic social teaching tries to avoid both the extreme of an individualism that denies the importance of shared institutions and the extreme of a collectivism that denies the importance of individual freedom. In a certain sense, the Catholic tradition has given priority in its teaching to the responsibility each individual has for the moral and spiritual integrity of one's own life; never far behind, however, is the teaching that people are social by nature and thereby responsible for the larger whole.

Gaudium et Spes finds the initial basis for interpersonal communion in the existence of men and women. In other words, the complementarity between two beings who are fundamentally the same and yet different provides a root meaning for human social relationships. The document names a growing interdependence as one of the characteristics of modern times; as society becomes more and more complex, people need each other more and more.

As human goodness is manifested both individually and socially, so too is human sinfulness. In *Gaudium et Spes* is to be found the beginnings of Catholic teaching about what is now talked of as sin imbedded in social structures:

> To be sure the disturbances which so frequently occur in the social order result in part from the natural tensions of economic, political, and social forms. But at a deeper level they flow from human pride and selfishness, which contaminate even the social sphere. When the structure of affairs is flawed by the consequences of sin, human beings, already born with a bent toward evil, find there new inducements to sin, which cannot be overcome without strenuous efforts and the assistance of grace. (*GS*, 25)

As is the case with dignity, so too with sin: The individual is given priority over the social. Catholic documents consistently teach that sin takes its roots in the individual human heart. Yet having acknowledged this, Catholic teaching also recognizes that the results of individual sins pervade our institutions in such a way that the institutions themselves are in an analogous sense "sinful" and help to lead individuals to sin.

One could exemplify this point with virtually any large institution or class structure. Take, for example, the educational systems, both private and public, in the United States. Although the U.S. strives to be the land of equal opportunity, the country is full of cities that have struggling inner-city schools surrounded by affluent suburbs with highly superior schools. In many cases, opportunities are not only not equal; they are not even comparable. Yet the great discrepancies in opportunity in this country are buttressed by the myth that everyone is given a fair chance and, if they do not make it, it is simply their own fault.

Of course, the issue of equal opportunity is much more complex than a brief mention of one system or institution will allow. Catholic teaching on the social nature of the individual attempts to spell out the proper balance between social obligation and individual freedom. Human persons take first place; people should acknowledge their many interdependencies and their responsibilities for each other; institutions must remain always at the service of human beings. Philosophies that place too much stress either on the need to look out for "Number 1" or on the need for individuals to be controlled by the state do not fit easily within a traditional Catholic outlook.

One Human Family

The other day during a long car trip, my seven-year-old son asked out of the blue if he was related to Joe Montana. I said no, he was not. "But aren't we all members of God's family?" he wanted to know. "Yes," I said, "I suppose that in that sense you are related to Joe Montana." My boys proceeded to list many people to whom they are related, including Michael Jordan and Abraham Lincoln. When one of them mentioned singer Debbie Gibson, the seven-year-old wanted to know if he could still marry her since they were related. This brought us to a distinction concerning different ways of being related; through blood/legal ties, and in the general sense of being part of the human family. The boys then used this distinction further to explain why they would not get free tickets to 49ers or Bulls games, even though they are related to star players.

My sons' discussion points up how clear the difference is between the very real concept of blood/legal ties and the ideal concept of one human family. And yet an important question to pose to Christians concerns the size and quality of the gap between the two. Jesus is portrayed several times in the New Testament as calling people beyond established boundaries of blood, nationality, and religion to take one's place as part of the larger human family. At one point when he is teaching, he is told that his mother and his brothers are outside. Jesus says:

> "Who are my mother and my brothers?" And looking around at those seated in the circle he said, "Here are my mother and my brothers. For whoever does the will of God is my brother and sister and mother." (Mark 3:34–35)

The famous parable of the Good Samaritan (Luke 10:29–37) illustrates a similar point in regard to nationality and religion. Since the Jews and the Samaritans tended to despise each other, it would have been shocking to Jewish ears to hear Jesus speak approvingly of the Samaritan who reached out to help his neighbor in need.

Vatican II taught clearly that all human beings are members of one family with God as their creator:

> God, who has fatherly concern for everyone, has willed that all human beings should constitute one family and treat one another in a spirit of brotherhood [and sisterhood]. (*GS*, 24)

In former documents such as *Humani Generis* (1950), the oneness of the human family had been taught mainly as a way to illustrate the universality of original sin and the universal need for redemption in Christ. Vatican II, however, emphasized human interconnectedness and personal responsibilities toward each other.

Gaudium et Spes referred to this interconnectedness of human beings as "solidarity." This term was picked up not only by the famous Polish labor union of that name, but also by the famous Pole, Pope John Paul II. John Paul explains solidarity as a recognition of interdependence, a readiness to serve others, a readiness to lose oneself, and a recognition of each other as persons. Traditionally, the highest Christian virtue has been called "charity" or "love." John Paul connects solidarity with love:

> Solidarity is undoubtedly a Christian virtue. In what has been said so far it has been possible to identify many points of contact between solidarity and charity, which is the distinguishing mark of Christ's disciples.

For the Pope to link solidarity with love and to suggest that it is an essential part of being a Christian is no small matter.

Gaudium et Spes links solidarity with the concept of one human family and the belief that God saves us not just as individuals but as members of a community:

> This solidarity must be constantly increased until that day on which it will be brought to perfection. Then, saved by grace, human beings will offer flawless glory to God as a family beloved of God and of Christ their Brother. (*GS*, 32)

This is one of several passages that suggest a link between the progress of the human family and the coming of the kingdom of God. It is balanced by other passages that emphasize that the two are not the same:

> Hence, while earthly progress must be carefully distinguished from the growth of Christ's Kingdom, to the extent that the former can contribute to the better ordering of human society, it is of vital concern to the Kingdom of God. (*GS*, 39)

Thus, at Vatican II, the mission of the church is spelled out both as the need to proclaim the gospel of Christ and the need to work for the betterment of human society. The underlying principles are that each human being is of tremendous worth and that we are all interconnected with each other in a growing solidarity.

Idealistic Fluff?

Some people think that these underlying principles are idealistic fluff. They are very nice to think about, but how do they apply in the real world?

Catholic social teaching rarely if ever gets very concrete and specific. By its nature it refers to basic attitudes and general orientations. Many documents, as well as the concluding chapters of _Gaudium et Spes_, attempt to apply these principles to particular issues, but even there the air stays pretty rarified.

But attitudes and orientations are crucial, much more crucial than most people would care to admit. Within each of us lies a Ruby Turpin diagram by which we judge others and ourselves. To be asked to give it up is a frightening thing. To accept from the start that other people, even those people whom we tend to rank low, share a basic dignity equal to our own, threatens our fragile sense of self worth. The great paradox is that when we do accept the basic dignity of all members of the human family, we find ourselves promoted to a new sense of our true worth that is not threatened by the goodness of others. When we can love others in spite of their terrible sins and rationalizations, we will find it easier to love ourselves in spite of our own.

Summary

In this chapter we have examined the basic principles that underlie Catholic social teaching: the dignity of the human person, the human person's social nature, and the ideal existence of one human family.

In the next chapter we will discuss the first of a series of specific social/cultural issues raised in _Gaudium et Spes:_ marriage and the family.

FOR FURTHER REFLECTION

1. Try to think of various types of standards according to which people tend to "rank" each other.

2. What is it that ultimately makes a person valuable and worthwhile?

3. Can the idea of "one human family" be taken too far? Are you at one with the scruffy people who panhandle on the city streets?

4. What objection can be raised to focusing too much on the sinfulness of social systems? What objection can be raised to not focusing on the system?

5. Is "solidarity" idealistic, or might it work to bring about social improvements?

SUGGESTED READINGS

Baum, Gregory. *Compassion and Solidarity.* Mahwah, N.J.: Paulist Press, 1990.

Bellah, Robert, et. al. *Habits of the Heart: Individualism and Commitment in American Life.* Berkeley: University of California Press, 1985.

Flannery O'Connor. *The Complete Stories of Flannery O'Connor.* New York: Farrar, Straus and Giroux, 1971, pp. 488-509.

Lamb, Matthew. *Solidarity with Victims: Toward a Theology of Social Transformation.* New York: Crossroad, 1982.

Marcel, Gabriel. *The Existential Background of Human Dignity.* Cambridge: Harvard University Press, 1963.

Moltmann, Jurgen. *On Human Dignity: Political Theology and Ethics.* Philadelphia: Fortress Press, 1984.

Sobrino, Jon and Juan Hernandez Pico. *Theology of Christian Solidarity.* Maryknoll, N.Y.: Orbis Books, 1985 [1983].

Stevenson, Leslie Foster. *Seven Theories of Human Nature.* 2nd Edition. New York: Oxford University Press, 1987 [1974].

CHAPTER 32

MARRIAGE AND THE FAMILY

S hakespeare's comedy, *Twelfth Night*, presents romantic couples who are madly and wildly in love with each other. They pledge their eternal love, and attribute their love to mysterious forces beyond their understanding or control. At the end of the play, however, one of the characters who was disguised as a boy turns out to be a girl (as the audience knew all along). All of a sudden, other romantic arrangements turn out to be more practical. The characters then prudently decide to plan marriages that reflect new loves; the original pledges are conveniently forgotten.

Shakespeare provided this play with an alternative title: *What You Will*. One strong theme is that love involves some degree of will or choice.

A common myth about romantic love in our culture is that personal choice has nothing to do with it. This is why we say that people "fall" in love. It is just something that happens. We have no control over it. You cannot make it happen.

Like many myths that structure the possibility for meaning in our lives, the myth of romantic love has potential for great good and for great ill. People really do fall in love. Falling in love is not real, however, if it has been manipulated simply for practical purposes. Many of the great things in life, such as love, are properly experienced as coming from "outside" of ourselves, as being "bigger than both of us." Many married couples believe, quite properly I think, that they have a "marriage made in heaven." Falling in love can even turn people away from meanness and selfishness toward an appreciation of the world beyond themselves.

At the same time, however, the myth of romantic love has a destructive side if it is detached completely from matters of choice and personal responsibility. Just as in traditional Catholic theology the overwhelming love of God still needs to be embraced through the will of the cooperating human being, so in romantic love the partners need to accept the burden of trust and commitment that has been thrust upon them.

Why is the film *Harold and Maude*, in which a very young man becomes romantically involved with a silver-haired older woman, such a cultural shocker? Why does this phenomenon not happen more often in real life? It is because romantic love is not simply something over which people have no say or control. There is indeed a great deal of personal choice involved, often subtly, when people are orchestrating the possibility of their falling in love and concocting schemes for making sure that it will happen in a way that they feel free of control or manipulation.

I do not say these things to belittle romantic love. Indeed, romantic love is a very important dimension of life. I simply wish to point to the sometimes crazy and paradoxical nature of such love, and how the experience of it as being like a gift from "outside of ourselves" does not relieve the partners of responsibility within the relationship.

This is one reason why seeking an annulment involves more than simply saying that one used to be "in love" but now is not any more. Those seeking an annulment are called upon to demonstrate that essential elements necessary for a marriage were lacking from the very time of the wedding. Annulments today are much more common and are granted for many more reasons than they were in the pre-Vatican II period. No longer being in love, however, is not in itself considered to be an acceptable reason.

A saying from Marriage Encounter, an organization that runs retreats for married couples, is helpful here: "Love is more something that you do than something you're in." Love is a great gift, but you cannot keep that gift unless you work at it. Successful marriages do not just magically happen.

Does this mean that those couples whose marriages are not successful are to be judged guilty and responsible? Far be it from anyone to make such a gross and insensitive generalization. Many things do happen in life that are beyond the control of individuals. Yet few marriages end without two people feeling a need to work through their responsibility for it. At the same time, in even the most successful marriages, both people can become aware of their own deep failings and of their need for improvement.

This Chapter

The chapter on family in *Gaudium et Spes* recognizes that married love involves personal choice and commitment:

> The intimate partnership of married life and love has been established by the Creator...and is rooted in the conjugal covenant of irrevocable personal consent....This love is an eminently human one since it is directed from one person to another through an affection of the will....(*GS*, 48, 49)

In this chapter we will explore themes concerning the family: the importance of family, love, and the domestic church. This material corresponds with chapter 1 of part 2 of *Gaudium et Spes.*

**The Importance of Marriage and Family
in Catholic Social Teaching**

For many theologians, the most dramatic characteristic of contemporary theology is its awareness of how deeply human culture influences religious experience and expression. Theology is not just an academic explanation of a religious tradition; it involves a true dialogue between a religious tradition and a culture. If this is the case, then why does the chapter on marriage and the family come before the chapter on culture in *Gaudium et Spes*? Would it not have been more logical to begin with the deeper issue of culture, and then to include family as one of the specific applications of how religion and culture interact?

The arrangement of chapters is no mistake, however. In the eyes of the authors of *Gaudium et Spes*, marriage and family are deeper and more foundational matters than particular cultural variations. True, every culture and society will have its own legitimate customs and variations; the basic unit of the family, however, will provide the underlying structure for any healthy society.

Many commentators today like to clarify that "family" in contemporary U.S. society is itself a diverse phenomenon. Some children today find themselves with several sets of relatives from various combinations of parents. One of my students recently made reference to all four of her parents. In addition to these "blended families" is the rise in the number of single-parent homes.

At the same time, there are also many people who for whatever reason do not live with any relatives and yet whose personal supports in life could be considered their "family." This situation has been highlighted recently in some cases of persons with AIDS whose friends and lovers have been more "family" than their blood relatives.

Some recent church documents have shown an openness to recognizing the familial nature of ongoing relationships of mutual support. At the same time, however, it is clear that in official church teaching the traditional family is to be taken as ideally normative even if it becomes no longer sociologically normative.

In the novel *Brave New World* (1932), Aldous Huxley describes a future time when all children are conceived in test-tubes, and sex becomes a recreational expression of temporary intimacy.[1] Catholic social teaching is diametrically opposed to such a future. The basic idea of family is that there is a mother and a father and their children. Variations on this theme may occur for many reasons, but they are not to be considered the norm.

Much of Catholic teaching on sexuality, such as that sex belongs exclusively in marriage and that marital love should be forever faithful, finds its roots in the underlying belief that marriage and the family form the basis of a healthy society. People who put all morality on a "personal" basis often miss the larger social implications of the freedoms that they grant themselves. Is there a relationship, for example, between the sexual freedoms that many adults today allow themselves and the dramatically high statistics on teenage pregnancy? I do not wish to ignore the many complexities of these issues, but I believe that there is such a connection. Catholic social teaching asks us to consider the larger question of what kind of a world we want to live in, not just if we are hurting someone in an immediate sense.

An Institution Worth Saving

Gaudium et Spes itself does not point to the benefits of various alternative lifestyles; rather, it points to factors that threaten marriage and the family:

> Yet the excellence of this institution is not everywhere reflected with equal brilliance, since polygamy, the plague of divorce, so-called free love and other disfigurements have an obscuring effect. In addition, married love is too often profaned by excessive self-love, the worship of pleasure and illicit practices against human generation. Moreover, serious disturbances are caused in families by modern economic conditions, by influences at once social and psychological, and by the demands of civil society. Finally, in certain parts of the world problems resulting from population growth are generating concern. (*GS*, 47)

These "signs of the times" are still very much with us. I recently asked students what threatened the family today, and then I wrote their answers on the board. What they said, although it was phrased differently, corresponded very closely with the factors listed in the document.

Why is it that marriage and the family are so important in Catholic teaching? One reason is the belief, based on the creation story in Genesis, that the unity between man and woman expressed in marriage is the most very basic unit of human community:

> But God did not create man to be alone, for from the beginning "male and female he created them" (Genesis 1:27) Their companionship produces the primary form of interpersonal communion. (*GS*, 12)

On this basis it is thought that marriage, the union of a man and a woman, is sacred in a way that is prior to the recognition of cultural variations.

Other reasons given for the importance of marriage are the procreation and education of children; the mutual sanctification of the spouses; and the link between healthy families and healthy societies.

Benefits of Marriage and the Family
reflects the order of creation
appropriate for raising children
helps spouses to grow spiritually
forms the basis of a healthy society

Although the document proclaims the value of marriage as the appropriate context for these social goods, the question still remains as to why. It is not simply because *Gaudium et Spes* proclaims that these values reflect the will of God as found in the Scriptures. Nor is it necessarily obvious that other social arrangements might not work just as well. Could not a healthy society be structured such that children could be cared for by institutions other than the family? Why is *Brave New World* such a bad idea?

A question like this touches on values so deep that they cannot be definitively established by rational arguments. How important to us are the concepts of mother, father, daughter, son, sister, brother? How much are we willing to shape our behaviors and commitments to support a world that continues to be based on these relationships? It is the collective judgment of church leaders interpreting the Christian tradition that "Christians, redeeming the present time and distinguishing eternal realities from their changing expressions, should actively promote the values of marriage and the family, both by the example of their own lives, and by cooperation with other people of good will" (GS, 52). For such crucial judgments of values, each of us must reach into the deepest part of our beings in order to say why we agree or why we do not.

The Domestic Church

The chapter on family contains many inspiring passages on the meaning of love and sex within marriage.[2] Far from seeing sex as negative, the document says that "the actions within marriage by which the couple are united intimately and chastely are noble and worthy ones." Yet it is recognized that the love between spouses "far excels mere erotic inclination, which, selfishly pursued, soon enough fades wretchedly away" (GS, 49).

In contrast, the love between spouses, "merging the human with the divine, leads the spouses to a free and mutual gift of themselves, a gift proving itself by gentle affection and by deed; such love pervades the whole of their lives: indeed, by its active generosity it grows better and grows greater" (GS, 49). A great stress is placed upon the interrelationship between married love and divine love. Marriage is a sacrament because it is one of the primary means by which Christ comes to dwell in the lives of the spouses. Married love is enriched with Christ's redeeming power to act as an aid in the partners' mutual quest to live lives of holiness. Married couples "should realize that they are thereby cooperators with the love of God the Creator, and are, so to speak, the interpreters of that love" (GS, 50).

In the encyclical, *Familiaris Consortio* (1981), John Paul II develops these ideas about the presence of God's love in marriage by calling the family the "domestic church." He explains how the mission of the family is related to the mission of the church:

> The spiritual communion between Christian families, rooted in a common faith and hope and given by love, constitutes an inner energy that generates, spreads and develops justice, reconciliation, fraternity and peace among human beings. In so far as it is a "small-scale church," the Christian family is called upon, like the "large-scale church," to be a sign of unity for the world and in this way to exercise its prophetic role by bearing witness to the King-

dom and peace of Christ, towards which the whole world is journeying. (section 48)

John Paul also compares the family to the church in that both are communities of love that give birth to and educate Christians. The family is to establish ideal patterns of relationships that anticipate the coming of the kingdom of God by giving expression to the mission of Jesus.

Why Aren't All Families Like This?

Church documents tend to speak in the language of ideals. One problem contributing to the large number of failed marriages is that people sometimes enter into them with unrealistic expectations. Although it mentions the sacrifices that accompany married life, *Gaudium et Spes* does not dwell on the difficulties that people often experience. Some might even think that the unqualified lofty language that the document uses could contribute to the naivete of Catholic newlyweds insofar as they expect marriage to be a continuous reflection of divine love.

Few married couples spend every waking moment feeling deeply in love. Indeed, many, many married couples experience serious problems in communication. Most marriages have their ups and downs, and the downs can be pretty low.

Can the sometimes harsh realities of married life be seen as compatible with the lofty ideals of *Gaudium et Spes*? I think that they can. Couples who are growing together in their marriage can recognize their own relationships being described through the analogies with divine love. High ideals can challenge and sustain people who grapple with the less than perfect realities of everyday life. St. Paul said, "Now we see as through a glass, darkly; but then we shall see face to face." *Gaudium et Spes* tries to reveal to us the true nature of married love, even though we sometimes experience it through our dark glasses.

I do not wish to overemphasize the struggles of married life. I simply want to make up somewhat for *Gaudium et Spes*'s neglect of them. I also like to encourage married people to be open to marriage counseling or other therapeutic opportunities at the first signs of trouble in communicating and relating. Many families develop patterns that are today labeled "dysfunctional"; various counseling techniques and self-help groups exist for dealing with these issues. Many groups, such as Adult Children of Alcoholics, Gamblers Anonymous, Emotions Anonymous, and Overeaters Anonymous, are based on the twelve step program of A.A. I also like to encourage married people to consider involvement with groups such as Marriage Encounter, which is designed not for "problem" marriages, but for taking good marriages and making them better. Love is bigger than all of us, but we still have to work at it.

Summary

In this chapter we have discussed the importance of marriage and family in Catholic social teaching, the family as domestic church, and the distance between the ideal and the real.

In the next chapter we will examine the church's position on the relationship between faith and culture.

FOR FURTHER REFLECTION

1. When two people "fall in love," how much is their choice and how much is just something that happens to them?

2. If you had to choose, which of the following would you most want to emphasize for today's society: the traditional family structure or the existence of many types of "families?"

3. Are marriage and the family worth saving? Would *Brave New World* be just as good?

4. Should one's vision of the ideal society influence one's personal sexual morality, or should sexual behavior really just be a matter of individual choice?

5. Are high ideals and expectations more helpful or more hurtful to making marriages work?

SUGGESTED READINGS

Greeley, Andrew M. *The Young Catholic Family: Religious Images and Marriage Fulfillment.* Chicago: Thomas More Press, 1980.

John Paul II, Pope. *Familiaris Consortio.* "On the Family." Washington, D.C.: United States Catholic Conference, 1981.

Martin, Thomas M. *The Challenge of Christian Marriage: Marriage in Scripture, History, and Contemporary Life.* Mahwah, N.J.: Paulist Press, 1990.

Roberts, Challon O'Hearn, and William P. Roberts. *Partners in Intimacy: Living Christian Marriage Today.* Mahwah, N.J.: Paulist Press, 1988.

Rossi, Albert S. *Can I Make a Difference? Christian Family Life Today.* Mahwah, N.J.: Paulist Press, 1990.

CHAPTER 33

CULTURE

E mily, a student of mine, wrote a paper about a Catholic religious sister from Africa who had been brought up in a polygynous family. In a polygynous family, there is one husband who has many wives. (Emily uses the more familiar but somewhat less accurate term, "polygamy," which refers to either a man or a woman having many spouses.)[1] Emily said of the sister:

> She came from a very large polygamous family and was grateful for it. Her biological mother did actually live with her father and the nun was very close to her. She explained that her family relationship was like the sun. Her natural mother was like the sun who shined on all her children just like our sun shines on all the earth. Although her mother, the sun, loved all the children and shined over all of them, the nun's relationship to her mother was special, like the sun shining at a strong angle. In a sense, this is like our relationship with God. We are all special and unique in his eyes.

Emily had strong but ambiguous feelings about this arrangement:

> At first I was shocked at this nun for being Catholic and advocating this lifestyle. But, I do realize that no matter how much she was influenced by being in the United States, she was still rooted in her culture. Her culture is not entirely bad because polygamy, strange as it may seem, does have value. I would not know how to draw the line on the church's position on culture.

This Chapter

Emily's own ambivalence reflects a personal wrestling with what has been one of the most important issues in theology in the twentieth century: the relationship between faith and culture. This is not only an issue in Africa; it is an issue everywhere in the world, including the United States. How can the gospel interact with the various social systems, beliefs, values, and behaviors ingrained within any particular cultural setting?

In this chapter we move from a reflection on the relationship between Christianity and various aspects of African culture to a discussion of the position on culture taken at Vatican II. This material is related to chapter 2 of part 2 of *Gaudium et Spes*.

Polygyny in Africa

Emily did not realize just how right she was when she indicated that polygyny has meaning and value within African culture. It is, however, not simply a matter of a meaningful relationship between a particular daughter and her mother; polygyny is part of the very fabric of the social structure in many traditional societies.

Among the Luo of Kenya and Tanzania, for example, the social status and economic security of a man and the members of his family has traditionally depended upon how many wives and children he has, as well as how many wives and children his sons have.[2] The extended family forms a broad-based community that provides identity, support, and meaning in the life of each individual. There are various hierarchies of relationship within a complex network of households. Included in these hierarchies are the deceased ancestors of the family members.

For many of the Luo, the coming of Christianity and its attendant industrialization and urbanization has meant the breakdown of traditional family ties and supports. Some individuals who would have had a clear and significant place within the extended family have now become "displaced persons" without meaningful status or function. A people who had no concept of money before the late nineteenth century are now acquainted with such sophisticated concepts as unemployment, alienation, and alcoholism.

The Ibo of Nigeria have a traditional family structure similar to that of the Luo. An Ibo friend of mine, Father John, was born to Christian, monogamous parents. His own father, however, was the first son of his grandfather's fifth wife. Father John has many relatives within his large extended family. He says that at times he does not know whether to call them cousins or half-brothers; there are often no strict English equivalents to describe the relationships.

Father John told me that soon after he was ordained he received a visit from one of his "cousins." The cousin told Father John that he now wanted to become a Christian. Father John said, "You know that you cannot do that. You have two wives." The cousin said, "Yes, but now that you are a priest you can fix things up." Father John had to explain to him that although he was now a priest he did not control the rules of the Catholic church. It was different from their traditional arrangements, where the holy man had the power to "fix things."

I asked Father John if he wished that he could change the rules and baptize his cousin. He laughed at first, and evaded the question. Upon being pressed, however, Father John first insisted that I realize that, as a Catholic priest, he supports the policies of the church on this matter. He would not advocate among his people that polygyny be recognized as acceptable among Christians. He said, though, that since we were two scholars talking with each other, he would share with me his personal opinion. He said very clearly that he does not consider his personal opinion to be on the same level as the official teaching of the church.

Father John distinguished between two levels of culture: Capital "C" Culture, which includes things that are universally human and thus apply to all people; and small "c" culture, which refers to things that are specific to particular peoples. He said that he thinks that monogamous marriage is ultimately better and should be acknowledged as belonging to Culture. Ideally, he believes, societies should at least move in the direction of recognizing that monogamy has worthwhile advantages, especially regarding the dignity of the woman. Problems of jealousy and domination often arise among the wives in a polygynous marriage, although he was quick to add that such is not always the case.

Concerning polygynous marriage, though, Father John expressed his personal opinion with great passion. He referred to Jesus' teaching against divorce, and suggested that Jesus would not approve of wives being cast aside. He spoke of the many wives of Abraham and of Solomon, and declared, "God spoke to them! God did not turn away because they had many wives!" Father John said that the Lord would not reject people on account of such a small thing as being rooted in a polygynous culture, nor would he force a man to divorce his wives, or wives to leave their husband.

In other words, Father John's opinion (which is similar to that of several other African Christian theologians), is that whereas those who are already baptized should remain monogamous, those who are already polygynous should be allowed to remain so and still be baptized.

Throughout Africa, many independent Christian sects have emerged that accept traditional ways of life, including polygyny. In recent years, some Christian denominations have begun to follow the policy recommended by Father John. Many other denominations, including the Catholic, will not officially baptize those involved in polygynous marriages. As might be expected, in some cases actual practice diverges from the official church policy.

Problematic Aspects of African Culture

Although Christian missionaries in Africa in the nineteenth and early twentieth century came from various countries and represented many denominations, most shared in common an answer to the question of how Christianity should relate to African culture. They thought that the European culture in which Christianity was rooted should replace African culture, which they perceived to be primitive and often barbarous. This is not to say that there were not some exceptional missionaries more sensitive to African culture; as a rule, however, Christian preaching and education were directed toward obliterating traditional beliefs and customs. At the same time, missionaries often failed to condemn European practices of war, exploitation, and slavery on the African continent.

Christian missionaries in Africa were not without some good reasons for wanting to make serious changes in traditional African practices. Although the tremendous variety of tribes and customs makes generalization difficult, some practices common to many peoples were repulsive to those with European values. One such practice is twin-killing. This practice rests on the belief that humans are unlike animals in that they give birth to one child at a time. Twins are an abomination, so when they are born they are killed. Some missionaries have set up clinics for the care of twins. In some cases natives have rioted over the apprehension and preservation of twins by missionaries.

Human sacrifice, though not common, has sometimes been practiced among some Africans. Much more common is the practice of procuring land and domestic animals through wars of vengeance against enemies. Such practices can lead to wealth and high social status for the victors.

The belief in spirits and magic is another dimension of traditional African life. This primitive style of religion, known as "animism," finds the presence of spirits throughout all of nature and the cosmos. These spirits must be appeased and sometimes manipulated for protection or to bring about desired results. Especially important are the spirits of ancestors who bring many blessings when pleased but who cause famine, illness, and death when angered. Some tribes believe that death is always the result of punishment by an ancestor. Also common is a belief in reincarnation. Children are told at an early age of whose spirit they are a reincarnation; they then develop their talents in accordance with what was known of that ancestor. Of course, the process of discerning whose spirit they contain involves already an assessment of the child's talents and temperament.

The above elements of African societies were unacceptable to Christian missionaries. A problem arose, however, in that the missionaries often tried to do away with all elements of the culture, both positive and negative. They themselves did not tend to think of European culture as just one culture among others; they thought of it as the high point of human civilization, as something that could be imposed on others without guilt or apology.

Positive Elements of African Culture

The late twentieth century is marked by a heightened awareness of cultural pluralism. Educated people are no longer likely to think of their own culture as offering a "one size fits all" manner of living. It is almost universally recognized that various constellations of meanings and values can constitute humanly acceptable ways for people to live their lives.

With these new attitudes have come new approaches among missionaries to African culture. There are significant attempts to integrate the positive dimensions of African lifestyles within a Christian framework.

African theologian Edmund Ilogu, an Ibo from Nigeria, discusses several traditional practices regarding extended family and lineage duties that he thinks could be acceptable: traditional burial rites, including "second burials," which are designed to smooth the relations between the newly deceased and other ancestors; celebrations connected with childbirth; initiation into masquerade societies and dance groups; keeping the "secrets" of the lineage groups; reverence to ancestors through animal sacrifice; tributes within clans of younger to elders on lineage days. Ilogu argues concerning the latter:

It is a means of recognizing the lineage tree when a line of seniority is clarified once a year by the exchange of these tribute gifts on the appointed day. Furthermore Christians should see in it an occasion for re-establishing their membership in the community of blood relationships. In these days of the growth of cities where children are born, who do not easily recognise their membership in the community, this yearly exchange of tribute no matter where people actually live will strengthen their sense of belonging to counteract the evil effects of the anomie of city life.

Belief in the continuity of the lineage through a link that connects the dead, the living, and the children of the future, is a very strong and healthy cultural feature of Iboland. Christianity has removed the irrational fear of ancestral spirits as the source of evils like sickness, barrenness, and some epidemics, especially when the ancestors have been neglected and the duties of allegiance to them fall by default. Yet Christianity has not been able to destroy the belief in some unexplainable link between us and our forefathers. But the question is, should Christianity destroy such a belief? Is there nothing in the Christian faith that echoes this belief?[3]

In other words, although Ilogu believes that Christianity has rightfully eradicated certain irrational or harmful Ibo beliefs and practices, he finds in family and ancestor duties not only strong community bonds but also a link with the Christian concept of the communion of saints. He says, "We cannot fully believe in the communion of saints and in the resurrection of the body without seriously thinking of our common humanity with those who have begotten us and yet knew not the Lord Jesus." Ilogu suggests that in Ibo towns, both Christians and non-Christians should agree to celebrate lineage day on All Saints Day.

The Shift at Vatican II

The chapter on culture in *Gaudium et Spes* represents a shift in official Catholic thinking from a "one size fits all" view of culture to an acceptance of cultural pluralism. Of course, the gospel is still given a priority, but its meaning can be distinguished from the cultures with which it has been associated historically. Various cultures are recognized as legitimate and necessary dialogue partners. This position has been called the "adaptation model" because it adapts the gospel to the customs and values of particular cultures.

The document distinguishes between a general sense of "culture" that refers to basic human capacities for producing social ways of living, and a more specific sense of "culture" that refers to diverse lifestyles, values, and customs. This is the same distinction that Father John referred to as capital "C" culture and small "c" culture. It is in this second sense of "culture" that the document speaks of a "plurality of cultures" (*GS*, 53). This distinction is important in the context of traditional Catholic theology, because it recognizes a level of being human in which all people share and to which the gospel must speak. That is, there are certain things common to all human beings; any presentation of the gospel should keep this in mind.[4]

The distinction between different meanings of "culture" is also crucial to contemporary Catholic theology, however, because of the clear way in which it recognizes cultural pluralism as legitimate. Explicit concern is expressed for the preservation of the heritage of various peoples:

> What is to be done to prevent the increased exchanges between cultures, which should lead to a true and fruitful dialogue between groups and nations, from disturbing the life of communities, from destroying the wisdom received from ancestors, and from placing in danger the character of each people? (GS, 56)

The richness of particular cultures is recognized in that "the customs handed down . . . form the patrimony proper to each human community" (GS, 53).

Gaudium et Spes thus wishes to protect particular cultures from being swallowed up as the new global community emerges. The document speaks hopefully of "a new age of human history" in which human beings have opportunities for building a more just world on a global scale (GS, 54). It attests to "the birth of a new humanism, one in which human beings are defined first of all by their responsibilities to their brothers [and sisters] and to history" (GS, 55). It cites also the tremendous potential of science and technology in contributing to human progress.

At the same time, however, while acknowledging the many positive values of contemporary culture, the document also points to the danger of taking either human science or human beings themselves as self-sufficient and thereby "no longer seek the higher things" (GS, 57). The positive values of culture, while accepted as good in themselves, are also seen as providing "some preparation for the acceptance of the message of the gospel" (GS, 57). While it is recognized that the word of God is to some extent already present in the very cultures themselves, the church is put forth as making a crucial contribution:

> The Gospel of Christ constantly renews the life and culture of fallen humanity; it combats and removes the errors and evils resulting from the permanent allurement of sin. It never ceases to purify

and elevate the morality of peoples. By riches coming from above, it makes fruitful, as it were from within, the spiritual qualities and traditions of every people and of every age. It strengthens, perfects and restores them in Christ. Thus the church, in the very fulfillment of her own function, stimulates and advances human and civic culture; by her action, also by her liturgy, she leads them to interior liberty. (*GS*, 58)

For the above reasons, the church recalls to mind that all culture is to be subordinated to the integral perfection of the human person. (*GS*, 59)

In the final analysis, the document presents the message of the gospel as enabling all of the positive elements of human culture to be directed to the integral perfection of the human person.

Another Vatican II document, The Decree on the Church's Missionary Activity, focuses on the metaphor of planting the gospel as a seed within a culture rather than replacing a "barbaric" culture with a "civilized" one:

The special end of this missionary activity is the evangelization and the implanting of the church among peoples or groups in which it has not yet taken root. All over the world indigenous particular churches ought to grow from the seed of the word of God, churches which would be adequately organized and would possess their own proper strength and maturity. (section 6)

Lumen Gentium likewise attests to the value of cultures:

Since the kingdom of God is not of this world the church or people of God in establishing that kingdom takes nothing away from the temporal welfare of any people. On the contrary it fosters and takes to itself, insofar as they are good, the ability, riches and customs in which the genius of each people expresses itself. (*LG*, 13)

At least in theory, then, the official policy of the Catholic church on cultural matters is one of openness.

Some scholars argue that although this new "adaptation model" represents welcome growth, it does not go far enough. Missionary theologian Aylward Shorter contends that rather than simply planting the seeds of the gospel in foreign soil, more attention should be given to the seeds of the gospel that already exist within a given culture. It is better to begin with the culture and then integrate Christianity within it rather than vice-versa.[5] A U.S. scholar, Robert Schreiter, has developed an elaborate flow chart to capture the complexities of inculturation.[6] He calls his theory the "contextual model" because it looks first to the cultural context within which Christianity must be integrated. Both of these scholars are more radically accepting of established traditional customs than is the current policy of the church.

Evangelization

In contemporary theology, the topic of culture is often linked with the topic of evangelization. A renewed concern for evangelization, the sharing of the good news of Christ, is one of the most important movements throughout the Catholic church today. Evangelization has commonly been thought of as the job of missionaries; today it is recognized as everyone's task. Other tools for church renewal, such as the order of Christian initiation, lay ministry, and building the local church, are seen as extensions of evangelization. Church policy no longer distinguishes clearly between those cultures that need to be evangelized and those that have already been evangelized; all cultures need ever to be brought anew into dialogue with the message of the gospel.

A church without a missionary outreach is not going to be very lively. As they say in Alcoholics Anonymous, "If you want to keep what you've got, you've got to give it away." At the same time, however, if you want to be able to give something away, you first have to get it. One of the beautiful things in the new concern for evangelization is the realization and admission that the proclamation of the gospel needs to begin at home. Christians must become "hearers of the Word" before they can become "sharers of the Word." We have come to realize that when we talk about missionary efforts to implant the seed of the gospel where it has not yet taken root, we need to talk first about ourselves. Respect for other cultures thus goes hand in hand with our ability to be self-critical about our own culture.

Summary

In this chapter we have explored the shift in attitude toward culture at Vatican II against the background of the relationship between Christianity and African traditions.

Relating the gospel and the culture remains a challenging issue. On the one hand, many elements of U.S. culture, from widespread addictions to teenage pregnancy to the high divorce rate to gross violence in the media, could stand some correction by the message of the gospel. On the other hand, some elements, such as our stress on tolerance, freedom, innovation, and participation, might challenge our manner of appropriating the Christian tradition in a positive way. These are extremely difficult issues, although perhaps they seem relatively simple when compared with polygyny in Africa.

In the next chapter we will discuss the teaching of Vatican II concerning economic justice.

FOR FURTHER REFLECTION

1. Do you think that Father John's polygynous "cousin" should be permitted to be baptized?

2. Does the teaching of Vatican II go far enough in promoting respect for various cultures? If not, what would be a better position?

3. Can concerns for "cultural pluralism" be taken too far?

4. What elements of U.S. culture need to be eradicated by the gospel message? What elements could make a positive contribution to the ongoing evolution of the Catholic church?

5. Do you see evidence in your own parish or church of the growing awareness that evangelization needs to begin at home?

SUGGESTED READINGS

Barnes, Michael H. _In the Presence of Mystery: An Introduction to the Story of Human Religiousness_. Revised Edition. Mystic, Conn.: Twenty-Third Publications, 1991 [1984].

Hater, Robert J. _News That Is Good: Evangelization for Catholics_. Notre Dame, Ind.: Ave Maria Press, 1990.

Ilogu, Edmund. _Christianity and Ibo Culture_. Leiden: E.J. Brill, 1974.

Jassy, Marie-France Perrin. _Basic Community in the African Churches_. Maryknoll, N.Y.: Orbis Books, 1973 [1970].

Luzbetak, Louis J. _The Church and Cultures: New Perspectives in Missiological Anthropology_. Maryknoll, N.Y.: Orbis Books, 1988.

Schreiter, Robert J. *Constructing Local Theologies*. Maryknoll, N.Y.: Orbis Books, 1985.

Shorter, Aylward. *African Culture and the Christian church*. Maryknoll, N.Y.: Orbis Books, 1974.

Shorter, Aylward. *Toward a Theology of Inculturation*. Maryknoll, N.Y.: Orbis Books, 1988.

ECONOMICS, POLITICS, PEACE, ECOLOGY

CHAPTER 34

ECONOMICS

I know three women in my neighborhood who have received significant amounts of government assistance. I'll call them Amy, Becky, and Cathy.

Amy is a divorced parent. Her two children live with her. She went on welfare for a time after her divorce. Eventually, she got an interesting but low-paying job with few benefits. She figured out that if she went back on welfare and worked odd jobs under the table, she would make more money and be able to keep her government medical card. Because of her basic honesty, however, Amy chose to quit her meaningful job to take on a physical labor job that paid more money. She could now use an operation on her knee, but she cannot afford it. Although the temptation is there to go back on welfare and get a medical card, she has not yet given into it.

Becky is a divorced parent recovering from alcoholism. She has many personal and social problems. Her three children live with their father, who has remarried. For a long time now, Becky has received government assistance along with a medical card. She sometimes does odd jobs for people. She reports whatever she makes to the welfare department. Becky is scrupulously honest. Sometimes she turns down odd jobs offered to her because her pay would exceed the amount that she is allowed to earn. As far as I know, Becky does not dream at this time of trying to become regularly employed. Besides lacking skills, she is also attached to her medical card.

Cathy lives with her boyfriend and his niece, whom they are raising. She has received government disability for an ailment for many years.

She also receives aid to families with dependent children and has a medical card for herself and the child. Cathy works at jobs for several different people and insists that she always be paid in cash so that she will not have to report her earnings. She prides herself for beating the system. In her perception, the system has not done much for her. She certainly does not live in high society, but she is able to support herself and her little girl while getting medical treatment. As far as I can tell, Cathy has no qualms about her lifestyle and no plans for making any changes.

These stories are intended to illustrate something that most people already have an inkling of: There are things about our social and economic and welfare systems that cry out for correction. These are complex issues; it seems, however, that we have been building a system that does not reward people for honesty and industriousness.

On the other side of the tracks is a friend of mine who is a lawyer. I'll call him David. A few years ago David told me of a big business client of his who decided to move his business from Ohio to Kentucky because of a rise in Ohio state taxes. I was somewhat taken aback by this. I expressed concern for all of the workers who would be affected by this move. David then expressed his outrage at the then governor of our state for driving businesses away. I defended the taxes on the basis of the social good to which they were put and questioned whether David should not rather be outraged at his client, who perhaps is callously throwing people out of work over a profit margin.

David then looked me in the eye and asked, "If it were going to cost you a quarter of a million dollars a year out of your own pocket, wouldn't you move?" I hesitated at this. I wondered what it must be like to make so much money that a small percentage drop in one's profit margin would cost a quarter of a million dollars. David clarified that the savings included not just taxes but material and labor costs. Still, it was clear that we were talking about an extremely rich man who made more money than most of us can imagine. I refused to agree that I would necessarily move on that account.

I cannot say that I would not move either. It is a complex issue. My only point is that in such a decision I would take human factors into account. I would not allow profit to be the sole determinant in my decision. Again, however, I was faced with the reality that some things about our economic system seem to be out of kilter. Injustice and even craziness seem to be almost built-in at some points.

This Chapter
Chapter 3 of part 2 of _Gaudium et Spes_ deals with economic and so-

cial issues. In this chapter we will examine some basic principles for economic justice, and then discuss the meaning of success and the place of material goods in a Christian's lifestyle.

Principles for Economic Justice

Gaudium et Spes articulates many principles that lie at the heart of Catholic teaching concerning economic justice. These are the principles that are applied more specifically in national and regional documents such as the U.S. Catholic bishops' *Economic Justice for All* (1986). What follows is my own summary of these principles.

1. *Human beings are the end of social and economic life.* Labor is not just another factor for figuring out spreadsheet calculations. Labor is performed by people, and people are ultimately to be served by institutions, not vice versa. People are not to be treated like numbers or like cogs in a machine. Profit is important, but human beings must also be taken into account when making economic decisions. Investments should be directed toward providing employment and other social goods. Economic development is good insofar as it serves human beings.

2. *Current gaps between rich classes and poor classes and between rich countries and poor countries are too great.* Catholic social teaching does not oppose the existence of classes whatsoever, but rather calls for harmony and cooperation among them. Increasing inequality, however, is a matter for concern. The document points out that whereas progress could mitigate social inequalities, instead "extravagance and wretchedness exist side by side" (*GS*, 63). It calls for "strenuous efforts . . . to remove as quickly as possible the immense economic inequalities, which now exist and in many cases are growing and which are connected with individual and social discrimination" (*GS*, 66).

3. *Economic development should follow the principle of subsidiarity, whereby decision making is done on the most local level possible and includes the participation of the people most directly involved.* International decisions should include all nations involved. National decisions should include all localities involved. Community problems should be addressed at the level of the community. Neighborhood problems are often best solved within the neighborhood. One should not make a federal case out of local issues. Workers, too, should participate as much as possible in the administration and profit-sharing of the enterprises where they are employed.

4. *Employment is the most important factor in considerations of economic*

justice. Work is the means by which people support themselves and their families, contribute to society, and express their identities. Through their work, people "unfold their own abilities and personality" (*GS,* 71). Workers have the right to form unions; at the same time, workers have a duty to contribute to the best of their ability. Jobs should provide sufficient wages, as well as time for rest and leisure.

5. *Ownership is a legitimate right, but not an absolute right.* The goods of the earth are intended for the use of all. Goods should be available in an equitable manner. People should regard their possessions not only as their own but also "as common in the sense that they should be able to benefit not only the owner but also others as well" (*GS,* 69). People who have more than they need have a duty to provide for the relief of the poor, "and to do so not merely out of their superfluous goods" (*G.S,.* 69). All are called to share their earthly goods.

6. *Neither pure socialism nor pure capitalism are morally acceptable alternatives.* In line with the larger tradition of Catholic social teaching, *Gaudium et Spes* rejects both the extreme that says that government control will create justice and the extreme that claims that the free market will create justice. Catholic social teaching calls for government to play a strong role, and yet to be only one factor among others in the achievement of a just society: "Growth is not to be left solely to a kind of mechanical course of economic activity of individuals, nor to the authority of government" (*GS,* 65). This is because it is believed that both systems taken to an extreme necessarily lead to gross injustices. Although Catholic social teaching does not propose any alternative system, any workable solution should land somewhere between the two extremes. In recent documents, Catholic teaching has found market systems to be acceptable starting points if implemented within a higher social vision.[1]

7. *Christians should grow beyond materialism and consumerism to embrace lifestyles of creative simplicity. Gaudium et Spes* laments that "many people, especially in economically advanced areas, seem, as it were, to be ruled by economics, so that almost their entire personal life is permeated with a certain economic way of thinking" (*GS,* 63). In the encyclical *Sollicitudo Rei Socialis* (1987), John Paul II asks us to distinguish between "being" and "having." Who we are is prior to and more important than what we own. John Paul writes, "This then is the picture: There are some people—the few who possess much—who do not really succeed in 'being' because, through a reversal of the hierarchy of values, they are hindered by the cult of 'having'; and there are others—the many who have little or nothing—who do not succeed in realizing their basic human vocation because they are deprived of essential goods" (section

28). Christians are called to value people more than things by loving their neighbors as themselves and being willing to alter their lifestyles accordingly.

8. *Attempts to transform social structures should be rooted in conversion of heart. Gaudium et Spes* calls Christians to live the spirit of the beatitudes, particularly the spirit of poverty. If we first seek the kingdom of God, we will be moved to perform "the work of justice under the inspiration of charity" (*GS*, 72). Working for justice purely out of a sense of outrage and self-righteousness is a dead end. We all have our own poverties and shortcomings; we are always to retain our humility and the awareness of our own need for God as we work to bring about needed change.

9. *Christians must be convinced that they can make a contribution to the improvement of economic and social conditions.* Catholics are not utopian dreamers who think that the kingdom of God will necessarily be here in its fullness overnight. Yet Catholics are called to maintain a realistic hope that true progress can be made when human beings work together in divine hope. No one is asked to do it alone or to carry the weight of the world on one's shoulders. We are asked simply to strive to do what we can in accordance with our station and our capacities in life.

The Successful Life

The majority of my students find Catholic teaching on economic justice to be inspiring and refreshing. I encounter a few students in most classes, however, who are put off by this teaching. Some of these students are disturbed because their core values have been challenged. They have placed material concerns at the forefront of their lives, and are either not ready or not willing to consider major changes. I can only hope that some day they will realize that materialistic values give them no real advantages but simply hold them back from living their lives to the fullest capacity.

Note that I say "materialistic values" and not "material values." There is nothing wrong with valuing material things as long as such values are put in their place below one's relationships with other human beings. There is nothing wrong with making a living, even a very good living. One should remain aware, however, of injustices in a social system that often denies interdependencies by promoting the myth that "successful" people make it all on their own and owe nothing to anyone.

For what is the meaning of "success"? If we could travel ahead to the moment of our death and look back over the life that we had lived, what would constitute a "successful" life?

The Russian novelist Leo Tolstoy tells the story of Ivan Illich, a judge who lived a selfish and corrupt life. Throughout his life, his only real concerns were for his personal wealth and social status. He would even make decisions as a judge based on his own political advantage. When Ivan Illich is on his deathbed, however, he is able to look back over his life and realize that the wealth and status he valued were really worth nothing. He then sees that things he had considered trivial, such as kindness and mercy to other human beings, were what he should have valued all along.

Gaudium et Spes makes a point similar to that of Tolstoy by recalling a scriptural injunction:

> Not everyone who cries, "Lord, Lord," will enter into the king-dom of heaven, but those who do the Father's will by taking a strong grip on the work at hand. Now the Father wills that in all human beings we recognize Christ our brother and love Him ef-fectively, in word and in deed. (*GS*, 93)

In other words, without discounting the value of material goods and the need for people to make a living, *Gaudium et Spes* is claiming that the truly successful life is lived by one who seeks the will of God above all. One who seeks the will of God will, in some sense, be called to a life of service to others, whether in the context of the business world, fami-ly life, religious life, science and technology, education, manual labor, or whatever combinations of options to which one is drawn.

A Specific Question

Most of my students are amenable to these suggestions, but they are left with many questions. A big one that is often asked (with infinite variations, of course) is: Is it O.K. to own a BMW? Now that is a specific question!

I do not know the answer. I suspect that it varies from case to case. I myself would feel uncomfortable owning any luxury car in the face of widespread poverty and unemployment in our country. Owning a lux-ury car would not be in harmony with my own commitment to live a life of creative simplicity.

However, I would feel even more uncomfortable declaring that no one should own a BMW or that BMWs should not exist. There is some-times a fine line between garish luxury and excellent quality. I am not in principle opposed to excellent quality.

At times I think that our society will be heading in the right direction when more and more people get sick to their stomachs in the face of garish luxury. Again, I do not know the answer to this question. I only know that within it there is a real issue with which people need to wrestle.

Traditionally, Catholic social teaching has distinguished between what a person needs to maintain one's station in life and what constitutes superfluous goods. It is not reasonable that a prince be forced to live like a pauper. If, like Francis of Assisi, a rich person embraces a life of poverty, that person is answering a higher call, not what is expected of everyone. I suppose that today it could be argued that it is not reasonable to say that a business executive should not own a BMW.

Yet Catholic teaching has also stressed that those with means have a duty to come to the aid of the poor, and that one should dig deeper than just one's superfluous goods. Of particular concern is the widening gap between the rich and the poor. This is a structural issue. It is a matter of seeking changes in the system. Yet changes in the system must be accompanied by changes in the hearts of people. If enough individuals act out of the attitudes and principles articulated in Catholic social teaching, positive changes can be accomplished.

Summary

In this chapter we have examined some basic principles of Catholic teaching on economic matters and have discussed some practical implications.

So what have I said in this chapter, other than that things within our system need to be changed? We all knew that already. Has Catholic social teaching offered any real concrete solutions?

By its nature, Catholic social teaching cannot be too concrete. The gospel is not full of specific advice for structuring economic systems. Yet it is easy to underestimate the real effects of general principles if people truly set about practicing them. To Amy, Catholic social teaching says, bravo, don't give up hope. To Becky, it says your honesty is appreciated; perhaps you can now start improving your willingness to work. To Cathy, it says that "beating the system" may not be the best approach; growth is gradual, but for starters you could use some basic honesty. Yet to all of them Catholic social teaching says that they are the victims of a system that is beyond their control, and that they should work in the hope of seeing changes in that system within their own lifetime.

To David, Catholic social teaching says that governors and big business people must keep human beings in mind when making large-scale economic decisions. All people share a basic dignity. We are all one human family who are in this together.

In the next chapter we will discuss Catholic teaching concerning peace and politics.

FOR FURTHER REFLECTION

1. Of the nine principles from *Gaudium et Spes's* chapter on economics listed in this chapter, which do you find to be the most important?

2. Which of the principles do you find to be the most disturbing?

3. Can we distinguish between excellent quality and garish luxury?

4. Do you personally believe that progress is possible in the realm of economic justice?

5. What in your opinion would constitute a life of creative simplicity?

SUGGESTED READINGS

Dorr, Donal. *Option for the Poor: A Hundred Years of Vatican Social Teaching.* Maryknoll, N.Y.: Orbis Books, 1983.

Finnerty, Adam Daniel. *No More Plastic Jesus: Global Justice and Christian Lifestyle.* Maryknoll, N.Y.: Orbis Books, 1977.

Gnuse, Robert. *You Shall Not Steal: Community and Property in the Biblical Tradition.* Maryknoll, N.Y.: Orbis Books, 1985.

Harrington, Michael. *The New American Poverty.* N.Y.: Holt, Rinehart, and Winston, 1984.

John Paul II, Pope. *Centesimus Annus.* May 1, 1991.

Lappe, Francis Moore, and Joseph Collins. *World Hunger: Twelve Myths.* New York: Grove Press, 1986.

Novak, Michael. *Freedom with Justice: Catholic Social Thought and Liberal Institutions.* San Francisco: Harper & Row, 1984.

U.S. Catholic Bishops. *Economic Justice for All.* Washington, D.C.: United States Catholic Conference, 1986.

Walsh, Michael, and Brian Davies, eds. *Proclaiming Justice & Peace: Papal Documents from Rerum Novarum through Centesimus Annus.* Mystic, Conn.: Twenty-Third Publications, 1991.

CHAPTER 35

PEACE AND POLITICS

O nce at a dinner I was seated next to a physician who had been a bomber pilot during World War II. He told me that he had flown five bombing missions over Germany.

When this doctor, a Catholic, found out that I was a Catholic teacher of religion, he expressed how furious he was at the letter on peace issued by the U.S. Catholic bishops (*The Challenge of Peace* [1983]). He was especially outraged by the bishops' teaching that the people of the U.S. need to develop a spirit of repentance regarding the bombings of Hiroshima and Nagasaki at the end of World War II:

> After the passage of nearly four decades and a concomitant growth in our understanding of the ever growing horror of nuclear war, we must shape the climate of opinion which will make it possible for our country to express profound sorrow over the atomic bombing in 1945. Without that sorrow, there is no possibility of finding a way to repudiate future use of nuclear weapons . . . . (*The Challenge of Peace*, 302)

The doctor believed that these bombings were fully morally justified. "The bishops shouldn't poke their noses into areas where they have no qualifications," he said. "They just don't know what they're talking about when it comes to war. In war, it's you against them. They're trying to kill you, and you're trying to kill them back. When you're in that situation, you do whatever you can to win. It's a matter of life and death. It's easy to sit back and make high moral pronouncements when it's somebody else's life on the line. The bishops are just too far away from what war is really about to have anything worthwhile to say on the subject."

My immediate reaction to the doctor was a somewhat defensive one. I said that there are two ways to not see a situation clearly. One way is to be too far away. The other is to be too close.

The doctor turned away and did not speak to me or in my direction the rest of the evening. I suppose that he did not want to get into a debate with someone who probably understood even less than the bishops. A little later, when he left the table, his wife mentioned that she was worried about him because he seemed obsessed with the topic of World War II. His main hobby was watching film clips of World War II combat and reading books about military strategy. He spent many hours absorbed in this hobby.

That helped me to convince myself that he was the one who owned the problem, but when I left the dinner party I felt uneasy about my own part in the conversation. After all, the doctor had a point. Things do look different when one is engaged in combat; if combat is to exist at all, the perspective of the combatants is not to be ignored. From that point of view, the position of the bishops is perhaps difficult to appreciate. These are indeed complex issues.

This Chapter

The position of the church, however, cannot be that "all is fair in love and war." It is the business of the church to interpret the gospel in response to the major issues of our times. In this chapter, we will examine the basic teaching of the Catholic church on matters of peace and politics. This material corresponds with chapters 4 and 5 of part 2 of *Gaudium et Spes*. The U.S. bishops' letter, *The Challenge of Peace*, will also be relevant.

A Just War?

On January 16, 1991, at 7:00 P.M. EST, after repeated warnings, Allied forces led by the United States began to bomb Iraq. The bombing severely weakened the Iraqi military so that the ground attack launched in February lasted only a few days. Estimates of the loss of Iraqi soldiers range from 80,000 to 200,000. Allied casualties were relatively few—in the hundreds.

Was this a just war on the part of the Allies?

The Catholic tradition offers some general criteria to help assess the morality of any particular war. It is important to understand that in the

Catholic tradition the presumption in any situation is in favor of peace. The Just-War Theory provides conditions that must be fulfilled if the presumption for peace is to be overridden. The classic criteria for a just war, as articulated in *The Challenge of Peace*, are as follows (in abbreviated form):

1. *Just Cause*: War is permissible only to confront a real and certain danger, i.e., to protect innocent life, to preserve conditions necessary for decent human existence, and to secure basic human rights.

2. *Competent Authority*: War must be declared by those with responsibility for public order, not by private groups or individuals.

3. *Comparative Justice*: Which side is sufficiently "right" in a dispute, and are the values at stake critical enough to override the presumption against war? Do the rights and values involved justify killing?

4. *Right Intention*: Right intention is related to just cause—war can be legitimately intended only for the reasons set forth above as a just cause. During the conflict, right intention means pursuit of peace and reconciliation, including avoiding unnecessarily destructive acts or imposing unreasonable conditions.

5. *Last Resort*: For resort to war to be justified, all peaceful alternatives must have been exhausted.

6. *Probability of Success*: This is a difficult criterion to apply, but its purpose is to prevent irrational resort to force or hopeless resistance when the outcome of either will clearly be disproportionate or futile.

7. *Proportionality:* The costs incurred by war must be proportionate to the good expected by taking up arms.

Before, during, and after the war, different voices in the United States cried out both in protest and in support of "Desert Storm." One side shouted, "No blood for oil." The other side shouted, "We support our troops." Among those who protested the war, many Christians referred to the Just-War Theory of the Catholic tradition. They tended to rely on criteria numbers 1, 3, 5, and 7 for their grounds that the war could not be justified. Archbishop Pilarczyk, head of the National Conference of Catholic Bishops, wrote a public letter to President George Bush before the attack urging that all peaceful means of settling the dispute be exhausted before resorting to violence. Once the attack was launched, however, Pilarczyk refused to condemn the action because it involved a prudential judgment that he considered to be beyond his competence. Several other Catholic bishops, however, did publicly denounce the war.

Other Christians, among them President Bush, used the Just-War Theory to defend the Allies' action. In an address to religious broadcasters, Bush analyzed Desert Storm point by point according to each principle of the Just-War Theory and proclaimed that the war was just. A few Catholic bishops concurred with Bush's judgment.

Principles and Applications

Does this mean that the Just-War Theory is useless because it can be made to mean whatever a person wants it to mean?

On one level, the question highlights the gap that always exists between ideal principles and concrete applications. Just because the concrete applications can be difficult does not mean that the ideal principles are wrong or useless.

On yet a deeper level, it can be contended that one side in this argument was clearly right, and that the other side really was engaging in gross rationalizations. To the extent that such was the case, it can be argued that simply because some people misuse the principles does not mean that the principles are useless when applied properly. Some who firmly believe that President Bush was among the greatest of rationalizers console themselves with the idea that at least he brought the Just-War Theory into public political discourse, and perhaps the presence of such principles will yield long-term peaceful results. It may be that in the future some leaders may use the Just-War Theory to help make a decision rather than simply to help justify what they may have decided to do on other grounds.

Pacifism, Military Service, and International Progress

There are many people who pay no attention whatsoever to the Just-War Theory. Some people might be described as "militarists"; that is, those persons who see military action not as a moral issue but simply as a means of defending oneself or even of procuring one's goals. Yet other people who reject the Just-War Theory are "pacifists"; that is, those persons who reject violence and killing under any circumstances.

Contemporary Catholic teaching rejects all forms of militarism. Pacifism, however, is recognized as a way that individuals may legitimately interpret the Christian tradition: "We cannot fail to praise those who renounce the use of violence in the vindication of their rights" (*GS*, 78). In other words, official Catholic teaching holds that individuals may decide for themselves whether they interpret pacifism or Just-War Theory as the more authentic path of following Christ. Governments, however, "cannot be denied the right to legitimate defense once every means of peaceful settlement has been exhausted" (*GS*, 79). Pacifists, of course, contend that no war can be justified. Some Catholic pacifists such as Philip Berrigan argue that killing cannot be justified by those who follow Jesus, who preached turning the other cheek, and who himself went to his death rather than contradict everything he stood for.

How does the Catholic church officially address the question of military service? The U.S. bishops quote from *Gaudium et Spes:*

> Millions of you are Catholics serving in the armed forces. We recognize that you carry certain responsibilities for the issues that we have considered in this letter. Our perspective on your profession is that of Vatican II: "All those who enter the military service in loyalty to their country should look upon themselves as the custodians of the security and freedom of their fellow-countrymen; and where they carry out their duty properly, they are contributing to the maintenance of peace." (*Challenge*, 309; *GS*, 79)

The bishops urge military professionals to understand their vocation as the defense of peace and to carry out their duties in that light. The bishops do not imply in any way that one cannot be a good Catholic and a good soldier too.

Issues of individual choices and commitments find their larger context within the Catholic vision of a global community, within which disputes can be mediated peacefully. *Gaudium et Spes* relates peace to "an international order that includes a genuine respect for all freedoms and amicable brotherhood between all" (*GS*, 88). To this end, the document supports the establishment of a universal public authority, although it does not specifically mention the name of the United Nations. The document links peace with justice, arguing that the two go hand in hand. The arms race is denounced as "an utterly treacherous trap for humanity, and one which ensnares the poor to an intolerable degree" (*GS*, 81). Yet the final appeal brings the issue back to individuals:

> The human family . . . cannot accomplish its task of constructing a world more genuinely human unless each person devotes oneself to the cause of peace with renewed vigor...(*GS*, 77). It is our clear duty, therefore, to strain every muscle in working for the time when all war can be completely outlawed by international consent. (*GS*, 82)

Mixing Religion and Politics?

Peace and war are political issues. The complaint is frequently made that the pope and bishops should not speak about such topics. The doctor referred to at the beginning of this chapter echoes the sentiment of many when he says that the church should stay out of politics.

This sentiment can be broken down into several basic issues: whether the bishops are qualified to speak in these areas, whether the gospel itself has any political implications, and whether church and state should not be completely separate from each other.

Concerning whether the bishops are qualified, the distinction between different levels of authority needs to be taken into consideration. The bishops are qualified to interpret the message of the gospel in a way binding for Catholics. They are qualified to make specific judgments about how the gospel might be applied, as long as they clarify that the binding power of their judgments becomes less and less as the judgments become more specific. Even when the bishops are quite specific, however, Catholics and people of good will should allow themselves to be challenged by what they say. It should also be taken into consideration that the writing of church documents on political matters involves hours and hours of in-depth consultation with people who are expert in various fields, as well as review and advice from such people through various stages of drafting.

Does the gospel itself have any political implications? Catholic teaching is clear that neither the gospel nor the church promotes any one particular political system. As stated in *Gaudium et Spes*:

> The church, by reason of her role and competence, is not identified in any way with the political community nor bound to any political system. She is at once a sign and safeguard of the transcendent character of the human person. (*GS*, 76)

The gospel, however, has clear implications concerning types of government that are unacceptable, given the freedom and dignity of the human person. Repressive totalitarian regimes, for example, are not acceptable. If the gospel can determine types of government that are not acceptable, it can also have something to say about necessary characteristics of governments that are acceptable. The gospel has even more implications for how political practices are to be carried out within particular political systems.

Several characteristics of acceptable forms and practices of government can be identified in *Gaudium et Spes*. Although these principles are very general, it should be kept in mind that many governments do not value them and many more do not live up to them.

Characteristics of Acceptable Governments

1. Recognize the rights of citizens, such as freedom of association, speech, and religion.

2. Foster participation in government decision making and in the economic and social life of the nation. Recognize the rights of minorities.

3. Seek the common good; it is the only purpose for which the political community exists.

4. Be pluralistic; recognize that different people have the right to prefer different solutions to common problems.

5. Rulers should be appointed through the free will of the citizens.

These ideals sound very much like the ideals of a representative democracy, such as we have in the United States and Canada. In his 1991 encyclical, *Centesimus Annus*, John Paul II, while strongly warning against the materialism and consumerism of the Western world, expressed a basic approval for market economies and democratic forms of government.

Church and State

Another issue within the area of church and politics is the popular belief that the separation of church and state should be absolute. The state should provide for religious freedom; the church should refrain from interfering with the concerns of the state.

A distinction is needed here between the church interfering with the state on the one hand, and the church teaching on matters that have political implications on the other. Although in the long history of the Catholic tradition the church has indeed often been inextricably intertwined within government affairs, *Gaudium et Spes* recognizes a legitimate autonomy to governments: "The church and the political community in their own fields are autonomous and independent from each other" (*GS*, 76). In this sense, official Catholic teaching can be read as supporting the separation of church and state, although it also supports the existence of countries whose official religion is Catholicism but that allow for religious pluralism.

Gaudium et Spes also teaches, however, that the church has a word to speak on political matters. This is because "the political community and public authority are founded on human nature and hence belong to the order designed by God..." (*GS*, 74). Political institutions are not somehow exempt from judgment according to moral and religious principles.

In *Under God: Religion and Politics in America*, political commentator Gary Wills demonstrates how deeply and subtly religion and politics have been intertwined throughout U.S. history, including the contemporary scene.[1] Of special interest is Wills' study of how two of the founders of the country, Jefferson and Madison, understood the separation of church and state. Both understood the concept differently; both fought for it vigorously; and yet neither in his wildest dreams thought for a moment that religion should not be a powerful force in the public arena.

When Catholic church leaders express particular opinions on political matters, they consider themselves to be adding their own voice to the public debate.[2] There have been exceptions to this, such as instances where particular bishops have supported or opposed political candidates because of their stand on abortion. Often this is done in a slightly indirect manner by naming the issue without naming the candidates. But the very sensitivity of such actions and the outcry that they raise demonstrates that most Catholics today expect church leaders to articulate basic guidelines but not in any way tell them how they have to vote. Many Catholics protest against what they label the "one-issue politics" that supports anti-abortion candidates no matter what their positions on other issues. Some Catholics argue that other issues are indeed important, but that abortion is so important that it rightfully takes a certain priority. It is clear that the basic principle of religious influence without undue interference gets played out in real life under circumstances that are often less than clear-cut.

Clear Distinctions

Sometimes my students ask why, if the church is so interested in politics, does it not allow priests and religious to run for and hold political office? Would not that be a good way for the church to help to bring about a better world? Did not Father Robert Drinan have more influence when he was also Congressman Drinan from Massachusetts? (Father Drinan resigned after the pope issued a general statement affirming church teaching on this matter.) Has it not been good that several members of the Sandinista government in Nicaragua have been Catholic priests, despite direct orders to the contrary from Nicaraguan bishops and from John Paul II?

The primary reason for the ban on priests and religious in politics is so that the church, through its official representatives, does not become overly involved with any particular government, political party, or social movement. Put simply, it is acceptable for a Catholic to be a Republican, a Democrat, or a member of any number of political parties. It would, I believe, be contradictory to Catholicism to be a Nazi or a Ku Klux Klan member. But beyond these anti-Catholic extremes, one is called only to follow one's conscience. Which party or platform holds the most promise for the common good? It is a difficult matter to move from the gospel to such a determination; such a decision must be left up to the individual Christian. Church teaching that restricts clergy from political office reflects the belief that such a degree of entanglement over-commits the church on a too specific political level.

Liberation theologian Leonardo Boff expresses this distinction as one between capital "P" Politics and small "p" politics. Capital "P" Politics addresses the ideals to which governments must aspire; small "p" politics involves the level of partisan platforms and particular interests. The official church should operate only on the level of Politics; lay members should find specific ways of living out the Christian life in the world of politics. At times Christians will diametrically oppose each other on political matters while at the same time doing the best they can to live out the same Politics of the Christian tradition.

Gaudium et Spes calls for yet another distinction:

> ...between the tasks which Christians undertake, individually or as a group, on their own responsibility as citizens guided by the dictates of a Christian conscience, and the activities which, in union with their pastors, they carry out in the name of the church. (GS, 76)

That is, the church encourages its members to band together to work for political and economic and social improvements. When church members do so, however, they are acting in their own name. Although they may be doing so out of the motivation of their Christian consciences, their group is not an official representation of the Catholic church.

Summary

In this chapter we have examined official Catholic teaching on matters of peace and politics. We discussed the Just-War Theory, pacifism, military service, and many aspects of the relationship between the church and political matters.

In order to carry out its mission to the world, the church must avoid either of two extremes: not getting involved in political matters at all, and getting too involved by taking sides on what are legitimately partisan concerns. The doctor in the opening story of this chapter, I believe, only grasped one side of this complex matter.

In the next chapter we will investigate some areas of intersection between ecology and Christianity.

FOR FURTHER REFLECTION

1. Does the bomber pilot/doctor have a point?

2. Can the Just-War Theory be a useful tool for deciding whether or not an operation such as "Desert Storm" was just?

3. Are you personally more inclined to be a pacifist or to accept some form of the Just-War Theory?

4. Should the Catholic church oppose candidates who support abortion?

5. To what extent should one's religious beliefs influence one's choice of a political party (or stance)?

SUGGESTED READINGS

Berrigan, Daniel. *To Dwell in Peace: An Autobiography.* San Francisco: Harper & Row, 1987.

Drinan, Robert F. *Stories from the American Soul: A Reader in Ethics and American Policy for the 1990's.* Chicago: Loyola University Press, 1990.

Foroohar, Manzar. *The Catholic Church and Social Change in Nicaragua.* Albany, N.Y.: SUNY Press, 1989.

Fox, Thomas C. *Iraq: Military Victory, Moral Defeat.* Kansas City: Sheed & Ward, 1991.

Kolbenschlag, Madonna, ed. *Between God and Caesar: Priests, Sisters and Political Office in the United States.* Mahwah, N.J.: Paulist Press, 1985.

McGinnis, James B., and Kathleen McGinnis. *Parenting for Peace and Justice: Ten Years Later.* Maryknoll, N. Y.: Orbis Books, 1990.

Merton, Thomas. *Thomas Merton on Peace.* New York: McCall Publishing Company, 1971.

Simon, Arthur. *Harvesting Peace: The Arms Race and Human Need.* Kansas City: Sheed & Ward, 1991.

U.S. Catholic Bishops. *The Challenge of Peace.* Washington, D.C.: USCC, 1983. See also *Building Peace,* an updated reflection issued in 1988.

Wills, Gary. *Under God: Religion and American Politics.* New York: Simon and Schuster, 1990.

CHAPTER 36

ECOLOGY

Few things that people do in public aggravate me to the extent that I would consider taking action. Yet I remember vividly a day a few years back when, sitting in my car, I saw a man in another car empty his overflowing ashtray in the middle of a parking lot, leaving a large pile of butts and ashes. This so disgusted me that I took off after him in hot pursuit. I have no idea what I intended to do if I caught up with him. I had two small children with me in the car, and, after a few moments, I simply trailed off, leaving me with only my anger and frustration.

With our new ecological awareness in recent years, fewer and fewer people would even dream of emptying an ashtray in the middle of a parking lot. Yet the current ecological crisis is not just about individual waste disposal; it is about the ozone layer, the rain forests, threatened species of plants and animals, the quality of available air and water, and the preservation of soil for farming.

Although a store employee could sweep up the butts and ashes in the parking lot, the larger butts and ashes of the systematic waste of human society are currently causing damage that may well be irreversible. Is it enough to get angry about it, but then trail off?

This Chapter

The final five chapters in *Gaudium et Spes* deal with "a number of particularly urgent needs characterizing the present age, needs which go to the roots of the human race" (*GS*, 46). Those issues include family, culture, economics, politics, and peace. In the conclusion of the document, the reader is told that the "conciliar program . . . will have to be followed up and amplified since it sometimes deals with matters in a constant state of development" (*GS*, 91).

If *Gaudium et Spes* were to be written today, I have little doubt that it would contain a separate chapter on ecology. At the time of Vatican II in the 1960s, what we now call "green movements" were sporadic and underground. In the 1990s, ecological concerns are at the forefront of important issues for people throughout the world. It is a global problem because the environment of the entire planet is perceived to be threatened. It is an urgent problem because time is such a factor. It is a social and personal problem because it calls for significant changes in people's lifestyles. It is a religious problem because it calls for changes in people's ways of thinking about their most basic relationship with God and with the rest of creation.

In this chapter we will discuss some of the theological issues related to ecology. Ecology deals with questions of the environment. It forces people to look more deeply at the contexts, including the ultimate context, within which life is lived. It poses the question of how everything fits together in the big picture. In that sense, ecology is an issue that naturally lends itself to theological reflection.

Dominion over All the Earth?

There is much debate today concerning the following passage from Genesis and the impact its interpretation has had on Christian attitudes toward the environment:

> Then God said: "Let us make man after our own image, after our likeness. Let them have dominion over the fish of the sea, the birds of the air, and the cattle, and over all the wild animals and all the creatures that crawl on the ground...God also said, "See, I give you every seed-bearing plant all over the earth and every tree that has seed-bearing fruit on it to be your food; and to all the animals of the land, all the birds of the air, and all the living creatur; that crawl on the ground, I give all the green plants for food. (Genesis 1:26, 29)

This passage reinforces the hierarchy established by the order of creation in the first of the two accounts of creation. Human beings are created by God last, as the final masterpiece to which all of the rest of creation was leading.

Gaudium et Spes expresses well the way in which Genesis has been interpreted by Christians as having universal application:

According to the almost unanimous opinion of believers and unbelievers alike, all things on earth should be related to man as
their center and crown. (*GS*, 12)

It should be noted that this view, which is here attributed to virtually all of humankind, is really most associated with Western monotheistic culture influenced by Judaism, Christianity, and Islam. It has not
been the dominant religious ideal either of Eastern religions or of the
religions of native peoples. For that reason, the first half of the statement can be considered *ethnocentric*, because it projects the view of one
portion of humankind on to everyone.

The second half of the statement, however, that human beings are
the center and crown of all creation, is even more deeply criticized for
being *anthropocentric*. That is, the statement proposes that humans have
the highest place in the created universe and that everything else is in
subordination to them. Nature exists not so much for its own sake but
for the use and service of human beings.

In a well-known essay published in 1967, historian Lynn White said
that "Christianity bears a huge burden of guilt" in regard to the ecology
crisis.[1] White held that the environmentally exploitative nature of contemporary science and technology finds its roots within the anthropo-
centrism of the Christian tradition. The belief that human beings have
mastery over nature had led human beings to justify their abusing the
environment without any regard for the environment itself. White,
himself a Christian, calls for the liberation of nature from the destructive
domination of human beings. In this sense, the ecological movement is
a liberation movement not unlike feminism or liberation theology.

In a 1985 article, theologian H. Paul Santmire revisits and evaluates
White's seminal essay.[2] Santmire reviews some of the vehement criticisms White's essay has received. Although in the end Santmire is very
sympathetic to White's major concerns, he offers the following points:

1. Religion has not been the only factor shaping Western attitudes
toward technology and the environment. Underlying economic
forces have also been especially important.
2. The anthropocentric strain in Christianity is complemented by
other strains that lead to concern for the environment. This is especially true of the theocentrism, or God-centeredness, that runs
deeper than the human-centeredness. It also applies to the basic
goodness of creation and to the cosmic dimensions of the redemption.

Santmire, therefore, gives the role of Christianity in shaping ecological attitudes a more mixed review than White does. Although Santmire is critical of White, he also takes to task other critics of White who have failed to appreciate the important challenge underlying White's thesis. Are Christians called to overthrow their attitudes of human dominance that have helped to justify the rape of the earth?

Santmire concludes with an openness towards White's idea that St. Francis of Assisi, because of his solidarity with creation, is a most appropriate model for Christians today. Santmire simply disagrees with White's implication that St. Francis necessarily contradicts the mainstream Christian tradition rather than representing an important strain within it.

Stewardship

Some attempts to articulate Catholic teaching in an ecologically sensitive manner have focused on the concept of stewardship. Stewardship is the idea that human beings are the "stewards" or caretakers of creation. God is the owner or master; human beings are left in charge. Stewardship makes clear the theocentric (God-centered) context of any anthropocentric tendencies within the Christian tradition. That is, the belief in the exalted place of human beings is contextualized by an emphasis on the subordination of human beings to God. Human beings were created not to do with the environment simply as they please, but to tend to the environment, to nurture it, and care for it. In the second story of creation, we are told: "The Lord God then took the man and settled him in the garden of Eden, to cultivate and care for it" (Genesis 2:15).

John Paul II expresses this contextualizing perspective in his encyclical *Sollicitudo Rei Socialis* (1987):

> The task is "to have dominion" over the other created beings, "to cultivate the garden." This is to be accomplished within the framework of obedience to the divine law and therefore with respect to the image received, the image which is the clear foundation of the power of dominion recognized as belonging to human beings as the means to their perfection. (section 30)

In other words, John Paul II is making clear that the charge of "dominion" must be understood within the context of human beings reflecting the image of their creator. Abuse of "dominion" is therefore the result of sin, not the result of Christians carrying out their proper purpose.

The Catholic bishops of the United States have recently released a statement on the environment, "Renewing the Earth," in which they make significant use of the metaphor of stewardship.[3] This concept allows them to be faithful to the traditional view that human beings are the high point of all creation while at the same time expressing the urgency of the ecological crisis.

Some proponents of the ecological movement do not believe that "stewardship" goes far enough. The God-centeredness may contextualize the human-centeredness, but the human-centeredness still runs too deep. Jay B. McDaniel, for example, holds that one should appreciate that all of the elements of creation, including animals, plants, rocks, and stars, have an intrinsic value that is independent of their relations with human beings.[4] Stewardship still makes human beings the focal point of the value of creation. This discussion will receive much attention in the coming years.

A New Way of Thinking

Thomas Berry, a leading thinker in the area of ecological spirituality, says that humankind is entering into an entirely new period in history, which he calls the Ecozoic period.[5] The planetary developments of the last 65 million years (the Cenozoic period), such as birds, insects, and mature flowers, are being systematically destroyed as human beings make permanent and devastating changes in the environment. Human beings will either choose to continue to destroy the environment and themselves along with it, or else will make radical changes in thoughts, values, and lifestyles. Such changes must come not only through a reliance on our religious traditions and science, but also through a new listening to the voices of nature, women, primitive peoples, and childhood dreams. Art, poetry, and dance are as important for survival as the latest environmental technologies.

The ideas of Thomas Berry and others are presented in a highly readable format by Michael Dowd in *Earthspirit: A Handbook for Nurturing an Ecological Christianity*. Dowd makes clear that what is being called for is a whole new way of thinking about the cosmos and the place of human beings within it. He describes the earth itself as a living organism with human beings as the self-reflective element of that organism:

> ...the fact that Earth is a living being just makes good, common sense. The physical structure of the planet—its core, mantle, and mountain ranges—acts as the skeleton or frame of its existence. The soil that covers its grasslands and forests is like a mammoth

digestive system, into which all things are absorbed, broken down, and recycled. The oceans, waterways, and rain function as a circulatory system that provides life-giving blood, purifying and revitalizing the body. The vegetation of the planet, the algae, the plants, and the trees, provide its respiratory system, its lungs, constantly regenerating the entire atmosphere. The animal kingdom provides the lower functions of the nervous system, a finely tuned and diversified series of organisms that are sensitized to environmental change and have provided the first stages for the advent of humanity. Humanity itself can be understood as the capacity of the planet for conscious awareness and reflexive thought. That is, the human enables Earth to reflect on itself and on the divine Mystery out of which it has come and in which it exists.[6]

This understanding of the earth as a living organism is known as the "Gaia theory." Dowd does not find this a mere metaphor; he believes that it is scientifically supportable and thus both literally and mythically true. He voices clearly the opinion of many leading thinkers in the ecological movement when he argues that true growth in our culture will occur only as human beings radically revise their understanding of the story of the cosmos and of the place of human beings within it.

Dowd believes that Christianity is not to be rejected; it is, however, to be reinterpreted in the light of the new cosmology such that basic teachings can be appreciated in a fresh way. What we have traditionally thought of as "sin" finds its roots in our lack of awareness of our true place in the cosmos and of our interconnectedness with all things. "Salvation" will come through telling the new story of creation and getting in touch with the most basic principles of the universe. To follow Jesus is to experience the kingdom of God through unconditional, self-expansive love. The kingdom of God is itself the "Reality" in which the whole universe participates. For our time, "eternal life" can be understood as the continued evolution of the planet with human beings providing reflective awareness.

These ideas are fresh, exciting, and challenging. The dialogue between traditional Christianity and ecological Christianity still has a long way to go, but these ground-breaking notions should prove valuable as the conversation progresses.

Denial

Making the environment a matter of special concern is not simply a benevolent concession. It is a matter of survival for the human race and for the planet. What will be left for future generations after present society gets done pillaging the earth?

Psychologists talk about the problem of "denial." Denial involves the conscious repression of things that we are aware of unconsciously. An alcoholic who will not admit to having a problem is in denial. But there are other more subtle ways of being in denial. A person who says, "I admit that I am an alcoholic," but who goes right on drinking or only slightly alters some peripheral habits is still enmeshed in a web of denial. That person is denying the seriousness of the problem and is failing to take appropriate measures.

That today we live in denial of our environmental problems is a possibility worth considering. We say that we admit to them, but we fail to acknowledge their true seriousness or to take the radical steps to really do something about them. Many of us are recycling some percentage of our trash and trying to buy reusable or biodegradable products, but most of us have not significantly altered our lifestyles to affect deeply the production and use of pollutants.

What would it take, for example, to reduce dramatically the first world's dependence (addiction?) on the use of oil as a source of energy? Are we willing to make alternative energy sources a top research priority? Are we willing to demand that our industries operate in an environmentally sound manner? Are we willing to change our diets to use food sources that do not harm the environment? Are we willing to seriously restrict the use of cars and to develop more extensive systems of mass transportation? What would it take to make truly significant improvements in the ways that human beings relate with the environment? This last question is currently receiving much study. To the extent that we are unwilling to do what it takes, we are in denial.

The Ecological Crisis as a Moral Issue

On the first day of the new decade of the 1990s, John Paul II issued a message on ecological concerns.[7] His main theme was that the widespread destruction of the environment is a moral as well as a technological problem. This is because a "lack of respect for life" underlies the ecological crisis. This is manifested first of all in a contempt for human beings that does not recognize the fundamental human "right to a safe environment." Destruction of the environment threatens the health and survival of human beings. The lack of respect for life is also seen in disregard for the harmonious order of the universe and for the beauty of creation. At the root of the problem is human greed, selfishness, and exploitation.

John Paul II argues that "we cannot interfere in one area of the eco-system without paying due attention both to the consequences of such interference in other areas and to the well-being of future generations." He cites especially the depletion of the ozone layer, the greenhouse effect, industrial waste, unrestricted deforestation, and the exhaustion of farming soil. The following advice can be gleaned from his message:

1. Cultivate respect for life, and above all for the dignity of the human person.
2. Grow in one's awareness of the beauty of creation.
3. Appreciate the earth as a common heritage, the fruits of which are for the benefit of all.
4. Develop a more internationally coordinated approach to the management of the earth's goods.
5. Work toward a new international solidarity, especially in relations between the developing nations and those that are highly industrialized.
6. Address the structural forms of poverty that exist throughout the world; rural poverty and unjust land distribution, for example, have led to subsistence farming and to the exhaustion of the soil.
7. Realize that today, any form of war on a global scale would lead to incalculable ecological damage.
8. Take a serious look at our personal lifestyles, especially in modern societies.
9. Become better educated concerning ecological responsibility.
10. Recognize the ecological crisis as the responsibility of everyone.

Concerning the change in lifestyles, John Paul II states:

In many parts of the world society is given to instant gratification and consumerism while remaining indifferent to the damage which these cause. As I have already stated, the seriousness of the ecological issue lays bare the depth of the human moral crisis. If an appreciation of the value of the human person and of human life is lacking, we will also lose interest in others and in the earth itself. Simplicity, moderation and discipline, as well as a spirit of sacrifice, must become a part of everyday life, lest all suffer the negative consequences of the careless habits of a few. (section 13)

Summary

In this chapter we have reflected briefly on the ecological crisis in relation to Christianity. Scholars debate the extent to which the relationship between Christianity and the environment has been positive or negative. Current Catholic teaching emphasizes the concept of stewardship, which interprets the special role of human beings in the universe within the context of our responsibilities to God and to creation. Some in the ecological movement call for more radical changes in our thinking about the cosmos. John Paul II has urged all to become more aware of the seriousness of the crisis, its moral dimension, and the need to change attitudes, values, and behaviors.

FOR FURTHER REFLECTION

1. On what occasions have you become outraged by the sight of someone littering, polluting, or otherwise destroying the environment?

2. Do you think that talk of the ecological crisis is either understated or overblown?

3. Is the concept of "stewardship" a good one, or do we need a whole new story of our place in the cosmos?

4. Is our society in denial about the ecological crisis?

5. Do you agree that underlying the ecological crisis is a moral crisis?

SUGGESTED READINGS

Berry, Thomas (with Thomas Clarke). *Befriending the Earth: A Theology of Reconciliation between Humans and the Earth.* Mystic, Conn.: Twenty-Third Publications, 1991.

Berry, Thomas. *The Dream of the Earth.* San Francisco: Sierra Club Books, 1988.

Carmody, John. *Ecology and Religion: Toward a New Christian Theology of Nature.* Mahwah, N.J.: Paulist Press, 1983.

Dowd, Michael. *Earthspirit: A Handbook for Nurturing an Ecological Christianity.* Mystic, Conn.: Twenty-Third Publications, 1991.

John Paul II. "The Ecological Crisis: A Common Responsibility." Washington, D.C.: United States Catholic Conference, 1990.

Lonergan, Anne, and Caroline Richards, eds. *Thomas Berry and the New Cosmology*. Mystic, Conn.: Twenty-Third Publications, 1987.

McDaniel, Jay B. *Earth, Sky, Gods & Mortals: Developing an Ecological Spirituality*. Mystic, Conn.: Twenty-Third Publications, 1990.

McDonagh, Sean. *The Greening of the Church*. Maryknoll, N.Y.: Orbis Books, 1990.

Murphy, Charles. *At Home on Earth: Foundations for a Catholic Ethic of the Environment*. New York: Crossroad, 1989.

Santmire, H. Paul. *The Travail of Nature: The Ambiguous Ecological Promise of Christianity*. Philadelphia: Fortress Press, 1985.

U.S. Catholic Bishops. "Renewing the Earth." *Origins* 12, December 1991.

NOTES

CHAPTER 1

1. *New York Times*, February 28, 1990: A14.

2. "Statement of Catholic Theological Society of America," *Origins* 3 (January 1991): 461-67.

3. "Vatican II: Promise and Reality." (Jamaica, N.Y.: Fellowship of Catholic Scholars [offices at St. John's University], September 20, 1990), pp. 20-21.

4. Dennis M. Doyle, Michael H. Barnes, and Byron R. Johnson, "Pluralism or Polarization? The Results of a CTS Survey," in *Raising the Torch of Good News*, edited by Bernard P. Prusak (Lanham, Md.: University Press of America, 1988), pp. 278-79.

5. William M. Shea, "A Response," in *Raising the Torch of Good News*, edited by Bernard P. Prusak (Lanham, Md.: University Press of America, 1988), pp. 287-90.

CHAPTER 2

1. Yves Congar, *Diversity and Communion* (Mystic, Conn.: Twenty-Third Publications, 1985 [1982]), pp. 92-3.

2. A collection of Marx's writings on religion can be found in K. Marx and F. Engels, *On Religion*, (Moscow: Foreign Languages Publishing House, 1955).

3. Freud's most concise critique of religion can be found in *The Future of an Illusion* (Garden City, N.Y.: Doubleday, 1957 [1927]).

4. A good introduction to Albert Camus' philosophical writings on religion is "The Myth of Sisyphus," in *The Myth of Sisyphus and Other Essays*, trans. Justin O'Brien (New York: Random House, 1955). A novel that captures some of his yet more mature thought is *The Plague*, trans. Stuart Gilbert, First American Edition (New York: Alfred A. Knopf, 1948).

5. "Pope John's Opening Speech to the Council," *The Documents of Vatican II*, ed. by Walter M. Abbott (New York: Guild Press, 1966), p. 715.

CHAPTER 3

1. For a concise yet detailed history of the composition of the various documents, see Hubert Jedin, "The Second Vatican Council," in *History of the Church*, ed. by Hubert Jedin, vol. 10: *The Church in the Modern Age*, pp. 96-151.

2. Gérard Philips, "History of the Constitution," in *Commentary on the Documents of Vatican II* (5 vols.), edited by Herbert Vorgrimler (New York: Herder and Herder, 1967-69), p. 106.

3. For a discussion of De Smedt's talk, see Avery Dulles, *Models of the Church* expanded edition (Garden City, N.Y.: Doubleday, 1987), p. 39.

4. Gérard Philips, "History of the Constitution," p. 110.

5. Donald R. Campion, "The Church Today," in *The Documents of Vatican II*, ed. by Walter M. Abbott (New York: Guild Press, 1966), p. 184.

CHAPTER 4

1. Avery Dulles, *Models of the Church*, Expanded Edition (Garden City, N.Y.: Doubleday, 1987). The original edition was published in 1974.

CHAPTER 5

1. Avery Dulles, *Models of the Church*, Expanded Edition (Garden City, N.Y.: Doubleday, 1987), p. 114.

CHAPTER 6

1. Clifford Geertz, "Religion as a Cultural System," *The Religious Situation 1968*, edited by D.C. Cutler (Boston: Beacon Press, 1968), p. 643.

2. Joseph Campbell, *The Power of Myth* (Garden City, N.Y.: Doubleday, 1988), p. 6.

CHAPTER 7

1. Lutheran-Roman Catholic Statement, "Martin Luther's Legacy," *Origins* 9 (June 1983): 65-69.

2. John Dillenberger, ed., *Martin Luther: Selections from His Writings* (Garden City, N.Y.: Doubleday, 1961), p. xxxiii.

3. See Thomas Halton, *The Church*. Message of the Fathers of the Church vol. 4 (Wilmington, Del.: Michael Glazier, 1985), pp. 70-73.

CHAPTER 8

1. Raymond Brown, *The Churches the Apostles Left Behind* (Mahwah, N.J.: Paulist Press, 1984).

2. Jean Comby, *How to Read Church History* (New York: Crossroad, 1985), p. 132.

3. Edward Day, *The Catholic Church Story* (Liguori, Mo.: Liguori Publications, 1978), p. 71.

4. For a good sample of Luther's writings as well as a good introduction to his life, see John Dillenberger, ed., *Martin Luther: Selections from His Writings* (Garden City, N.Y.: Doubleday, 1961).

CHAPTER 9

1. Heinrich Fries and Karl Rahner, *The Unity of the Churches: An Actual Possibility* (Philadelphia: Fortress Press, 1985 [1983]).

2. Cardinal Joseph Ratzinger, *Church, Ecumenism, and Politics* (New York: Crossroad, 1988), especially Part II, pp. 65-142.

3. Avery Dulles, "Eucharistic Sharing as an Ecumenical Problem," in *The Resilient Church* (Garden City, N. Y.: Doubleday, 1977), pp. 153-71; Wolfhart Pannenberg, "The Lord's Supper—Sacrament of Unity," in *The Church* (Philadelphia: Westminster Press, 1983), pp. 116-23.

4. For a review of such dialogues, see Cardinal Johannes Willebrands, "Ecumenical Dialogue Today: An Overview," *Origins* 28 (January 1988): 565-73.

5. "Observations on the Final Report of ARCIC," *Acta Apostolicae Sedis* 74 (1982): 1063-74; "Observations on 'Salvation and the Church,'" *Origins* 15 (December 1988): 429-34.

6. Raymond Brown, *The Churches the Apostles Left Behind* (Mahwah, N.J.: Paulist Press, 1984), pp. 72-73.

7. Max Thurian, ed., *Churches Respond to BEM* (Geneva: World Council of Churches, 1986-), 6 vols. to date.

8. S. Mark Heim, "The WCC Faith and Order Plenary Session in Budapest," *Ecumenical Trends* 19 (January 1990): 10-12; followed by the WCC report: 12-14.

9. "Baptism, Eucharist, and Ministry: An Appraisal," *Origins* 19 (November 1987): 401-16.

CHAPTER 10

1. Francis Sullivan, *Magisterium* (Mahwah, N.J.: Paulist Press, 1983). See especially chapter 5.

2. "An Archbishop Wronged," *Commonweal* October 10, 1986: 515-17.

3. "The Cologne Declaration," *Commonweal* February 24, 1989: 110-14.

CHAPTER 11

1. Lawrence Cunningham, *The Catholic Heritage* (New York: Crossroad, 1983), p. 193.

2. Kenan Osborne, *Priesthood: A History of the Ordained Ministry in the Roman Catholic Church* (Mahwah, N.J.: Paulist Press, 1988).

3. Dean R. Hoge, *The Future of Catholic Leadership: Responses to the Priest Shortage* (Kansas City: Sheed & Ward, 1987).

4. Philip Murnion, "Commentary," pp. 81-84 in *Research on Men's Vocations to the Priesthood and the Religious Life*, by Dean R. Hoge, Raymond H. Potvin, and Kathleen M. Ferry (Washington, D.C.: United States Catholic Conference, 1984).

CHAPTER 12

1. See Bernard Lonergan, *Method in Theology* (New York: Seabury, 1972), especially his chapters on "Meaning," pp. 57-99 and "Doctrines," pp. 295-333.

2. Bernard Lonergan, *Method in Theology*, p. 295.

3. Monika Hellwig, "Tradition in the Catholic Church—Why It's Still Important." *A Catholic Update*, St. Anthony Messenger Press, October 1981.

4. Francis Sullivan, *Magisterium* (Mahwah, N.J.: Paulist Press, 1983), pp. 169-70.

CHAPTER 13

1. Pope John Paul II, *Christifideles Laici*, in *Origins* 9 (February 1989): 563.

2. *Christifideles Laici*, p. 563.

CHAPTER 14

No notes for this chapter

CHAPTER 15

1. John Paul II, *Laborem Exercens* (On Human Work) (Washington, D.C.: United States Catholic Conference, 1981).

2. G.K. Chesterton, *St. Francis of Assisi* (New York: George H. Doran Company, 1924), pp. 141-42.

CHAPTER 16

1. Thomas Aquinas, *Summa Theologica* II-II, Q. 19, A. 11.

2. Rudolf Otto, *The Idea of the Holy* (London: Oxford University Press, 1923).

3. Daniel C. Maguire, "A 'New' View of Sin," *Catholic Update*, August 1981: 4.

CHAPTER 17

1. The idea for this interpretation of Jesus as "breaking the cycle" came to me when listening to a paper given by David M. Hammond, "The Genesis of Bernard Lonergan's Social and Historical Understanding of Christ's Redemption," given at the annual meeting of the College Theology Society, New Orleans, 1 June 1990.

2. Today many scholars raise many legitimate questions about exactly what Jesus taught and how accurately the gospels communicate his teaching. In this chapter, I ascribe to the basic belief that the gospels, although not literal news reports, give us a fairly good picture of how Jesus was remembered by the early Christian communities. On that basis, I will talk about "what Jesus taught," but it should be understood that I am more directly talking about how the teaching of Jesus is portrayed in the gospels.

CHAPTER 18

1. Bernard Lonergan, *Method in Theology* (New York: Herder and Herder, 1972), pp. 237-43.

2. For Lonergan on this topic, see *Method in Theology* (New York: Herder and Herder, 1972), pp. 101-07. For Rahner, see *Foundations of the Christian Faith*, translated by William V. Dych (New York: Crossroad, 1982 [1976], pp. 51-71.

3. See, for example, Raimundo Panikkar, *The IntraReligious Dialogue* (Mahwah, N.J.: Paulist Press, 1978) and William Johnston, *The Mirror Mind* (New York: Harper & Row, 1981).

CHAPTER 19

1. John P. Meier, *The Vision of Matthew* (Mahwah, N.J.: Paulist Press, 1979), pp. 136-41.

2. For a discussion of martyrs and ascetics, see Lawrence Cunningham, *The Catholic Heritage* (New York: Crossroad, 1983), chapters one and two.

3. Joan Chittister, *Winds of Change* (Kansas City: Sheed & Ward, 1986), pp. 116-18, 132-34.

CHAPTER 20

1. Robert Burns, "To a Louse." *The Complete Poetical Works of Robert Burns.* Cambridge Edition (Boston: Houghton Mifflin, 1897).

2. Leonardo Boff, *Church: Charism and Power* (New York: Crossroad, 1985).

3. Boff, *Church: Charism and Power*, p. 22.

4. Boff, *Church: Charism and Power*, p. 64.

5. Robert E. Rodes, Jr., "Law, History, and the Option for the Poor," *LOGOS* 6 (1985): 68.

6. Boff, *Church: Charism and Power*, p. 135.

CHAPTER 21

1. Arthur McGovern, "Liberation Theology Adapts and Endures," *Commonweal* November 3, 1989: 589.

2. Arthur F. McGovern, "Latin America and Dependency Theory," pp. 106-32 in *Liberation Theology and the Liberal Society*, ed. by Michael Novak (Washington, D.C.: American Enterprise Institute, 1987).

3. John R. Pottenger, *The Political Theory of Liberation Theology* (Albany: SUNY Press, 1989), pp. 3-4, 187-89.

4. For a discussion of the history of "utopia" and how it functions in contemporary theological discussion, see Dennis M. Doyle, "Utopia and Utopianism," *New Catholic Encyclopedia*, update volume 18 (Washington, D.C.: The Catholic University of America, 1989), pp. 527-29.

5. Novak's most comprehensive evaluation of liberation theology can be found in *Will It Liberate? Questions about Liberation Theology* (Mahwah, N.J.: Paulist Press, 1986); Novak's clearest outline of his argument against utopianism is in *Freedom with Justice* (San Francisco: Harper & Row, 1984), pp. 16-38.

6. Karl Mannheim, *Ideology and Utopia* (New York: Harcourt, Brace, 1959 [1929]).

7. Gustavo Gutierrez, *A Theology of Liberation* (Maryknoll, N.Y.: Orbis Books, 1973 [1971]), pp. 232-39.

8. *Origins* 13 (September 1984): 193ff.

9. *Origins* 17 (April 1986): 713-28.

10. Richard Ostling, "A Lesson on Liberation," *Time* April 14, 1986: 84.

11. Juan Luis Segundo, *Theology and the Church: A Response to Cardinal Ratzinger and a Warning to the Whole Church* (Minneapolis: Winston Press, 1985), especially pp. 152-56.

12. Rosino Gibellini, *The Liberation Theology Debate* (London: SCM Press, 1987 [1986]), p. 60.

13. Leonardo Boff, *Church: Charism and Power* (New York: Crossroad, 1985), p. 1.

14. Patrick Brennan, *Re-Imagining the Parish: Base Communities, Adulthood, and Family Consciousness* (New York: Crossroad, 1990).

CHAPTER 22

1. Having said this, I felt compelled to look it up. A discussion of the history of the Stations of the Cross can be found in Fred Krause, "A Humanizing Expression of the Faith: The Stations of the Cross" *Liturgy* 1 (1980): 49-54.

2. Wilfred Cantwell Smith, *Toward a World Theology* (Philadelphia: Westminster Press, 1981), pp. 5-6.

3. A Latin and English text of the *Syllabus of Errors* and the encyclical to which it was appended can be found in *Dublin Review* 4 (April 1865): 500-29.

4. John Courtney Murray, "Religious Freedom," in *The Documents of Vatican II*, edited by Walter M. Abbott (N.Y.: Guild Press, 1966), p. 673.

5. International Theological Commission, "On the Interpretation of Dogmas," *Origins* 17 (May 1990): 4.

6. Philip Hughes, *A Popular History of the Catholic Church* (New York: Macmillan, 1947). Hughes is also the author of the three volume *A History of the Catholic Church* (New York: Sheed & Ward, pp. 1935-47).

7. Hans Küng, *The Church* (Garden City, N.Y.: Doubleday, 1967), p. 184.

8. Monika Hellwig, "Tradition in the Catholic Church—Why It's Still Important." A *Catholic Update*, St. Anthony Messenger Press, October 1981.

CHAPTER 23

1. James Joyce, *A Portrait of the Artist as a Young Man* (New York: Viking Press, 1964 [1916]). The sermon on hell is found interspersed between pp. 110-33.

2. William P. Frost, *Following Joseph Campbell's Lead in the Search for Jesus' Father* (Lewiston, N.Y.: Edwin Mellen, 1991), pp. 145-79.

3. Thorton Wilder, *Our Town* (New York: Coward-McCann, 1938).

4. T.S. Eliot, *Four Quartets* (New York: Harcourt, Brace & World, 1943), p. 17.

5. Thomas J.J. Altizer, *Total Presence* (New York: Seabury Press, 1980). p. 108.

6. Elie Wiesel, *Night* (New York: Hill & Wang, 1960 [1958]).

7. Gustavo Gutierrez, *A Theology of Liberation* (Maryknoll, N.Y.: Orbis Books, 1973 [1971]).

8. See S.D. Hayes, "Beatifications and Canonizations," in *New Catholic Encyclopedia*, update volume 18 (Washington, D.C.: Catholic University of America, 1989), pp. 31-35, for a list from 1978 to 1988.

9. Leonardo Boff, *Church: Charism and Power* (New York: Crossroad, 1985 [1981]), p. 123. See also Boff's *St. Francis: A Model for Human Liberation* (New York: Crossroad, 1984 [1982]).

CHAPTER 24

1. This translation is from the 1969 version of *The New American Bible* rather than from the more recent *New American Bible with Revised New Testament*, which is otherwise used throughout this book.

2. Schillebeeckx's theology can be found in his trilogy, *Jesus: An Experiment in Christology; Christ: the Experience of Jesus as Lord;* and *Church: The Human Story of God* (New York: Crossroad, 1981, 1981, 1990 [1974, 1977, 1989]).

3. Joseph Ratzinger (with Vittorio Messori), *The Ratzinger Report* (San Francisco: Ignatius Press, 1985), p. 45.

4. Ratzinger, *The Ratzinger Report,* p. 46.

5. For a study of liberal-moderate-conservative positions among Catholic theologians and parishioners, see Dennis M. Doyle, Michael H. Barnes, and Byron R. Johnson, "Pluralism or Polarization: The Results of a CTS Survey," in *Raising the Torch of Good News,* ed. by Bernard P. Prusak (Lanham, Md.: University Press of America, 1988), pp. 275-296.

6. "The Final Report," *Origins* (1985): 448.

7. "The Final Report," p. 445.

CHAPTER 25

1. Some biblical scholars strongly challenge traditional interpretations that blame Eve for the Fall. See Phyllis Trible, *God and the Rhetoric of Sexuality* (Philadelphia: Fortress Press, 1978). See also Elaine Pagels, *Adam, Eve, and the Serpent* (New York: Random House, 1988).

2. David Macaulay, *Cathedral: The Story of Its Construction.* Unicorn Projects Inc., 1985. Words spoken by Caroline Berg. Distributed by Dorset Video.

CHAPTER 26

1. Gerda Lerner, *The Creation of Patriarchy* (Oxford: Oxford University Press, 1986), pp. 8-9.

2. I constructed the following chart from an article by Char McKee, "Beliefs about Reality in Patriarchal and Feminist Imagination," reprinted from *Woman of Power* magazine.

3. Mary Daly, *The Church and the Second Sex* (San Francisco: Harper & Row, 1968). This work was reissued in 1975 with a new introduction by the author.

4. Mary Daly, *Beyond God the Father: Toward a Philosophy of Women's Liberation* (Boston: Beacon Press, 1973).

5. Mary Daly, *Gyn/Ecology: The Metaethics of Radical Feminism* (Boston: Beacon Press, 1978).

6. Mary Daly, *Pure Lust: Elemental Feminist Philosophy* (Boston: Beacon Press, 1984).

7. Elisabeth Schüssler Fiorenza, *In Memory of Her* (New York: Crossroad, 1984), p. 346.

8. Anne E. Carr, *Transforming Grace: Christian Tradition and Women's Experience* (San Francisco: Harper & Row, 1988), p. 200.

9. Rosemary Radford Ruether, *Women-Church: Theology and Practice of Feminist Liturgical Communities* (San Francisco: Harper & Row, 1985), p. 59.

10. Fiorenza, *In Memory of Her*, p. 351.

11. Ruether, *Women-Church*, p. 61.

12. Ruether, *Women-Church*, p. 39.

13. Mary Jo Weaver, *New Catholic Women* (San Francisco: Harper & Row, 1985), p. 201.

14. Una M. Cadegan and James L. Heft, "Mary of Nazareth, Feminism, and the Tradition," *Thought* LXV (June 1990): 169-89.

CHAPTER 27

1. "Partners in the Mystery of Redemption: A Pastoral Response to Women's Concerns for Church and Society." (Washington: United States Catholic Conference, 1988).

2. "One in Christ Jesus: A Pastoral Response to the Concerns of Women for Church and Society," *Origins* 5 (April 1990): 717-40.

3. "*Inter Insigniores*," in *Vatican II: More Post-Conciliar Documents*, ed. Austin Flannery (Collegeville, Minn.: The Liturgical Press, 1982), pp. 331-45.

4. John Paul II, "*Mulieris Dignitatem*," *Origins* 6 (October 1988): 279.

5. Elisabeth Schüssler Fiorenza, *In Memory of Her: A Feminist Theological Reconstruction of Christian Origins* (New York: Crossroad, 1984).

6. Vincent Branick, *The House Church in the Writings of Paul* (Wilmington, Del.: Michael Glazier, 1989), p. 103.

7. Leonardo Boff, *Ecclesiogenesis* (Maryknoll, N.Y.: Orbis Books, 1986 [1977]), p. 47.

8. Boff, *Ecclesiogenesis*, pp. 95-96.

9. Boff, *Ecclesiogenesis*, p. 96.

10. Sara Butler, "Second Thoughts on Ordaining Women," *Worship* 63 (March 1989): 157-65.

11. See Bishop Kenneth Untener, "Ordination of Women: Can the Horizons Widen?" *Worship* 65 (January 1991): 50-59; Charles Meyer and Sara Butler, "Responses to Bishop Kenneth Untener," *Worship* 65 (May 1991): 256-68; John Sheets, "The Ordination of Women," *Worship* 65 (September 1991): 451-61.

CHAPTER 28

1. For this version of the story I am indebted to a children's book by John Ryan, *One Dark and Stormy Night: The Legend of St. Christopher* (London: Bodley Head Ltd., 1986).

2. An interesting discussion of biblical themes in art history can be found in two volumes by Richard Mühlenberger: *The Bible in Art: The Old Testament* (New York: Moore and Moore Publishing, 1991) and *The Bible in Art: The New Testament* (New York: Moore and Moore Publishing, 1990).

3. Karl Rahner, "Toward a Fundamental Theological Interpretation of Vatican II," *Theological Studies* 40 (December 1979): 716-27.

4. "The Final Report," *Origins* (1985): 449.

CHAPTER 29

1. Robert Coles, *The Spiritual Life of Children* (Boston: Houghton Mifflin, 1990), p. 279.

2. This is true not only throughout *Gaudium et Spes* but also in *Lumen Gentium* chapter four, which discusses how the laity in their work in the world participate in the very salvific mission of the church.

3. Karl Rahner's own best summary of his position on God can be found in *Foundations of the Christian Faith* (New York: Crossroad, 1982 [1976]), especially the first four chapters. See also Joseph Donceel, "Rahner's Argument for God," *America*, vol. 123, October 31, 1970: 340-42.

4. Rahner, *Foundations of the Christian Faith* (New York: Crossroad, 1982), pp. 69-70.

CHAPTER 30

1. Michael Sheehan, *Apologetics and Catholic Doctrine*. Part 1. (Dublin: M.H. Gill and Son, 1939), p. 167.

2. Raimundo Panikkar, *The Intra-Religious Dialogue* (Mahwah, N.J.: Paulist Press, 1978).

3. A good place to begin reading Wilfred Cantwell Smith is his *Religious Diversity* (New York: Harper & Row, 1976). See also *Towards a World Theology* (Philadelphia: Westminster Press, 1981).

4. Edward Schillebeeckx can be observed in dialogue with other religious traditions in *Christ: The Experience of Jesus as Lord* (New York: Crossroad, 1981 [1977]), pp. 672-723; his statement of belief in Jesus can be found in *Interim Report on the Books Jesus and Christ* (New York: Crossroad, 1981 [1977]), pp. 125-43.

CHAPTER 31

1. Flannery O'Connor, *The Complete Stories of Flannery O'Connor* (New York: Farrar, Strauss and Giroux, 1971), pp. 488-509.

CHAPTER 32

1. Aldous Huxley, *Brave New World* (N.Y.: Time, Inc., 1963 [1932]).

2. This chapter also contains passages regarding Catholic teaching regarding abortion and birth control. Abortion and infanticide are called "unspeakable crimes." (51) Catholics are told to follow present regulations concerning birth control, but that the question is under study. In 1968 Paul VI reasserted the traditional Catholic ban on artificial contraception.

CHAPTER 33

1. Some Africans reject the term "polygamy" as being potentially prejudicial because it does not express how the phenomenon of polygyny is an integral part of a complex social system.

2. For my information about the Luo, I rely on Marie-France Perrin Jassy, *Basic Community in the African Churches* (Maryknoll, N.Y.: Orbis Books, 1973 [1970]).

3. Edmund Ilogu, *Christianity and Ibo Culture* (Leiden: E.J. Brill, 1974), p. 218.

4. Edward Schillebeeckx discusses what he calls "anthropological constants," by which he means things that all human beings hold in common, in *Christ: The Experience of Jesus as Lord* (New York: Crossroad, 1981 [1977]), pp. 733-43.

5. See Aylward Shorter, *Toward a Theology of Inculturation* (Maryknoll, N.Y.: Orbis Books, 1988); also *African Culture and the Christian Church* (Maryknoll, N.Y.: Orbis Books, 1974).

6. Robert Schreiter, *Constructing Local Theologies* (Maryknoll, N.Y.: Orbis Books, 1985), p. 25.

CHAPTER 34

1. See John Paul II, *Centesimus Annus*, 1 May 1991, especially chapter 4.

CHAPTER 35

1. Garry Wills, *Under God: Religion and American Politics* (New York: Simon and Schuster, 1990).

2. See for example, the U.S. bishops' *Economic Justice for All*, #27: "...we want to add our voice to the public debate about the directions in which the U.S. economy should be moving."

CHAPTER 36

1. Lynn White, Jr., "The Historical Roots of Our Ecologic Crisis," *Science* March 10, 1967: 1203-07.

2. H. Paul Santmire, "The Liberation of Nature: Lynn White's Challenge Anew." *The Christian Century*, May 22, 1985: 530-33.

3. U.S. Catholic Bishops, "Renewing the Earth," *Origins* 12 (December 1991): 425-32.

4. See, for example, Jay B. McDaniel, *Earth, Sky, Gods & Mortals* (Mystic, Conn.: Twenty-Third Publications, 1990), pp. 24-25.

5. See Thomas Berry, with Thomas Clarke, *Befriending the Earth: A Theology of Reconciliation between Humans and the Earth* (Mystic, Conn.: Twenty-Third Publications, 1991); also Thomas Berry, *The Dream of the Earth* (San Francisco: Sierra Club Books, 1988).

6. Michael Dowd, *Earthspirit: A Handbook for Nurturing an Ecological Christianity* (Mystic, Conn.: Twenty-Third Publications, 1991), p. 19.

7. John Paul II, "The Ecological Crisis: A Common Responsibility." Washington, D.C.: United States Catholic Conference, 1990.

Index